Air University

AU-2
Guidelines for Command

A Handbook on the Leadership of Airmen for Air Force Squadron Commanders

Prepared by

Air Command and Staff College

Air University Press
Air Force Research Institute
Maxwell Air Force Base, Alabama

Project Editors
Belinda Bazinet
Jeanne K. Shamburger

Cover Art, Book Design, and Illustrations
L. Susan Fair

Composition and Prepress Production
Nedra O. Looney

Print Preparation and Distribution
Diane Clark

AIR FORCE RESEARCH INSTITUTE

AIR UNIVERSITY PRESS

Director and Publisher
Allen G. Peck

Editor in Chief
Oreste M. Johnson

Managing Editor
Demorah Hayes

Design and Production Manager
Cheryl King

Air University Press
155 N. Twining St., Bldg. 693
Maxwell AFB, AL 36112-6026
afri.aupress@us.af.mil

http://aupress.au.af.mil
http://afri.au.af.mil/

AFRI / AU PRESS
AIR FORCE RESEARCH INSTITUTE

Library of Congress Cataloging-in-Publication Data

Air University (U.S.). Air Command and Staff College.
AU-2 guidelines for command : a handbook on the leadership of airmen for Air Force squadron commanders / prepared by Air Command and Staff College. — Second edition.
pages cm
Includes bibliographical references.
ISBN 978-1-58566-251-7
1. United States. Air Force—Officers' handbooks. 2. United States. Air Force—Rules and practice. 3. Command of troops—United States. I. Title.
UG633.A523 2013
358.4'1330410973—dc23
2013013228

Published by Air University Press in March 2015

Disclaimer

Contents

Preface

Squadron command is often described as the best job in the Air Force. It is also one of the most demanding. Commanders are entrusted with incredible power—in terms of legal authority and personal influence—and it is critical you honor that trust by commanding effectively with balance, purpose, and dedication. As the commander, it is your responsibility to set the tone, establish priorities, and take the lead. As you meet your daily challenges, remember that ultimately command is not about you or how skilled you are in your Air Force specialty. Command is about accomplishing the mission and taking care of your Airmen. This guide will help you on your way.

There is no "all-encompassing" checklist or "how-to guide" for command—no manual could hope to be so comprehensive. How you lead your squadron depends on your experience, ideas, goals, values, and willingness to learn. Your past performance has demonstrated that you are up to the task—if not, you would not have been selected for command. Even so, you will not know everything before you start, and the job will always be a learning endeavor. You can, however, take advice and learn from other commanders' experiences to make you a better, more effective leader. That is the intent of this publication—to advance the practice of command.

This edition of AU-2, *Guidelines for Command*, is not a full re-creation of the previous edition. Instead, it is the result of the research project from the 2011 Air Command and Staff College (ACSC) Commanders Connection team members, most of whom are former commanders. The team turned the previous edition into an online wiki on the Commanders Connection website (currently not active). This allowed AU-2 to become a living document, enabling commanders to give immediate feedback about its content, acceptability, and relevance. While this edition includes much of the previous edition's content because it is still valid, it also contains revised and updated information. Thanks to the responses of many commanders with expertise in their fields and the 2011 Commanders Connection team, this edition is fine-tuned and up to date at the time of publication.

The following articles and "tips for success" are not regulations you must follow, nor should they be your sole source of information. They are only guidelines based on the experiences and lessons learned from a diverse group of Air Force leaders. Used properly—and supplemented with other sources—this handbook will help to prepare you to effectively meet the needs of the mission while also taking care of your people.

We greatly appreciate the support of the following Air University organizations at Maxwell AFB, Alabama: ACSC; the Commanders' Professional

Development School, Ira C. Eaker Center for Professional Development; and Air University Press for their assistance in making this revised publication a reality. Without their support this project would not have been possible. Good luck in your command!

Commanders Connection Team

ACSC Class of 2011

- Maj (Lt Col, USAF, retired) Jeffrey A. Baldwin, Aircraft Maintenance
- Maj (now Lt Col) Dona L. Byron, Force Support
- Maj (now Lt Col) Kenneth D. Dewlen, Force Support
- Dr. Lynn M. List, Instructional Systems Specialist
- Maj (now Lt Col) Louis J. Marnell, Aircraft Maintenance
- Maj (now Lt Col) Tracy L. Parrish, Force Support
- Maj Ryan D. Sullivan, Operations

Air Command and Staff College Faculty Support

- Lt Col Mike Hower, USAF, retired, Commanders Connection program manager
- Lt Col Michael Hills, PhD, Commanders Connection instructor
- Lt Col Gonzalo Reyna, Commanders Connection instructor

Chapter 1

Taking Command

What Is Command?

Original Author: Maj Shannon Smith
14th Security Forces Squadron (SFS) Commander

“Command is the best job in the Air Force!” I heard this statement echoed at countless change-of-command ceremonies, mentoring sessions, and training courses. When my own change of command was just two months away, I began to ponder the following question: What is command? My research showed me there is no easy answer. There's the legal authority aspect of command, the mission aspect of command, and the people aspect of command. With these three pillars comprising the heart of the discussion, let's take a closer look at the concept of command.

Legally speaking, command is the authority given an officer to direct subordinates to attain military objectives. Commanders have legal authority by virtue of rank and written appointment. While tasks can be delegated to subordinates, command responsibility cannot—it must remain with one individual entrusted to direct the mission. Additionally, commanders are granted specific legal authority under the *Uniform Code of Military Justice* (*UCMJ*) to ensure good order and discipline. Commanders may independently impose reductions in rank, monetary fines, and restrictions on subordinates' freedoms to encourage behaviors that support mission success. Commanders may also refer the most egregious offenders to courts-martial, which could result in significantly greater penalties. While anyone with written appointment can command by exercising legal authority, only the best leaders will truly excel. These leaders focus on the mission.

Mission-focused commanders hold themselves and their subordinates accountable to high standards of performance. They clearly communicate and live the Air Force core values. They set the standards for others to emulate and never ask their Airmen to do something they are unwilling to do themselves. When Airmen fail to uphold standards, mission-focused commanders are not reluctant to hold them accountable for their actions. Commanders without the fortitude to do this will likely not be successful.

Mission-focused commanders also understand their unit's role in the big picture and clearly articulate this role to their Airmen. They understand the squadron's relationship to its higher headquarters (HHQ), its sister squadrons, and other units. Mission-focused commanders may disagree with leadership when necessary; however, once a legal order is received they communicate and execute that order with vigor and passion, regardless of personal feelings or beliefs. Mission-focused commanders also fully train and equip their Airmen for success in combat. They become budget experts—learning creative ways to stretch a dollar to its maximum value—because sending Airmen into harm's way without the right equipment is wrong. They also understand the necessity to train their Airmen for combat, even when that means driving the squadron hard.

Mission-focused commanders know their jobs inside and out. They are technical experts. They know how to communicate—both verbally and in written form. They develop themselves professionally through reading. While it is not necessary for commanders to be subject-matter experts in every area, it is essential that they understand every aspect of their squadron's operations to effectively organize, train, and equip their units to perform the mission. Without a mission focus in these three areas, commanders are impediments, not enablers, of mission success. This mission focus, however, must be balanced with the needs of the Airmen under their command.

Command is about people and inspiring them to do things they never thought they could do. It is about motivating Airmen to go above and beyond on a daily basis. It is about rewarding the best performers and providing incentives for those who are less than outstanding to improve their game. People-focused commanders understand that while some members of a squadron have more responsibility than others, every Airman has a valuable role to play in ensuring mission success. They are servant leaders—serving their subordinates as much, or more, than they serve their bosses. People-focused commanders get out from behind their desks; they learn and address the needs of their Airmen and take care of them like family. Helping Airmen and their families makes command not only one of the most challenging jobs in the Air Force but also the most rewarding experience that many officers have during their Air Force careers.

Authority, mission focus, and people are the three pillars of command and, when considered collectively, provide a substantive and formidable response to the question posed at the beginning of this essay: What is command? It is authority, legal and implied. It is a focus on the mission and the responsibility to organize, train, equip, and lead a unit to mission success. It is caring for people—helping Airmen and their families meet their needs, enabling them to grow and focus on the mission. Too much mission focus without regard to the needs of the people can quickly burn out a squadron and lead to disastrous results in combat. Too much emphasis on people without regard for legal accountability or mission success will lead to a happy unit in the short term but will ultimately result in a squadron incapable of accomplishing even the simplest objectives. The truly exceptional commander understands the necessity of striking a good balance between these three areas.

Tips for Success

- Recognize the difference between being in command and just being a leader.
- Fully understand the responsibilities associated with command.
- Remember, you've been entrusted with the safety and welfare of your squadron members. Fully accept that responsibility, and take it seriously.
- Hold your subordinates and yourself to high standards. Administer disciplinary action when necessary, but always direct it toward a desired outcome.
- Know the mission and stay focused.
- Lead by example.

Additional Resources

- *Taking Charge: A Practical Guide for Leaders* by Maj Gen Perry Smith
- *Sharing Success and Owning Failure* by Col David Goldfein
- *Commanding an Air Force Squadron in the Twenty-First Century: A Practical Guide of Tips and Techniques for Today's Squadron Commander* by Lt Col Jeffry F. Smith

Making the Most of Your Preparatory Time

Maj Tracy L. Parrish
2011 Commanders Connection Team

> *By three methods we may learn wisdom: First, by reflection, which is noblest; second, by imitation, which is easiest; and third by experience, which is the bitterest.*
>
> —Confucius

Congratulations on your selection for command! Your leadership challenge is about to begin, and your incredible journey starts the moment that you accept the guidon. Now is the time to learn lessons from your peers, figure out your plan of attack, and contribute your experience and lessons learned for others. Make the most of your time in the months or weeks prior to taking command. Any time-stressed commander will be quick to point out that you will never have more time than you do now and that playing catch-up in the early stages of command is not where you want to be. Take the time now to prepare early; consider the following wise advice from past commanders to equip you for success. Good luck as you venture on this exciting chapter of your career!

Tips for Success

Original Author: Maj Shannon Smith, 14th SFS Commander

- Educate yourself about your squadron and its mission. Study the unit and wing missions and how they fit together.
- Call your gaining boss and let him or her know you are looking forward to the opportunity for command.
- Call your squadron's incumbent commander.
    - Ask questions, but don't be too aggressive. For example, confine your questions to those items related to changing command, reporting dates, and base housing.
    - Some incumbent commanders prefer not to share details about current squadron issues, especially if the change of command is still weeks away. Respect their prerogative.
    - Avoid contact with members of your new unit unless you discuss it first with the incumbent commander.
    - Ask for access to your squadron's Air Force Knowledge Now community of practice (if any) or SharePoint page (if possible) to familiarize yourself with unit processes and procedures.
- Identify issues on which you need further information—budget status, squadron morale, last inspection results, quality initiatives, safety records, and so forth.
- Make a clean break from the old assignment. Close out all the paperwork. You won't have time to take care of old business in your new assignment.
- Begin a study of publications related to disciplinary actions such as *The Manual for Courts-Martial* and *The Military Commander and the Law*—the more you understand *UCMJ* issues, the more effective you will be when making disciplinary decisions.
- Review any major command (MAJCOM), wing, or group supplements and directives concerning your new unit's mission as well as any current squadron operating instructions (OI), policy letters, and inspection reports.
- Evaluate your fitness level. If you don't think your current appearance and fitness level set a good example, develop a plan to get in shape before the change of command.

- Attend your annual MAJCOM's conference (if possible). If you do, keep a low profile, take plenty of notes, and get to know the MAJCOM staff that will support your unit.
- Make the most of your MAJCOM's squadron commander's course. Build a network with those in your class who are headed to your base.
- If married, talk to your spouse about the role he or she may play during your command.

The Change-of-Command Process

Original Author: Maj Dan Sheesley
43rd Comptroller Squadron Commander

Your level of involvement in your change of command will vary depending on the location of your new unit, the amount of protocol and public affairs (PA) support available, and a host of other unique circumstances. No two changes of command are exactly alike. You must strike a balance between what you will manage versus what the incumbent commander will handle. Together, you should sort out the details of the ceremony. Remember that this is not only your big day, it is also the incumbent's last official act in command. He or she may want certain things to happen during the ceremony. Be flexible.

Tips for Success

Touch Base with the Ceremony's Point of Contact

- Begin a dialog on specific requirements for the ceremony.
- Provide complete contact information (phone numbers and address, if known) so you can be reached at home, at work, or in transit to your new station.
- E-mail your biography and official photo and spouse's and children's names.
- Keep your point of contact (POC) apprised of changes as soon as they happen.
- Provide the POC your recommendations and desires regarding location (indoors or outdoors), headgear (on or off), formations, and uniform for participants and guests.
- Work with your POC to obtain information on local policies, advice on guests, and ideas for planning your reception.

Contact Protocol

- Contact the local protocol office and introduce yourself.
- Allow the incumbent commander to work with the protocol office to plan the ceremony; provide assistance when requested.

Deconflict the Date and Time

- Provide the incumbent commander with preferred dates and times.
- Be patient. The sitting commander and POC must coordinate the function with the presiding officer and deconflict with the base/wing schedule.

Determine Your Invitees

- Provide ranks or civilian titles, names (go-by names), positions, and addresses of your invitees to the POC. Clearly identify any distinguished visitors (DV) on your list.
- Ensure the POC sends DV information to the protocol office.
- Ensure the POC sends your invitees a formal invitation to the ceremony with an RSVP date.
  - o Ensure the POC tracks RSVPs.
  - o Provide RSVPs you received directly to the POC.

Keep Your Future Supervisor Informed

- Ensure you establish a dialog with your future supervisor and keep him or her in the loop with any significant changes. Your goal: to prevent surprises for your future boss.

Develop Your Change-of-Command Speech

- Shorter is better; aim for less than three minutes.
- Don't
  - o Expound on your personal leadership philosophy or your specific goals for the squadron—save that for your first commander's call.
  - o Deliver a list of historical military references or metaphors.
- Do
  - o Be humble, thankful, and appreciative for the opportunity to command.
  - o Thank your new boss, DVs, group commanders, fellow squadron commanders, guests, and the outgoing squadron commander
  - o Thank the POC and others who organized the ceremony.

- o Give kudos to the squadron for its successes; the wing historian is a great source of this type of information.
- o Tell your Airmen you look forward to working with them.

Plan Your Reception

- Determine reception location with the POC—the closer to the change-of-command site the better.
- Provide input on the type and amount of food and beverages to purchase, and work with your POC for payment. Special funds may be available through the protocol office to offset costs.

Additional Resource

- *Commanding an Air Force Squadron in the Twenty-First Century: A Practical Guide of Tips and Techniques for Today's Squadron Commander* by Lt Col Jeffry F. Smith (12–13, 172–74)

Making the Right First Impression

Original Author: Maj Shannon Smith
14th SFS Commander

The first impression made on a squadron sets the tone for success in command. Commanders who excel start strong right out of the gate. There is no formula for a good first impression, but successful commanders do a few things consistently well during the first few days and weeks of command. The tips below should get you started on the right foot.

Tips for Success

- Live the Air Force core values. Go even further and be able to tie all activities in the organization back to the mission and core values.
- Set the standards and hold your team accountable to those standards.
- Be courteous! You are under scrutiny from the moment you arrive on base. Be polite to gate guards, commissary and base exchange personnel, and everyone you encounter—bad "episodes" with new commanders quickly become known basewide.

- Look sharp! Put a little extra effort into your uniform and haircut. Your Airmen pay special attention to your personal appearance.
- Make a concerted effort to shake hands with every Airman you meet during your first week in command.
- Be positive! You set the tone in the unit.
  - Focus on turning something poor into something average, average into good, good into excellent, and excellent into outstanding.
  - Don't underestimate the power of positive thinking.
- Make sure you understand your boss's vision. You will lose valuable time and credibility if you take your unit in a direction not consistent with your boss's priorities.
- Spend time getting to know your key leaders—officers, senior noncommissioned officers (SNCO), senior civilians, and senior contractors.
- Get your hands dirty: fly, stand watch, sit a post, work the customer service desk. These actions will win your Airmen's loyalty.
- Visit the spouses of your deployed Airmen with your first sergeant. Let them know the unit will support them during tough times.
- Set and enforce high standards from the start—it is much easier to loosen standards than to tighten them later.
- Be on time. Meet or beat suspenses. Show up for meetings on time, and don't keep your team waiting.
- Train your squadron leadership to lead. Things should still run smoothly when you're not in the office.
- Communicate effectively. Make sure your guidance is clear, concise, and understood.
- Serve your people! They are the reason you are in command!

Additional Resource

- *First Things First* by Stephen R. Covey offers practical insights for effective leadership.

Key Leadership Positions within Your Squadron

Original Author: Maj Kathy Goforth
898th Munitions Squadron Commander

References

Air Force Instruction (AFI) 36-2113, *The First Sergeant*, 19 December 2007.

AFI 36-2618, *The Enlisted Force Structure*, 27 February 2009.

AFI 38-101, *Air Force Organization*, 16 March 2011.

Air Force Manpower Standard (AFMS) 10S100, *Squadron Orderly Room*, 10 April 2013.

HQ USAF Program Action Directive (PAD) 02-05, "Implementation of the CSAF of the Air Force Direction to Establish a New Combat Wing Organization Structure," 20 June 2002.

The majority of the following information is excerpted directly from the above references.

As commander, you are at the helm of your squadron, guiding your Airmen to accomplish the mission. This job is not easy. Fortunately, you are not alone. Several key leaders within your squadron can assist you in managing your unit. Get to know the incumbents in these positions; they will greatly help you in your command. Keep in mind that not all of these key leadership positions are assigned to every Air Force unit. Based on ongoing personnel reductions, some of these positions may be consolidated within your group.

Operations Officer

- Assists the commander in overseeing the daily operations of the squadron.
- Ensures day-to-day suspenses and mission products are tasked to the unit staff and completed/submitted in a timely manner.
- Ensures manpower and levels of supervision are equally distributed for duty periods based on manning and workload.
- Enforces strict adherence to applicable technical data, Air Force directives, MAJCOM guidance, and local procedures.
- Ensures adherence to AFI 91-series safety directives.

- Where applicable, coordinates with other units to develop and execute a rotation plan for all applicable Air Force specialty codes (AFSC) to balance grade, skill level, and experience between units.
- Ensures a sufficient number of Airmen are qualified to perform the mission.
- Trains and mentors subordinate officers.
- Establishes a method to distribute inspection crosstalks and crosstells, policy announcements, technical data, and other important information.
- Reviews applicable support agreements triannually (or as required) and makes recommended changes.
- Reviews status of resources and training system (SORTS) and air and space expeditionary force (AEF) reporting tool (ART) information.
- Ensures unit manning document (UMD) complies with organization structure in AFI 38-101.
- Maintains current copy of unit personnel manpower roster.
- Monitors workforce availability.
- Coordinates permanent-change-of-assignment (PCA) actions.
- Distributes projected gain or loss lists to all work centers and establishes suspenses for updates.

First Sergeant

(Assigned to units with over 75 military personnel)

- Works directly for and derives authority from the unit commander.
- Provides a critical link to the commander in standing up a mission-ready enlisted force to execute the unit mission.
- Serves as the commander's advisor on personnel programs, career progression, family needs, financial matters, family and unaccompanied housing, details, personnel readiness management (PRM), recognition programs, and any additional needs the commander requires.
- Ensures the enlisted force understands the commander's policies, goals, and objectives.
- Provides advice to commander concerning health, morale, welfare, discipline, mentoring, well-being, recognition, and professional development of enlisted members.
- Administers the unit award programs.

- Serves as focal point within the unit for enlisted issues.
- Exercises general supervision over assigned enlisted Airmen.
- Performs various actions associated with disciplinary procedures, and ensures enlisted discipline is equitable and effective.
- Ensures base support agencies are responsive to needs of unit members.
- Responds to the needs of unit members (enlisted and officers) 24 hours a day, seven days a week.
- Conducts quality-force reviews and ensures timely processing of enlisted performance reports (EPR), awards, decoration recommendations, promotions, classification actions, quality control, and disciplinary actions.

Squadron Superintendent

- Usually the ranking enlisted member in your squadron, other than the first sergeant.
- Generally taken out of hide as the position is typically not authorized per AFMS 10S100, *Squadron Orderly Room*.
- Same responsibilities as operations officer but from an enlisted perspective.
- Subject matter expert (SME) on enlisted technical issues.
- Provides substantial institutional, operational, and functional experience as well as strong leadership skills.
- Trains and mentors enlisted personnel.
- Assists the commander in stratifying SNCOs.
- Provides valuable information concerning enlisted force promotions, EPRs, decorations, discipline, and training.

Additional-Duty First Sergeant

(Assigned to units with 75 or fewer military members)

- Same responsibilities as first sergeant (see above listing) but not a full-time job. Often wears two hats—first, additional-duty first sergeant and, second, normal SNCO assigned roles/responsibilities.
- Must be a SNCO; however, in units without SNCOs, commanders can assign a lower-ranking member.

- For Air Force Reserve Command (AFRC) and Air National Guard (ANG), must be an E-7 and uphold the same professional profile and criteria required for a full-time first sergeant.

Squadron Section Commander

As of final implementation of program budget decision (PBD) 720, all squadron section commander positions were removed from the UMD. (Historically, squadron section commanders were assigned only to units with over 250 military members.)

Some organizations may choose to maintain a squadron section commander out of hide, but they are currently not authorized manpower positions. This, however, is subject to change as the Air Force continues to reorganize. When a squadron section commander is appointed, he/she will have the following responsibilities:

- Manages commander's programs including leave, recognition, performance reporting, disciplinary actions, and others as assigned.
- Responsible for the morale, welfare, and safety of personnel.
- Usually a junior officer; requires mentoring and guidance from the commander and first sergeant.

Tips for Success

- Conduct one-on-one meetings with each of your unit's key leaders.
  - Clarify responsibilities and establish goals for each position.
  - Provide your expectations for the unit and how each leader fits into accomplishing them.
- These key leaders are your command team. Solicit input and request feedback on your actions and decisions. Don't work in a vacuum.
- Provide frequent feedback.
- Train the operations officer to do your job. Period.
- Learn from the first sergeant and superintendent.
- Mentor the section commander. If one is appointed out of hide, consider delegating all Airman and noncommissioned officer (NCO) evaluations and decorations to the section commander—this is a good learning opportunity for that individual.

- Remember, the command chief master sergeant (CCM) is available for advice regarding your first sergeant and superintendent, as well as for manning assistance, when it comes time to rotate these key leaders out of your unit.

Additional Resource

- *Commanding an Air Force Squadron in the Twenty-First Century: A Practical Guide of Tips and Techniques for Today's Squadron Commander* by Lt Col Jeffry F. Smith, 66–81.

Familiarizing Yourself with Base Agencies

Original Author: Maj Kathy Goforth
898th Munitions Squadron Commander

References

AU-2, *Guidelines for Command*, 2003.

Department of Defense Directive (DODD) 6495.01, *Sexual Assault Prevention and Response (SAPR) Program*, 23 January 2012 (incorporating change 1, 30 April 2013).

AFI 31-201, *Security Police Standards and Procedures*, 30 March 2009.

AFI 35-101, *Public Affairs Responsibilities and Management*, 18 August 2010.

AFI 36-2706, *Equal Opportunity Program, Military and Civilian*, 5 October 2010.

AFI 38-101, *Air Force Organization*, 16 March 2011.

AFI 51-201, *Administration of Military Justice*, 21 December 2007 (incorporating change 1, 3 February 2010).

Air Force Manual (AFMAN) 51-204, *United States Air Force Judiciary and Air Force Trial Judiciary*, 18 January 2008.

AFI 90-301, *Inspector General Complaints Resolution*, 15 May 2008.

The majority of the following information is excerpted directly from the above references.

Commanders must be aware of the various resources they have supporting them in performing the mission and in taking care of their Airmen and their families. This section provides a brief overview of units and agencies available on most Air Force bases to help you in your daily duties. As a commander, you must build working relationships with these agencies early in your command tour. The network you cultivate will assist you when a problem arises in your unit.

American Red Cross

The American Red Cross (ARC) supports and supplements Air Force activities involving morale, health, and welfare of Airmen and their families. Its representatives are the emergency communications link between members and their families when direct communication is impossible.

Air Force Office of Special Investigations

The Air Force Office of Special Investigations (AFOSI) provides professional investigative services to all Air Force commanders. The AFOSI identifies, investigates, and neutralizes criminal, terrorist, and espionage threats to Air Force and DOD personnel and resources. AFOSI personnel remain independent of your base's chain of command to ensure unbiased investigations. The AFOSI agents' primary duties include threat detection, criminal investigations, economic crime investigations, information operations, and technology protection.

Area Defense Counsel

The area defense counsel (ADC) provides legal defense services for military members. This certified judge advocate (JA), or military attorney, serves as counsel in all actions under the *UCMJ* and in administrative discharge actions. Additionally, the ADC advises members referred for nonemergency mental health evaluations and represents the member in other adverse actions.

Tips for Success

- As a commander, you must support the ADC to ensure the military justice system is not only fair but also perceived as fair. Whenever a unit member receives administrative or nonjudicial punishment, encourage the member to make an appointment with the ADC to ensure he or she understands his or her rights regarding how to best respond to any punishment.
- Important tip: If it is necessary to read an Airman his or her rights, do so before sending him or her to the ADC.

Office of the Staff Judge Advocate

The office of the staff judge advocate (SJA) advises commanders on military justice and disciplinary matters as well as civil, contract, and environmental law. Judge advocates prosecute courts-martial and represent the government in administrative separation hearings. Additionally, JAs provide legal aid, tax assistance, and claims support for military relocation. One of the key functions of the SJA is to manage the wing commander's status of discipline meeting. All unit commanders and first sergeants attend this regular briefing that provides an opportunity to gauge disciplinary actions across the wing. Most SJA offices also host regular squadron commander and first sergeant legal training courses to prepare you for your responsibilities associated with military law.

Tip for Success

- Consult the SJA before taking any disciplinary actions. Early SJA involvement can ensure your actions are legal and have the desired effect.

Comptroller Squadron

As a commander, you will need operating funds to perform your mission. You must ensure that your annual budget is based on mission requirements, submitted on time, and monitored. The comptroller, as the principal financial advisor to all commanders, will assist you in meeting these requirements. Your link to the comptroller and the comptroller squadron (CPTS) is your unit's resource advisor (RA), who will keep you updated on your budget status. The CPTS—in addition to managing the basewide leave, government purchase card (GPC), and government travel card (GTC) programs—is also responsible for overall financial planning, economic analysis, funds execution, military and civilian pay transactions, in- and out-processing, funds certification, funds authorization, and audit of pay or travel documents, as well as coordinating with the Defense Finance and Accounting Service (DFAS).

Tips for Success

- Soon after taking command, have your RA contact the CPTS training officer to schedule your budget training.
- Regularly meet with your RA to ensure proper execution of your budget.

Chaplain

Chaplains provide spiritual care and ethical leadership. They administer the wing's religious programs, provide religious ministry to Airmen and their families, and offer counseling. Chaplains are the primary advisor for commanders concerning religious accommodation issues. The chaplain is the only person on base who offers total confidentiality outside of the attorney-client relationship. Chaplains are noncombatants and will not be placed in a duty status that compromises their status as noncombatants.

Inspector General

The inspector general (IG) is responsible to the wing commander for assessing and improving unit operational readiness, nuclear surety programs, and mission support effectiveness of all assigned units. The IG is also responsible for establishing and directing the Air Force complaints and fraud, waste, and abuse (FW&A) programs. In essence, the IG serves as the "eyes and ears" of the wing commander, providing an independent fact-finding body to conduct investigations and serving as an honest broker in complaint resolution. The IG is only an investigative body; it neither determines guilt or innocence nor makes recommendations for punishment or remediation—it exists to provide information to the chain of command for decision making.

Tips for Success

- Encourage unit members to use the chain of command to resolve issues, but avoid giving the perception that members are restricted from going to the IG with a complaint.
- Stress that many matters are not appropriate for IG resolution and should be handled through the chain of command or other helping agencies. The following are examples: *UCMJ* issues, unprofessional relationships, performance report appeals, and equal opportunity (EO) issues.

Equal Opportunity Office

The EO office provides formal and informal complaint processing, counseling, conflict resolution, information referral, and other assistance to military and civilian members who believe they have experienced sexual harassment or unlawful discrimination based on color, race, religion, sex, or national origin. The EO staff conducts unit climate assessments (UCA) for commanders at all levels to assess their organizations' equal opportunity and treatment climate. Additionally, the EO office provides educational classes to all military and civilian personnel on various human relations subjects.

Public Affairs Office

The PA office advises and assists commanders in communicating Air Force messages to military personnel and the public. PA also helps you identify and manage communications issues that affect your unit as it conducts its mission. PA consists of three main areas: community relations, media relations, and internal information. Community relations initiatives develop understanding and acceptance of the Air Force in local communities. As a commander, you interact with PA for community relations when you support base tours, speaking engagements (and the local base speaker's bureau, if established), community events, open houses, flybys, and air shows and when you answer public inquiries. Media relations programs keep the public informed about Air Force issues. Your unit speeches, statements, interviews, news or feature stories, photographs, or hometown news releases must go through PA for media release. Internal information efforts are designed to keep your Airmen (and their families) fully informed about the Air Force mission, ensuring high morale, productivity, and retention. At the squadron level, you can take advantage of these PA programs by advertising squadron events, publicizing good news, and recognizing outstanding performance through your local base paper or website.

Tips for Success

- Appoint a unit public affairs representative (UPAR) to work closely with the PA office on internal information and community relations campaigns.
- Judiciously use the base newspaper and/or bulletin to publicize your unit.
- Encourage your Airmen to complete a hometown news release.
- Contact PA before speaking to any media outlet.
- Read the USAF Public Affairs Center of Excellence guide *Communication Excellence*, November 2013, http://www.au.af.mil/au/spaatz/pace.

Safety Office

The safety office develops, implements, executes, and evaluates your base's flight, ground, and weapons safety programs. Safety personnel manage space, system mishap prevention, and nuclear surety programs to preserve combat readiness. The safety office also develops and presents safety and operational risk management (ORM) education programs for your use.

Tips for Success

- Appoint a unit safety officer to oversee your unit's safety program.
- Meet with your unit safety officer periodically to identify trends in your unit.
- Include the safety officer in your commander's calls to promote safety throughout your unit.

Sexual Assault Response Coordinator

The sexual assault response coordinator (SARC) is part of a DOD-wide program designed to offer support services to victims of sexual assault. The Sexual Assault Prevention and Response Program assists victims of sexual assault in their physical and emotional recovery. Each base has a SARC to help victims and to provide advice and training to base personnel. The SARC accomplishes this mission with the help of victim advocates (VA) who are volunteers from different units across the base.

Tip for Success

- Identify and support personnel in your unit who are interested in volunteering as a VA.

Wing Plans

The wing plans office plans, schedules, and conducts realistic, timely, and integrated contingency response and combat employment training. This is accomplished through local contingency and major accident response exercises. The plans office obtains feedback, identifies shortfalls, benchmarks, and takes action to improve combat readiness. Your unit will be tasked to provide exercise evaluation team (EET) members and trusted agents to support base-wide exercises. The plans office also manages and monitors the status of all plans and taskings for the wing and its subordinate units; some may affect your unit.

Civil Engineering Squadron

The civil engineering squadron (CES) is responsible for maintaining all real property and real property installed equipment on your base. Most CESs consist of seven or eight flights that manage all base support including base operations, family housing, physical plant engineering, environmental support, explosive ordnance disposal (EOD), fire protection, and readiness training.

Communications Squadron

The communications squadron (CS) acquires, manages, operates, and maintains the base communication and information systems. These systems include airfield equipment, fixed telephones, cell phones, land-mobile radios, secure-communications equipment, personal computers, and the basewide local area network. The CS is also responsible for tracking all automated data processing equipment (ADPE) on the installation. Your unit will have an ADPE account custodian assigned. In addition, CS operates the base information transfer system (BITS) that picks up and delivers your unit's mail.

Contracting Squadron

The contracting squadron (CONS) provides local-purchase support to assigned units. Local purchase is a method to acquire parts, supplies, and services outside of the normal supply system. Your unit will make these purchases via an Air Force Form 9, Request for Purchase, or by using your unit's GPC. Your unit resource advisor will work closely with CONS to execute your purchases.

Logistics Readiness Squadron

The logistics readiness squadron (LRS) operates and maintains the vehicle fleet and manages supplies, equipment, and fuels to support all base organizations. It also provides aircraft parts for maintenance, directs the traffic management functions of the base (e.g., cargo movement and household goods shipment), manages readiness assets and war reserve materiel, and leads the base deployment mission.

Force Support Squadron

The force support squadron (FSS) provides manpower, personnel, and services support to commanders, military members, families, Reservists, guardsmen, civilian employees, and retirees. The FSS commander or deputy is the base mortuary officer. Several key functions of the FSS are highlighted below.

Sustainment and Community Services Flights. These flights provide activities to enhance your Airmen's quality of life. They manage almost all base support functions, including lodging, child development centers, youth centers, fitness centers, dining facilities, theaters, and bowling centers. In addition, they provide outdoor programs and discount tickets and travel through the information, tickets, and travel (ITT) office. At some bases, they also provide an auto hobby shop, horse stables, a FamCamp, recreational vehicle storage, and a marina.

Military Personnel Section. The military personnel section (MPS) provides a full range of personnel services to individuals on active duty, Reservists, and dependents, including relocation, promotion, separation, retirement, and casualty service actions. The MPS staff helps with passports, identification cards, the Defense Enrollment Eligibility Reporting System (DEERS), military personnel records review, citizenship and naturalization questions, and survivor benefits. The MPS also hosts your base's Individual Newcomer Treatment and Orientation (INTRO) program.

Civilian Personnel Office. The civilian personnel office (CPO) recognizes, plans for, and efficiently responds to the civilian personnel management and administration needs of serviced employees and managers. The CPO staff assists managers in classifying vacant and encumbered positions, managing civilian resources, and assisting supervisors in implementing discipline and administrative action for civilian employees. The CPO is responsible for staffing civilian positions to ensure they are filled with the best qualified candidates. It also provides advice and counsel concerning labor management and employee relations issues and provides or makes available educational and training opportunities for civilian employees and their supervisors.

Airman and Family Readiness Center. The Airman and family readiness center (A&FRC) provides your Airmen and their families with the skills needed to deal with the unique demands of military life. High deployment and temporary duty (TDY) requirements cause frequent family separations and increased pressures on single parents and dual-working families with children. The A&FRC strives to keep the military member focused on the mission through predeployment education and family support programs. It can assist with financial counseling, transition and relocation, and costs associated with personal emergencies.

Professional Development Flight. The professional development flight provides resources for education and training for the base. It oversees library operations and off-duty education opportunities at the undergraduate and graduate levels. Through the First Term Airman Center (FTAC) and Airman Leadership School (ALS) courses, it prepares Airmen for leadership roles. Additionally, it provides information about commissioning opportunities and implements professional military education (PME), the Weighted Airman Promotion System (WAPS), the College-Level Examination Program (CLEP), and Defense Activity for Nontraditional Education Support (DANTES) testing.

Manpower and Organization Section. The manpower and organization section provides workforce and organizational management services and evaluations, management advisory services, and wartime manpower support. This office also maintains and provides UMDs to commanders upon request.

Airman Professional Military Education Flight. The Airman professional military education flight prepares Airmen for leadership roles through ALS.

Security Forces Squadron

The SFS provides air base defense, law enforcement, and information security support to protect Air Force personnel, property, and weapons systems. The SFS provides unit security manager training to help you safeguard classified information and material through information, personnel, and industrial security programs. It also provides combat arms training and maintenance training to your Airmen prior to deployment. Due to increased operations tempo, SFS units often rely on contracted security personnel and military augmentees to accomplish base defense and entry control duties. Your unit may be tasked to support this program.

Tips for Success

- The SFS manages all personally owned firearms on base. Any member of your unit who lives on base and owns a firearm must register it with the SFS.
- Occupants of base housing may keep firearms in the provided quarters. Firearms are prohibited in dormitories, bachelor quarters, and lodging. Airmen who live in these areas must store weapons in the SFS armory.

Medical Resources Group

Medical services vary by base. Most bases provide daily operational medical support to the military members of your base. Additionally, the group normally provides primary health care to patients enrolled in TRICARE Prime and assigned to your base's clinic. Most clinics provide primary and specialty care on a space-available basis to other eligible beneficiaries. Some bases offer only an outpatient clinic with 24-hour ambulance transport service. The services not offered on base are provided through the TRICARE network that includes other military facilities and local medical providers.

Vision

Original Authors: AU-2 Research Seminar, 2001

Reference

- Air Command and Staff College (ACSC), AU-2, *Guidelines for Command*, 2008

The majority of the following information is excerpted directly from the above reference.

Man's mind, stretched by a new idea, never goes back to its original dimensions.

—Oliver Wendell Holmes

Commanders must have vision that empowers, inspires, and challenges. This same vision must motivate followers to commitment and performance. It is crucial that commanders understand what vision is and what it is not.

What Is Vision?

Vision is the rudder that keeps a ship on course. All decisions return to the basic vision. Vision is very broad and helps people believe they can accomplish their goals while moving toward a better future through their own efforts. Vision also conveys inspiration. Two examples of this are Franklin D. Roosevelt's announcement in May 1940 that he had set a production goal of 50,000 planes a year and John F. Kennedy's challenge to the United States to put a man on the moon and then return him safely to Earth within the decade. At the time, both goals were breathtaking, yet they were achieved. No one can doubt that the dramatic announcements and the infectious inspiration they bred led to the achievement of each goal. A key aspect of these visions—which holds true for most visions—is that they would come to fruition well beyond the tenure of their own leadership time frame. It took over eight years from Kennedy's speech before we landed on the moon, yet he supported his vision because that was the direction he felt we needed to go. A shortcoming of most leadership is preoccupation with the present at the expense of the future. Remember that a vision is about the future and direction of the force, not the accomplishments of command within a few years' time.

As a leader you must constantly anticipate influences, trends, and demands that affect vision over the next month, year, or decade. Effective commanders will direct and then delegate current operations while remaining aware of the details. This ensures time to focus on long-term issues, operations, and unit direction. Leaders with vision see the future without being farsighted and remain rooted in the present without being nearsighted. Tom Peters states in *Thriving on Chaos* that "effective visions prepare for the future. . . . Look to your prior experiences. . . . Look to the future and clarify the vision over time."[1] Vision must be logical, deductive, plausible, simple, and understandable to have realistic value. It must be specific, providing real guidance to people, yet vague enough to encourage initiative and remain relevant to a variety of conditions. Organizations whose leaders have no vision are doomed to follow tradition. They cannot prosper because they keep doing things as they always have. In the words of Prof. Peter Kreeft of Boston College, "To be a leader you have to lead people to a goal worth having—something that's really good and really there. That is vision."[2]

How to Implement the Vision

Senior leadership has the authority and responsibility to change the system as a whole. But leaders at all levels can direct the attention of both superiors and subordinates to tasks more appropriate to the challenges of the new age. Commanders must consider the visions of the Air Force, the wing, and the group as well as their own unit's vision within this context. Commanders must envision where their unit will be when their tenure ends, where they want it to be, and what they see as their legacy after their departure. Personnel of all ranks and occupations have excellent ideas for developing and implementing visions that dovetail into the Air Force's vision. By soliciting suggestions and promoting participation, commanders prepare their organizations for change while disarming those who would resist change. In addition, experience their people gain will prove invaluable as they progress into more responsible, high-level leadership positions and continue the vision. Finally, leaders must communicate their vision to the people in the unit. Leaders are responsible for bolstering their subordinates' courage and understanding. Launching a vision is not a solo effort. Burt Nanus draws a colorful parallel in his article "Visionary Leadership": "If you isolate yourself and hope to present your vision to the organization like Moses descending from Mount Sinai, [then] you are simply asking for skepticism and resistance."[3]

The Downside

Even a clearly articulated and achievable vision may flounder if appropriate resource management and effective leadership do not accompany it. Another possible consequence is that vision can become an obsession and adversely affect the leader's and follower's judgment. Crucial to the vision is not its originality but instead how well it serves mission requirements, unit goals, and parent and subordinate organizations. A frequent mistake that organizations make is embracing long-term planning in place of a conceptual vision. Such an approach results in counterproductivity or "wheel spinning." This does not mean that planning is not important; in fact, the very exercise of forward thinking and application of military planning principles encourages creativity and innovation throughout the organization. The motto of Canada's joint planning staff serves as an appropriate reminder: "Plans are useless; planning is vital."[4]

Maintain the Vision

Leaders must instill a vision that is enduring and invites total organizational commitment. Although a vision may be appropriate at the time of its implementation, eventually it will need amending to maintain currency. There is no regular schedule for modifying a vision. If the current vision is working and consistent with development in the internal and external environments, affirm and support it. However, a wise leader does not wait for the alert before thinking of alternatives. The vision-forming process should be continuous.

The Power of Vision

Dr. Lynn M. List, 2011 Commanders Connection Team

The human brain has the ability to form and translate mental images of the future into reality through leadership and action. Science says that the human mind cannot tell the difference between a vividly imagined event and the real thing.[5] Many great athletes attest to the power of vision. Visualization is an often-taught mental rehearsal technique in sports. There is a well-known research experiment conducted at the University of Chicago involving basketball players.[6] Dr. Judd Blaslotto had basketball players measure their abilities as a baseline and then divided them into three groups. The first group practiced free throws every day for an hour. The second group simply visualized themselves making baskets, and the third group did nothing at all. After 30 days the groups were measured again. The first group improved by 24 percent. The second group improved by an amazing 23 percent. The third group, as expected, showed no improvement. Having a vision triggers our creative powers in our subconscious mind. Once we can see it, we start to believe it is achievable.[7] Once we see ourselves achieving the goal, actually doing it becomes easy because we've already done it once—in our minds. This is the power of vision!

Tips for Success

- Develop a clear vision for your squadron; vision distinguishes leaders from managers.
- Make the vision logical, deductive, plausible, and simple enough to easily remember it.
- Make the vision specific, but leave room for initiative.
- Keep the Air Force, wing, and group visions in mind when developing a vision for your squadron.

- Solicit input from your unit; make the process participative.
- Ensure the vision aligns with mission requirements.
- Articulate the vision often.
- Support the vision with appropriate resources.
- Review the vision periodically, and revise as required.

Notes

1. Tom Peters, *Thriving on Chaos: Handbook for a Management Revolution* (New York: Alfred A. Knopf, 1987), 489.
2. Quoted in Neil H. Snyder and Michelle Graves, "Leadership and Vision," *Business Horizons* 37 (January–February 1994): 1.
3. Bert Nanus, "Visionary Leadership: How to Re-vision the Future," *The Futurist* 26 (September–October 1992): 23.
4. Motto displayed in the Canadian National Defence Headquarters, J-3 Plans Division.
5. Lynn M. List, *Changing Your Life by Changing Your Mind: The Power of Expectation* (Denver, CO: Outskirts Press, 2010), 148.
6. Ibid.
7. Ibid.

Squadron Goals

Dr. Lynn M. List
2011 Commanders Connection Team

> *The reason most people never reach their goals is that they don't define them, learn about them, or even seriously consider them as believable or achievable. Winners can tell you where they are going, what they plan to do along the way, and who will be sharing the adventure with them.*
>
> —Denis Waitley

Many success strategies recommend setting and writing goals, and some recommend converting those goals into affirmations.[1] Keeping some specific guidelines in mind can be helpful in making your goals tangible. A well-developed goal is clear, concise, specific, realistic, measurable, and action oriented. A goal should also be challenging yet achievable. Goals that are easy to achieve fail to motivate improvement; goals too difficult demoralize your Airmen and cause them to give up. A well-written goal should be creative and show action so it is easy to remember and creates a picture that links back to your overall vision. Goals are easily converted into affirmations by writing them in the present tense as if they are occurring now.[2]

Goals help define your unit, give direction and focus, and avoid confusion. Goals can help motivate members by communicating what the unit is striving for and what is valued. Goals also provide a basis of recognizing accomplishments and celebrating successes. Units that set well-defined goals are more effective.

As a squadron commander, you are responsible for setting and achieving unit goals. Involve your unit in the development of these goals as much as possible. You will already have guidance from HHQ and your long-range plan for command. Your goals will naturally be in line with your vision and mission. The following tips will help to get you started.

Tips for Success

- Brainstorm a list of potential goals as a group. True brainstorming means all ideas are initially accepted even if they are far-fetched.
- Choose from the brainstorming list those in line with your mission and vision. Be sure your goals are integrated with HHQ goals and either directly or indirectly support wing and MAJCOM goals.
- Prioritize.
- Write goals down and create objectives. Use plain and concise yet creative language.
- Create S.M.A.R.T. goals.[3]
    - **S**pecific—To set a specific goal, you must answer the six "W" questions (who, what, where, when, which, why).
    - **M**easurable—Establish concrete criteria for measuring progress toward the achievement of each goal.
    - **A**ttainable—Ensure the goal is feasible.
    - **R**ealistic—Evaluate whether the team is both *willing* and *able* to strive toward a goal.
    - **T**imely—Develop a timeline for goal accomplishment.
- Determine assessment—establish metrics and an appropriate system to track your progress.
- Communicate your goals effectively—display your goals in areas where your Airmen will see them daily. Reinforce your goals and relay progress toward achieving them at staff meetings, daily roll calls, and commander's calls.
- Follow through by regularly reviewing, evaluating, and revising.
- Celebrate and reward success!

Notes

1. Lynn M. List, *Changing Your Life by Changing Your Mind: The Power of Expectation* (Denver, CO: Outskirts Press, 2010), 53.
2. Ibid.
3. Top Achievement, online self-improvement and personal development community, http://www.topachievement.com/smart.html.

Your First Commander's Call

Original Author: Maj Dan Sheesley
43rd Comptroller Squadron Commander

Now that your change of command is behind you, it's time to get to work. Plan a commander's call as soon as is practical. This first commander's call is critical in establishing your relationship with your squadron. Everyone in your new command is curious about you. Your first commander's call sets the stage for your command tour. Get it wrong or wait too long to bring your unit together, and you may play catch-up for the next two years. Every action you take, or do not take, as a commander communicates a message to your squadron. Use this commander's call to your advantage to communicate—early, clearly, and directly—the plan for your command.

When Do You Have Your First Commander's Call?

While some commanders prefer to hold their first commander's call within a day or two of the change of command, some prefer to wait a week or so to meet everyone and complete an initial assessment of the unit. Whichever you choose, do not delay longer than two weeks—waiting too long inadvertently sends the message that you are not interested in communicating with your Airmen. Additionally, a long delay puts you behind the power curve in implementing your policies and emphasizing your approach to maintaining standards and administering discipline. This first commander's call is your most pivotal opportunity to prevent problems before they happen. Do not delay it!

What Do You Say at Your First Commander's Call?

Your first commander's call is where you deliver the message you didn't have time to say at your change of command. This is not the time for a massive information update or touchy-feely award presentations; those things are more suited for a routine commander's call. Your tone, whether it is directive or informative, depends on your leadership style and the state of the unit you have inherited. If, prior to the change of command, your unit had leadership issues or suffered from high-visibility *UCMJ* violations, you may choose a very directive tone to set the stage. If this is not the case, a more informative or casual approach may be adequate. Along with choosing an approach, it is critical for you to tell your squadron who you are, what you believe in, and what they can expect from you during your command. Be clear so there is no confusion as to your policies and approach. Your Airmen have the right to know what you expect from them and how to work successfully under your command. If you need to have more than one commander's call due to unit size or duty schedules, ensure you say the same thing at each presentation. Consistency eliminates confusion and builds trust.

Be Prepared

Plan what you are going to say and how you are going to say it well in advance. Develop your ideas before your change of command, and check with your operations officer, superintendent, and first sergeant to refine your ideas. These key leaders can help you determine what to emphasize in your presentation and how to deliver your message. Finally, even if you are a great public speaker, you should practice your delivery. Remember, during this first, critical presentation, all eyes are on you—there is no room to "wing it."

Tips for Success

- Hold your first commander's call within the first two weeks of your command.
- Introduce yourself—who you are, what you believe, what you expect, and what you will (or won't) tolerate.
- Be consistent.
- Be prepared.

Assessing Your Squadron's Strengths and Weaknesses

Original Author: Maj Shannon Smith
14th SFS Commander

One of the more difficult tasks new commanders face is accurately assessing the health of their squadrons. Since command tours are normally only two years, it's important to make accurate assessments in a timely manner so that goals can be established and problems fixed as quickly as possible. It is critical that new commanders make correct assessments of their unit strengths and weaknesses, or they could spend the bulk of their command tour "fixing" the wrong problems.

Be Objective

Commanders must be objective when making their initial unit assessments. Regardless of how strong (or weak) the unit's reputation is, don't jump to conclusions. Most commanders probably prefer inheriting "poor" units with much room to improve over units that are "outstanding." After all, commanders who resurrect broken units tend to get more credit than commanders who make already outstanding units more outstanding. However, commanders who hastily judge a unit as substandard risk alienating their Airmen by labeling their past efforts as inadequate, without proper justification or evidence. This could cause motivational problems.

While underestimating the unit's strength is a concern, overstating the unit's greatness in the first few weeks is also problematic. While commanders should set a positive tone early in their command, they must be wary of sharing glowing assessments—such as "You folks are great; keep up the good work, and I'll try to not get in your way!"—in an attempt to curry favor with the unit. If a positive assessment is overstated, two concerns arise. First, commanders lose credibility with their unit's top performers. The best and brightest are looking for commanders to support them with fixing problems, not to tell them everything is great. Secondly, commanders who inaccurately deem their squadrons to be in great shape at first glance may have a tough time motivating their Airmen to fix problems if time reveals major deficiencies. Airmen will wonder why they are being pressured to fix things never perceived as broken.

Meet the Staff and Ask Pointed Questions

One way to quickly assess the organization is to talk to the members of your leadership team. Within the first two weeks of command, meet with all the key leaders in the squadron (deputy, operations officer, flight commanders, superintendents, and the first sergeant) to solicit their input on the organization. Ask them pointed questions about the organization:

- What do you see as our organization's strength?
- What are our organization's weaknesses?
- What ideas do you have for immediate improvements in the squadron?
- What do you see as realistic long-term improvements we can effect in our squadron?

The responses to these questions will provide the new commander with a good sight-picture of the organization's strengths and weaknesses to complete an accurate assessment.

The Bottom Line

Commanders must use caution when judging or assigning merit to individuals, sections, or an entire unit within the first few weeks of taking command. While it is important to be complimentary if the squadron has made a good first impression, commanders should save more substantial assessments until they make an educated evaluation based on quantitative facts and subjective opinions from key leaders after a few weeks in command.

Tips for Success

- Begin your unit assessment by reviewing squadron metrics and performance data.
  - Mission-oriented metrics.
  - Self-inspection results.
  - Unit compliance inspections and operational readiness reports.
  - Customer feedback and survey results.
  - Disciplinary action history.
  - Training status such as career development courses (CDC).
  - Ancillary training completion reports.
  - Unit fitness status.
  - Equipment status.
  - SORTS and ART reports.
  - Most recent climate assessment.
  - Recent unit and individual awards.
- Schedule one-on-one meetings with key personnel (operations officer, flight chiefs, etc.) to get their take on the unit's condition.
- Take your predecessor's opinion with a grain of salt—the pride of ownership can lead to a skewed assessment.
- Review the facts as much as possible before sharing a big-picture assessment.
- Avoid making overly general positive or negative statements regarding the unit during the initial days in command.
- Don't make any major changes during the first couple weeks of command unless absolutely necessary.

Additional Resource

- *The Goal: A Process of Ongoing Improvement* by Eliyahu Goldratt and Jeff Cox.

Making a Difference: Leaving a Legacy

Original Author: Lt Col Jim Grant, 60th Supply Squadron/ 60th Logistics Readiness Squadron Commander

What you leave behind is not what is engraved in stone monuments, but what is woven into the lives of others.

—Pericles

There are different ways to approach a command tour. Some view it as an opportunity to finally use their leadership skills—to be in charge, create and pursue a vision, and motivate others toward a common mission. Others may see it as a chance to interact closely with a wide group of people or as long hours and many decisions. All of these are true, but there is another way to view command: as an opportunity to make a difference. When the difference you make in the mission or in people's lives has a lasting effect, it is sometimes referred to as a legacy. The legacies with the most impact occur when the focus is not on you but on your people and the mission instead. As a commander, if your attention is centered on what legacy you will leave, you've missed the point. But if you focus on improving mission effectiveness and developing your Airmen, you're on your way to making a difference and leaving a positive legacy.

What is meant by "leaving a legacy"? A legacy is more than the projects you accomplished or the awards the squadron won. Legacies, both tangible and intangible, are the lasting impact you have on the organization and especially the people. On the tangible side, you will have the opportunity to affect changes in procedures in your organization that could continue long after you depart. For example, improving efficiency by consolidating processes or reorganizing functions could be one example of a tangible legacy. However, remember that change for change's sake is a legacy no one wants to leave.

The other form of legacy is the intangible side. This involves the lasting impact you have on the people in your squadron. In this respect, your legacy "can be seen in the thoughts and actions of the people who have worked with or for you long after your professional affiliation has ended."[1] We can also define this type of legacy as "the sum total of the difference you make in people's lives, directly and indirectly, formally and informally."[2] In other words, when you turn over command to the next person, what attitudes or ways of thinking have you instilled into the squadron that will continue after you are gone? The fact that your unit earned an outstanding on an inspection is not a legacy; a legacy is the commitment to excellence and attention to detail you developed in the squadron that resulted in the outstanding rating. The inspection results are a one-time occurrence; the qualities that produced it will live on in the people who made it possible. That's a legacy.

Every leader leaves a legacy.[3] However, leaving a positive legacy doesn't happen automatically; it requires focus. Before taking command, think about the impact you want to have on your squadron and especially its members—not for you, but for them. What qualities do you want them to carry on after you depart? Do you want to instill in them a commitment to excellence, integrity, and safety; a pride in the unit; a teamwork atmosphere? Do you want them to recognize the importance of training, attention to detail, and thoroughness, as well as taking care of each other and oneself? The legacy you leave will be the way the organization functions after you're gone. "The challenge is how to live in a way that creates a legacy others want to be a part of, too. . . . A legacy is built moment by moment in small interactions. How you live your legacy can uplift people's spirits and inspire them to live or perform better than they thought possible."[4] Begin thinking now about the impact your leadership style will have on your squadron and what type of legacy will ensue. You will be able to watch it unfold over your command tour.

Tips for Success

- Go slow with regards to changing processes—make sure you fully understand current procedures before making any changes.
- Concentrate on three or four specific qualities you want to instill in the individuals in your squadron.
    - o How will you instill these qualities in your unit members?
    - o What will you emphasize?
- Assess early what actions you should stop, start, continue, or avoid to produce the legacy you want to create.[5]
- "Dare to be a person, not a position" (be honest, take responsibility, and keep your ego in check).[6]
- "Dare to connect with people" (talk one-on-one, and listen intently).[7]
- "Dare to drive the dream" (stay committed to a dream, be optimistic, and have fun).[8]

Notes

1. Robert M. Galford and Regina F. Maruca, *Your Leadership Legacy: Why Looking toward the Future Will Make You a Better Leader Today* (Boston: Harvard Business School Press, 2006), 14.
2. Marta Brooks, Julie Stark, and Sarah Caverhill, *Your Leadership Legacy: The Difference You Make in People's Lives* (San Francisco: Berrett-Koehler Publishers, Inc., 2004), xi.
3. Galford and Maruca, *Your Leadership Legacy*, 3.
4. Ibid., 14.
5. Ibid., 121.

6. Brooks, Stark, and Caverhill, *Your Leadership Legacy*, 76–77.
7. Ibid., 76.
8. Ibid., 77.

Commander's Transition Checklist

Compiled by the Faculty of Air Command and Staff College

The following list of items will assist you, as a new commander, in making a smooth transition into your squadron. Some areas can be addressed prior to taking command, whereas others must wait until after the change-of-command ceremony. Since this list is extensive and all items are important, you will need to prioritize them to use your time wisely.

Plans, Policies, Programs, and Budgets

- What is the squadron's mission?
- What is the squadron's mission statement? Vision statement?
- What is *your* vision for the squadron? Does it match the current vision statement?
- What are the squadron's goals (short and long term)?
- What are the squadron's priorities?
- In what plans (MAJCOM, wing, and group) does the squadron currently play a role?
- What policy letters does the squadron have? Are they still current? Do they match your policies? What changes are necessary? What policies do you need to implement?
- What is your command philosophy? When and how do you plan to articulate it to the squadron?
- What are your zero-tolerance areas?
- What programs is your squadron responsible for within the group or wing?
- Who manages the following programs, and how effective are they: security, safety, environmental, fitness, GTC, training and rotation, readiness and deployment, self-inspection?
- Discuss budget with your RA. What is his or her experience level?
    - o Current budget status and spend plan?

- o Unfunded requirements?
- o Furniture, facility, and computer upgrade plans?
- o Who are the GPC holders? When was the last GPC staff assistance visit (SAV); what were the results?
- o End-of-year plan? Do you have your requirements ready for end-of-year fallout funds?
- o What contracts does the squadron use? Are they funded?
- o What are the projected TDY and training requirements?
- o Is the budget centrally managed by the RA, or do the flights have their own budgets?

Facilities, Grounds, and Equipment

- What organizations are in the same building? What's the relationship and interaction? Any shared space?
- Who is the building custodian?
- How are janitorial services accomplished? How often?
- Computers? How many computers does the squadron own? Who has them, and when do they need to be upgraded? Who are the ADPE custodians? Are they trained and effective?
- Who are the equipment custodians? Are they trained and effective?
- Who is the work group manager?
- Who obtains supplies and equipment for the squadron? How?
- Any logistics problems? Supply shortages?
- Walk through all squadron facilities. What is their condition? What improvements need to be made? Review projects currently in work and outstanding work orders.
- Physically view all major equipment items. What is the condition? How is the equipment maintained? How is the maintenance funded?
- Is all equipment properly accounted for by the equipment custodians?
- Does everyone have the equipment and tools needed to do the job? If not, why not?
- Who accomplishes landscaping, mowing, sweeping, snow removal, and so forth? How often?

- How many vehicles does the squadron own versus the number authorized? What is their condition? Are they adequate to meet mission requirements? Who is the vehicle control officer? Is he or she trained and effective?

Organization

- What are the size and structure of the squadron?
- What is the relationship to the group, wing, and base?
- Are you responsible for supporting or leading any geographically separated units (GSU)?
- Review the UMD. Numbers authorized? Assigned? Inbound? Outbound? Attached? On loan? Assigned for flying?
- What flights and sections make up the squadron?
- Do you have training and readiness flights?
- Who are members of the commander's support staff? Do they understand their functions?

Leadership

- Who is the boss? What type of communication does he or she prefer? Expectations? Recurring suspenses? Pet peeves?
- What is his or her leadership and management style?
- Staff meetings? When? Who attends? Format? Deliverables?
- How often do the bosses visit?
- Does the squadron or group have any mentorship programs? What levels? Who leads them? What is your role?
- Does the first sergeant understand his or her role and responsibility? Who is the backup first sergeant? Are they trained?
- Do you have a section commander? Are his or her role and responsibilities clearly understood?
- What is the relationship among the members of the squadron leadership team? Between the commander and the leadership team?
- Who is the dorm manager? How often do you plan to visit the dorm? What projects are in work for the dorm?
- Who leads the Top 3? How often do they meet? What are their plans and objectives?

- Is there an Airmen's council? Who leads it?
- When do you plan to meet with your leadership team to discuss your vision and expectations?

Personnel

- Who are the key personnel in the squadron? What are their strengths and weaknesses?
- Of the key personnel, who has an assignment action in work? Who is on the vulnerable to move list (VML)?
- What are the assignment preferences of your key personnel?
- When are the next promotion boards? When will the next promotion results be released? What is the squadron procedure for notifying and recognizing promotees?
- Review the additional duty roster. Who maintains it?
- Are there any disciplinary actions pending resolution?
- Are there currently any IG or military equal opportunity (MEO) issues in work? Any past complaints?
- Are there any health problems in the squadron? Anyone on profile? Are there any issues with alcoholism or drug abuse?
- When was the last driving under the influence (DUI) incident in the squadron? What is the squadron's plan for reducing DUIs?
- What are the demographics of the squadron?
    - Officer, enlisted, civilian, and contractors.
    - Education levels, PME completed, skill levels.
    - Manpower data system (MDS) history.
    - Flight qualification and flying hours.
    - Duty history (overseas, staff, joint, short, career broadening).
    - Deployment history.
    - Race.
    - Religion.
    - Marital status, number of dependents, and single parents.
    - Who lives on base (dorms or family housing)? Off base?

  - o Newlyweds or recently divorced.
  - o Married couples working in the squadron.
  - o Non-US citizens.
- Are there Guard or Reserve personnel assigned to or working in the squadron?
- Review personnel information files (PIF), unfavorable information files (UIF), and control rosters.
- Who manages the fitness program? What is the schedule for group fitness activities? When is the next fitness assessment? What were the results of the last assessment? Who is in the fitness improvement program?
- What is the squadron leave policy (radius, sign-out log, safety briefs, holiday time off, etc.)?
- Who monitors use-or-lose leave status? Have leaves been projected for the rest of the year?
- Who monitors the GTC? Is the use policy clear to all members?
- Is there anyone with low income, high debt, or pay advance concerns?
- Does the squadron have personnel involved with the base honor guard?
- Does anyone perform off-duty employment? Has it been properly approved and documented?

Communications

- When do you plan to meet informally with individual squadron groups (officers, SNCOs, NCOs, Airmen, civilians) to obtain their thoughts about the squadron?
- When do you plan to meet with the squadron union representative?
- When is your first commander's call? How often do you plan to conduct commander's calls? Plan to schedule one soon after the change of command to clearly present your vision for the squadron, command philosophy, and expectations.
- Does the squadron have a newsletter? Read file? Who is responsible for these?
- Is e-mail used extensively? How effectively does it distribute information?
- Which base organizations and individuals should you briefly visit (e.g., other squadron commanders in your group, legal, ADC, OSI, IG, MEO,

CPO, CES, financial management [FM], CS, ARC, A&FRC, chaplain, services [SVS], FSS, medical)?

OPRs, EPRs, Awards, PRFs, Decorations, Feedback, and Civilian Appraisals

- Who reports directly to you? Why? Why not others?
- When is their next feedback due? Is it on your calendar?
- How well is feedback conducted in the squadron? How is it tracked? By whom? How is feedback conducted for civilians?
- Who tracks officer performance reports (OPR) and EPRs? How are they tracked? Any currently late? Who reviews them for quality? Is the status reviewed at the group or wing level?
- What are the current group or wing policies regarding senior rater endorsements?
- What is the procedure for promotion recommendation forms (PRF)?
- How are your officers and SNCOs currently stratified?
- Does the squadron have an active awards program? Who were the last wing winners? Who manages the program for the squadron? What functional awards do squadron members compete for? When are the next awards packages due? How are squadron winners recognized?
- Does the squadron have in-house awards or special recognition programs (e.g., sharp troop, star performer, and commander's coins)?
- What are the wing, group, or squadron policies on end-of-tour decorations? Does the wing publish a decorations guide?
- When are civilian appraisals due? Who has the lead for managing these? What are the wing policies and procedures? Are supervisors fully aware of their responsibilities?

Morale and Family Issues

- Who is currently deployed or preparing to deploy? Do those individuals have family members in the local area? How does the squadron support them?
- Does the squadron have a booster club? Who leads it? How often does it meet? What are its plans and objectives?
- What social gatherings does the squadron conduct?

- Does the squadron celebrate birthdays, babies, or weddings?
- Do the officers occasionally meet informally, such as at the officers' club on Fridays?
- Does the squadron have an active spouses' group? Who leads it? How often does it meet? What are its plans and objectives? Does the base have a key spouse program? Does the squadron participate?
- When was the last climate assessment conducted? What were the results?
- Any organizational or personnel skeletons in the closet?
- How effective is the squadron INTRO program? Do welcome packages contain a letter from the squadron commander? If so, you will need to sign a new letter.
- How does the squadron recognize incoming and outgoing personnel?
- How does the squadron raise funds? Who leads the effort? Has it been successful? How much money is currently on hand? How is it managed? Are proper guidelines followed?
- How are families involved in the squadron? How often?
- What are the emergency leave procedures and policies?
- Are family care plans up to date?
- Is next-of-kin notification information up to date for squadron members?
- Who is the squadron chaplain? How often does he or she participate in squadron events?
- Are there currently any family medical issues in the squadron? Do any families have special needs? Is anyone assigned for humanitarian reasons?
- Who is the squadron PA officer? Are hometown news releases and letters to parents regarding special events (e.g., reenlistments, promotions) accomplished?
- Who is the sports representative for the squadron?
- What intramural teams does the squadron have? When is the next game?

Readiness

- What operation plans (OPLAN) does the squadron support? What are the responsibilities of the squadron?
- What requirements are found in the designed operational capability (DOC) statement? Is it current? Have you reviewed it and signed it?

- Who prepares the SORTS and ART reports for the squadron? Review the most recent reports. Does the group commander require a monthly briefing on these reports before submission?
- What are the squadron responsibilities according to the installation deployment plan?
- Who is the squadron unit deployment manager (UDM)? Is he or she trained and effective?
- How does the UDM select personnel for deployments?
- What AEFs are squadron members assigned to?
- Are squadron personnel ready for deployments? What are the requirements (wills, immunizations, training, family care plans, etc.)? How is personnel readiness tracked? Is readiness tracked at a level above the squadron?
- Where is the squadron unit control center (UCC)? Who manages it? Is he or she effective? Is the UCC the focal point for receiving and disseminating critical information during exercises and contingencies? If not, how is information disseminated?
- Obtain a squadron recall roster. Who ensures the recall roster is current? How effective was the last recall?
- What is the wing exercise schedule?
- Who are the squadron EET representatives? Are they trained and effective?
- What squadron personnel are assigned to the resource augmentation duty (READY) program? Does the squadron receive any READY augmentees?
- Who are the squadron disaster control group members?

Operations and Flying

- Who handles scheduling? What are the procedures? How are personnel notified?
- What are the alert procedures?
- What are the training and currency requirements for the squadron? Are there any MAJCOM or wing-directed training requirements? Are you current on the aircraft in this squadron?
- Review other training requirements (life support, chemical warfare defense equipment, etc.).
- When are training meetings held? Who conducts them?

- Who conducts the operations meetings? What is the schedule?
- How is mission planning conducted and by whom?
- What is the upgrade policy for the squadron?
- How did you deal with delays? Maintenance group versus operations group issues? What are the procedures for assigning delay codes? Who briefs delays and in what forum?
- Review aircraft commander trip and mission reports. Look for issues.
- Meet with functionals to discuss your standardization and evaluation policy.
- Meet with the chief of the Air Force operations resource management system (AFORMS) to discuss any aircrew and mission flight documentation issues.

Standards

- Regarding the following inspections, when were the last ones conducted, what were the results, and when is the next one scheduled?
  - o MAJCOM inspections (e.g., operational readiness inspection [ORI], unit compliance inspection [UCI], national security information).
  - o Wing safety inspection.
  - o Wing security inspection.
  - o Wing Environmental Compliance Assessment and Management Program (ECAMP) inspection.
  - o Wing records inspection.
  - o Squadron self-inspection.
  - o Who is the safety representative for the squadron? Is he or she trained and effective? How does he or she ensure personnel follow safety requirements?

Heritage

- What is the history of the squadron? How are squadron personnel made aware of their history?
- Does the squadron have a mascot or a cheer?
- What are the squadron's recent major accomplishments?

Questions for the Outgoing Commander

- What initiatives did you try that worked well? Not so well?
- What initiatives are still in work?
- What initiatives were you not able to start?
- What does the boss like or dislike?
- What disciplinary actions are still in work?
- What was your schedule like?
- How and when did you schedule your priorities?
- What meetings did you attend?
- What are the toughest problems and issues I should expect to face during the first few months?
- Which areas do you recommend I focus on initially?
- Who are the key informal leaders in the squadron?
- Who are your "go to" people (inside and outside the squadron)?

Chapter 2

Leading and Developing Airmen

A basic yet essential responsibility of command is leading people. Today's environment requires commanders who know the difference between leading and managing and when and how to use both. Today's commanders must merge the art and science of leadership to guide people in times of change. But commanders must do more than just lead; they must develop the individuals entrusted to them, thus ensuring capable forces to perform the mission. To help with the task, this chapter includes subjects such as professional development, promotions, evaluations, mentoring, leadership, and feedback. Developing officer, enlisted, and civilian personnel is a critical commander responsibility and a privilege of command.

Leading versus Managing

Original Author: Maj Terri Sheppard
Cadet Squadron 17 Commander

Additional Contributions: Dr. Lynn M. List
2011 Commanders Connection Team

> *If you pick the right people and give them the opportunity to spread their wings—and put compensation as a carrier behind it—you almost don't have to manage them.*
>
> —Jack Welch

Leading and managing are significantly different, and effective command requires both. Leading is a delicate art that requires people-oriented attributes to inspire and motivate others toward a common mission, while managing is a science that calls for controlling and directing resources. Even though leadership can be elusive and difficult to develop, you can learn and foster these attributes by study, application, and determination. You, as the commander, can give your subordinates orders, and they will follow out of obedience—obedience based on command authority. However, leadership strives for inspiration and motivation.

Professor and leadership researcher Warren Bennis observes that "management is getting people to do what needs to be done, while leadership is getting people to want to do what needs to be done."[1] Field Marshal Sir William Slim, British Fourteenth Army leader during the reconquest of Burma during World War II, describes leadership as "of the spirit, compounded of personality and vision" and management as "of the mind, more a matter of accurate calculation, statistics, methods, timetables, and routines."[2] To command successfully, you must lead and manage. You must administer, maintain, and control as well as motivate, develop, and inspire as you steer your organization toward desired goals.

Lead by Example

You are probably familiar with the old adage "practice what you preach." It is never truer than when you are a commander because everyone is watching you. Consistency and integrity are the foundation of your credibility. Integrity is doing the right thing when no one is looking. As an officer and a commander, integrity is your most precious and powerful tool. If you strive to do the right thing, it does not matter if someone is watching. Your actions speak louder than words. The best way to lead by example is to be you and never try to be someone else. Your experiences, personality, and perspective make you unique. Be yourself, but be your best self possible.

Accountability is a key aspect of leading by example. It includes doing what is right—even if it is not popular or politically correct—and begins with setting standards and holding yourself responsible. You must take responsibility for your actions as well as those of your subordinates. Gen Robert E. Lee provided an example of this attribute after the failure of Gen George Pickett's charge at Gettysburg when he said, "All this has been my fault. It is I who have lost this fight, and you must help me out of it the best way you can."[3] Accountability often requires courage, but it is essential for effective leadership.

Tips for Success

- Maintain these key attributes as you command:
  - Positive attitude—your subordinates will reflect your enthusiasm.
  - Devotion—your desire to lead and achieve a mission.
  - Encouragement—motivate, inspire, and touch the hearts and minds of your subordinates.
  - Trust—give trust and be worthy of trust; make tough decisions when needed.
  - Integrity—always do the right thing.
  - Honesty—builds trust and respect.
  - Competence—know your job, and be confident enough to ask when you don't know.
  - Character—it is what you are in the dark.

  - o Compassion—show empathy for your people.
  - o Courage—both physical and moral.
  - o Sense of humor—be willing to laugh at yourself, but avoid sarcasm.
  - o Credibility—walk the talk.
- Lead and manage to maximize your squadron's success.
- Always do the right thing—everyone is watching the commander.

Additional Resources

- *The Leadership Challenge* by James M. Kouzes and Barry Z. Posner is a useful study of leadership with many examples.
- *My American Journey* by Colin Powell, with Joseph Persico, is a great read about Powell's experiences in the Army and as chairman of the Joint Chiefs of Staff (CJCS).
- *Taking Charge: A Practical Guide for Leaders* by Perry M. Smith offers insights and ideas (particularly see chap. 1 on 20 fundamentals to remember).
- *American Generalship: Character Is Everything: The Art of Command* by Edgar F. Puryear Jr. offers views about the essence of leadership based on hundreds of interviews with general officers.
- *Lincoln on Leadership: Executive Strategies for Tough Times* by Donald T. Phillips provides enduring ideas of how to motivate people and get results. It is an easy read with lots of nuggets.

Notes

1. Warren G. Bennis, *An Invented Life: Reflections on Leadership and Change* (Reading, MA: Addison-Wesley Publishing Co., 1993), 104.
2. Ibid., 89.
3. Robert L. Taylor and William E. Rosenbach, eds., *Military Leadership: In Pursuit of Excellence* (Boulder, CO: Westview Press, 1984), 45.

Leading by Walking Around

Original Author: Maj Shannon Smith
14th SFS Commander

> *People do not care how much you know until they know how much you care.*
>
> —John C. Maxwell

Technology has become an intricate part of every business and military office. People sit next to each other in a cubicle but still send an e-mail instead of speaking directly to one another. In this highly technological age, the idea of leading by walking around has an even greater meaning. Over 30 years ago, the idea of "leading by wandering around" began as an idea introduced by Hewlett-Packard. This concept was made popular in the book *In Search of Excellence* by Tom Peters and Robert Waterman Jr. Their research showed that the most successful companies' leaders stayed personally close to the people doing the work; they learned how to make the organization better from them.[1] In this technologically savvy world, the act of leaders getting out and connecting with their people is more important than ever. In fact, for commanders, this is the art of leadership by walking around.

Leadership by walking around is a simple enough concept—it embodies commanders engaging their people in their work settings. This simple concept gives people a sense of value and belonging and shows that a commander personally cares about the people. It is tough for leaders to cultivate the right environment for mission success when they refuse to leave their offices. Highly effective commanders make an effort to go out and see their Airmen on the job as much as possible. They ask questions about families and educational pursuits and solicit suggestions for improvement at all levels of unit operations. These visits are tremendous morale boosters. Done correctly, they are usually a great deal of fun, serving to break up the litany of never-ending paperwork. Additionally, visits to work centers keep people on their toes. Even the most unmotivated Airman will work a little harder if he or she thinks the boss could drop by without notice. Coordinate visits with your superintendent or first sergeant when possible. It is good for Airmen to see key squadron leadership on the same page and that intermediate supervisors welcome the commander's visit. Ensure that your visits are not viewed as spying trips or an attempt to micromanage.

Tips for Success

- Determine how you can help improve work efficiency. Solicit input, and ask for feedback. Encourage ownership by empowering your Airmen to fix the problems they identify.
- Take the opportunity to hand out "attaboys" and commendations.
- Think safety! Are your work centers neat and organized? Are they safe?
- Think communication. Is your internal information program working (professional and up-to-date bulletin boards, current photos, etc.)?
- Think professionalism. Do your Airmen present a professional appearance?
- Think personal. Do any of your Airmen have children with medical issues? Is there an easy way to know if someone has a birthday? Who is enrolled in school?
- Lead! It is easy to be viewed as a micromanager if your visits are all about work improvement. Use the opportunity to show your subordinates that you care about what they do and who they are!

Note

1. Tom J. Peters and Robert H. Waterman Jr., *In Search of Excellence* (New York: Harper and Row, 1983), 159–99.

Leading in the Midst of Change

2011 Commanders Connection Team

> *There is nothing more difficult to take in hand, more perilous to conduct, or more uncertain in its success, than to take the lead in the introduction of a new order of things.*
>
> —Niccolo Machiavelli
> *The Prince* (1532)

A sluggish economy, a new direction for political leadership, future guidelines for health reform, changes in policies, reduction in forces, and "doing more with less" make it clear that a key part of leadership is leading through change. A more accurate description may be finding solutions in the midst of constant change. Our Air Force continues to adjust based on a revolving door of change. Increased funding constraints and a constantly fluctuating world situation will strain your squadron. Demands on military units remain high. Your mission may adjust, adapt, or outright change daily. Managing this change effectively is a critical leadership skill. The mad rush to improve performance and pursue excellence has multiplied the demands on you and your squadron. We can count on mission increases even though resources will remain the same or decrease. Weapon systems have grown more technically sophisticated, organizational structures have become leaner and flatter, and multinational forces embrace diverse cultures and values. Therein lies the challenge—how does a leader effectively manage this continual change?

Your primary task when leading through change is prioritization. You must determine the most important tasks that need to be accomplished. You are responsible to set priorities. Are the things your squadron is doing in line with your vision? Your second task is to make job components and processes easier. You need to decide if a process or a document is absolutely necessary. Are you requiring data or reports that are not used or useful? Is there an easier method to obtain the information you need? Are you requiring extra work just because "that's the way it has always been done"? Are you running interference to protect your troops when possible? Are there processes in place that made sense in a nontechnical world but are cumbersome and time-consuming with a technologically well-versed organization? Streamline processes when possible. Facilitate your own changes to make things better.

Another challenge in guiding and leading high-pressure change is to maintain morale and motivation despite the constant pressure to do more with less. First, accept and embrace change as reality. Second, comprehend the increasing rate of change, and embrace it through a responsive and flexible vision. You must be proactive and innovative to bring new ideas, methods, and solutions to challenges your squadron will face. Innovation means change, and effective change requires leadership.

As the chief transformation officer within your squadron, your attitude is paramount. You must understand, facilitate, and envision change, including the inevitable emotions, uncertainty, chaos, and fear that accompany all change. You must turn insecurity and fear into hope through realistic optimism. Putting new processes in place is the easy step. Motivating people to accept and support the new values and beliefs demanded by change is more difficult.

Tips for Success

Original Author: Maj Terri Sheppard, Cadet Squadron 17 Commander

- Prioritize workload and streamline processes.
- Communicate—fully explain the reasons for change to all members of the unit, control rumors, and keep channels open.

- Be positive—your attitude and presentation matter; offer and encourage opportunities for new ideas, creativity, and innovation.
- Involve your people in the process—assign change-related tasks and roles to help them understand what the future holds.
- Facilitate change—you cannot force, but can guide, positive change.
- Be open-minded—let go of old ideas, and experiment with alternative concepts.
- Seek and accept feedback.
- Think about how you can alter the situation instead of simply matching your actions to situational needs and personal limitations of subordinates.
- Never become complacent—think ahead, and change before circumstances force change.
- Never lose your temper unless it is your intention.

Additional Resources

- *Who Moved My Cheese?* by Spencer Johnson, MD, is a humorous but hard-hitting book about dealing with change and is less than 100 pages.
- *Organizational Culture and Leadership* by Edgar H. Schein is a helpful source for understanding the relationship among organizational culture, change, and leadership.

Leadership and the Self-Fulfilling Prophecy

2011 Commanders Connection Team

High achievement always takes place in the framework of high expectation.

—Jack Kinder

The self-fulfilling prophecy has been referred to as the Pygmalion effect. This comes from the story of Pygmalion, an ancient king in Greek mythology. He carved a statue in the shape of what he considered his ideal woman, whom he called Galatea. His sculpture was so perfect that he could not help himself—he fell hopelessly in love with her. His love was so strong that his will, and the intervention from the Greek goddess Aphrodite, brought the statue to life. The concept of a leader's expectations affecting the outcome of a subordinate's performance became associated with the mythology of Pygmalion.[1]

The implication of the self-fulfilling prophecy for commanders is important. Commanders must realize that even subtle nuances at all levels can convey either a positive or a negative self-fulfilling prophecy. Commanders who convey positive expectations over time transform their Airmen into individuals who are intrinsically motivated to succeed, much like the statue of Galatea was transformed into a living being. The phenomenon is often so subtle as to appear almost magical. This is the *art* of leadership.

Robert Merton first coined the phrase "self-fulfilling prophecy" in 1948 in a 17-page essay. In 1968 Merton told a story of the Last National Bank and the events that led to its failure during the Great Depression.[2] Business was unusually brisk one morning, and people viewed this suspiciously as a run on the bank, so they withdrew their money, fearing disaster. The bank had a prosperous era until a rumor began to circulate that it was about to collapse. Although the bank was viable, hundreds of people withdrew their money, which led to its closure. The expectation of a disaster, although not originally true, created the disaster. It was the expectation, or prophecy, that produced the failure of the bank. Stock market crashes begin in much the same way. Higher-than-usual selling on a particular stock raises suspicion that causes other holders to sell; the expectation that a crash is coming results in a crash.

In one experiment from business, the impact of a leader's expectations on followers' performance was examined.[3] The supervisors of the employees were told erroneously that certain employees would show marked improvement. Fourteen new trainee employees were picked at random and designated as high-aptitude personnel (HAP).[4] The leaders were told that the HAPs would show training and development improvements during the training period. The results showed that not only did the HAPs perform at a higher level but that they also took less time to learn and were viewed more positively by their peers. The leaders/trainers truly believed that they treated all the employees the same way.

Bottom Line

There are thousands of similar experiments. Self-fulfilling prophecy in leadership has been studied in a wide variety of global and social concerns from economic issues to medicine and politics. Studies show that the self-fulfilling prophecy can be positive or negative, but not neutral. The key conclusions of the studies indicate: (1) what leaders expect from subordinates and how they treat them largely determines performance; (2) good leaders can create high performance expectations that followers will fulfill; (3) poor leaders do not develop these expectations; and (4) followers appear to accomplish what they believe they are expected to accomplish. What do you expect from your Airmen? What you expect is what you will get!

Tips for Success

- Expect the best of your Airmen.
- Treat your Airmen kindly and respectfully even when administering discipline.
- Challenge your Airmen by setting goals slightly above their known ability.
- Keep a positive attitude—even subtle gestures or glances can display a negative expectation.
- Communicate your expectations clearly and positively—your Airmen will do what they believe you expect them to do.
- Give feedback and follow up, but trust your Airmen to exceed your expectations.
- Encourage your Airmen by voicing your confidence in them—motivate, inspire, and push your Airmen.
- Reward success.

Notes

1. P. Jordan (producer) and Ron Underwood (director). *Productivity and the Self-Fulfilling Prophecy: The Pygmalion Effect* (Del Mar, CA: CRM/McGraw-Hill Training Systems, 1987), video.
2. Ibid.
3. Ibid.
4. J. Sterling Livingston, "Pygmalion in Management," *Harvard Business Review* 81, no. 1 (January 2003): 97–106.

Enlisted Specialty Training

Original Author: Maj Terri Sheppard
Cadet Squadron 17 Commander

Reference

AFI 36-2201, *Air Force Training Program*, 15 September 2010 (incorporating change 1, 8 March 2011).

The majority of the following information is excerpted directly from the above reference.

Though we may be learned by another's knowledge, we can never be wise but by our own experience.

—Montaigne

As a commander, you must ensure all personnel receive the required training to accomplish their mission. For enlisted training, you must rely heavily on the expertise of the unit superintendent, your unit training manager (UTM), and immediate supervisors to guide and execute training to meet mission and individual needs. Your support and active involvement ensure the success of your unit training program and start with selecting a competent and capable UTM. UTMs are typically consolidated at the group level; however, as the squadron commander, you are responsible for appointing one of the group UTMs as your squadron's UTM. Each UTM is required to receive training through the base education and training flight. AFI 36-2201 outlines the Air Force training program.

Key Components

The Air Force enlisted training program is comprised of technical training courses and on-the-job training (OJT). Career development courses are a part of OJT. The awarding of skill levels is dependent upon rank and completion of upgrade training (UGT), which may include some or all of these components.

Technical Training

- Foundation of enlisted specialty training.
- Initial technical training courses are usually completed prior to an Airman's first duty assignment.
- Cross-trainees may not attend initial training prior to assignment.

On-the-Job Training

The Air Force OJT program consists of three components: (1) job knowledge, satisfied through CDCs; (2) job proficiency, satisfied through hands-on training provided on the job; and (3) job experience, gained during and after upgrade training.

- It is a unit conducted and documented hands-on training portion of UGT.
- It is specific to an individual's assigned duty position.
- Supervisors and the career field education and training plan (CFETP) identify specific requirements.
- Certification is based on proficiency in specific duty-position tasks.

Key Personnel and Responsibilities

Base Training Manager. The base training manager (BTM) resides in the base education and training flight (part of the force support squadron [FSS] in the mission support group [MSG]).

- Develops, implements, and manages training policies and procedures.
- Coordinates and disseminates training policy and program changes.
- Assists commanders, unit personnel, and training activities with developing training programs.
- Conducts a SAV every 24 months on unit training programs and submits a written report with strengths, weaknesses, and recommendations.
- Reviews and supplements OIs, training plans, schedules, documentation, and evaluation procedures supporting unit operations, mission priorities, and CFETP requirements.
- Provides guidance to commanders and the UTMs on all CDC-related matters.
- Conducts quarterly training meetings.
- Instructs the Air Force Training Course, and trains personnel to teach it.
- AFI 36-2201, par. 6.4, lists BTM responsibilities.

Unit Training Manager. Ensures supervisors conduct and document initial training evaluations within 60 days of an Airman's assignment.

- Ensures trainers and certifiers meet the minimum grade, skill, and training qualifications.
- Implements and manages training programs, policies, and procedures.
- Develops, manages, and conducts training in support of home station and expeditionary mission requirements.
- Advises and assists the commander and unit personnel in executing their training responsibilities.
- Initiates AF Form 623, On-the-Job Training Record (when required by the Air Force career field manager), or its approved electronic equivalent, for all trainees entering UGT for the first time and provides the documentation to the supervisor.
- Reviews OJT records of trainees submitted for upgrade.
- Compares OJT records against the master task list for additional requirements such as CDC completion or special certification.

- Ensures all duty-position requirements (circled items in AF 623) and applicable core task requirements are trained or certified, as required.
- Conducts a SAV of unit training programs every 24 months (36 months for AFRC) and at least six months after the last base SAV to ensure corrective action implementation on deficient areas addressed in previous base SAV reports.
- Coordinates formal training.
- AFI 36-2201, par. 6.6, outlines UTM responsibilities.

Commander. Ensures an effective training program is in place.

- Appoints a UTM in writing and ensures he or she has adequate training, resources, and support to fulfill UTM duties.
- Along with the UTM, closely tracks:
  - Number of personnel in UGT by skill level.
  - CDC pass rates (including one- and two-time failures).
  - CDC reactivations and reenrollments.
  - 7-level school cancellations, reschedules, and no-shows.
  - Personnel withdrawn from training.
  - Training progress review results (within 24 months of training start date results).
  - Trainees beyond 24 months (36 months for ANG only).
  - Survey return rates.

Tips for Success

- Budget and allocate resources to support training requirements.
- Direct your UTM to provide a monthly status of training (SOT) briefing to include requirements in AFI 36-2201, par. 6.5.2.1.
- Ensure self-inspection programs and unit SAVs are meaningful and in-depth—take appropriate action to resolve any noted shortcomings.
- Ensure training is planned and scheduled according to operational or deployment requirements, personnel assigned, and equipment availability.
- Ensure the UTM is on the squadron in- and out-processing checklist.
- Ensure the UTM appropriately identifies and schedules formal training requirements.

- Ensure supervisors, assisted by the UTM, develop a master training plan (MTP) for each work center to ensure 100 percent task coverage.
- Withdraw Airmen from training who fail to progress, and take timely administrative action.
- Ensure the CDC program is administered in accordance with (IAW) Air Force Institute for Advanced Distributed Learning policies.
- Establish a training recognition program to highlight outstanding trainee performance and supervisory involvement, as appropriate—consider tangible rewards, such as a three-day pass for Airmen scoring 100 percent on the CDC end-of-course test.
- Periodically visit work centers, evaluate OJT, and meet with the UTM, supervisor, and BTM.

Enlisted Professional Military Education

2011 Commanders Connection Team

References

AFI 36-2301, *Developmental Education*, 16 July 2010.

AFI 36-2110, *Assignments,* 22 September 2009 (incorporating through change 2, 8 June 2012).

The majority of the following information is excerpted directly from the above references.

The Air Force enlisted developmental education (DE) program is central to the continuum of learning that spans an enlisted Airman's career. Education complements training and experience to prepare professional war-fighting Airmen to perform in progressively more demanding supervisor, leader, and manager positions. Enlisted PME is a four-level program that prepares Airmen for positions of increased responsibility by broadening their followership, leadership, management, and military professional skills. AFI 36-2301, *Developmental Education*, describes the courses and eligibility requirements. The command chief master sergeant, career assistance advisor (CAA), commander, first sergeant, force support squadron, and immediate supervisors play critical roles in recommendations to attend in-residence PME.

Airman Leadership School

- Basic DE.

- Airmen attend at their assigned bases.
- Rank of senior Airman (SrA) with 48 months total active federal military service (TAFMS) or staff sergeant (SSgt)-select.
- In-residence attendance required prior to sewing on SSgt.

NCO Academy

- Primary DE.
- Noncommissioned officers attend regional locations.
- Technical sergeant (TSgt) or TSgt-select.
- Individual bases may have additional local policies for prioritizing NCO Academy (NCOA) attendance among eligible candidates—check with the CCM for your base's policy.
- Resident NCOA attendance required prior to sewing on master sergeant (MSgt).

Senior Noncommissioned Officer Academy

- Intermediate DE.
- Part of the College for Enlisted Professional Military Education, Maxwell AFB–Gunter Annex, Alabama.
- Senior master sergeant (SMSgt), SMSgt-selects, and a select number of MSgts (local policies for selecting attendees vary; check with the CCM for your base's policy).
- Resident attendance required prior to sewing on chief master sergeant (CMSgt).

CMSgt Leadership Course

- Senior DE.
- Completion of CMSgt Leadership Course (CLC) is required for all CMSgt selects within one year of promotion selection.

Tips for Success

- Monitor PME status of your Airmen; know who is not current and why.
- Ensure your Airmen complete the appropriate PME courses.

- Ensure Airmen selected for PME courses are eligible to attend and are not
  - o on the control roster,
  - o under investigation, or
  - o charged with a *UCMJ*-punishable offense.
- Meet with NCOs selected to attend NCOA and Senior NCO Academy (SNCOA) prior to their departure—emphasize the significance of the course.
- Attend Airman and NCO PME graduations and recognize their accomplishments within the unit.
- Identify and recommend highly qualified nominees for PME instructor duty (AFI 36-2110 has criteria).

Enlisted Promotions

Original Author: Maj Serena Armstrong
48th Services Squadron Commander

References

AFI 36-2502, *Airman Promotion/Demotion Programs*, 31 December 2009.

AFI 36-2605, *Air Force Military Personnel Testing System*, 24 September 2008.

Air Force Pamphlet (AFPAM) 36-2241, *Professional Development Guide*, 1 October 2013.

The majority of the following information is excerpted directly from the above references.

AFPAM 36-2241 states that the enlisted promotion system provides a visible, relatively stable career progression opportunity over the long term. Promotions for Airman through SrA are based on time in grade (TIG), time in service (TIS), and commander recommendation criteria. For SSgts and above, Airmen promotions are earned either through the Weighted Airman Promotion System (WAPS) or Stripes for Exceptional Performers (STEP).

Weighted Airman Promotion System

Airmen compete and test under WAPS in their control Air Force specialty code (CAFSC). WAPS promotions use the following factors to determine an overall score that is compared to other eligible Airmen.

- SSgt through MSgt
  - o Specialty Knowledge Test (SKT)—100 points max.
  - o Promotion Fitness Examination (PFE)—100 points max.
  - o TIS—40 points max (2 points for each year of TAFMS up to 20 years).
  - o TIG—60 points max (1/2 point for each month in grade up to 10 years).
  - o Decorations—25 points max (decoration point value is based on order of precedence; see AFI 36-2502 for additional information).
  - o Enlisted Performance Report—135 points max (five years of EPRs rated as "5" earn maximum points; see AFI 36-2502 for additional calculations).
- SMSgt and CMSgt
  - o USAF Supervisory Exam—100 points max.
  - o TIS—25 points max (1/2 point for each month of TAFMS up to 25 years).
  - o TIG—60 points max (1/2 point for each month in grade up to 10 years).
  - o Decorations—25 points max (decoration point value is based on order of precedence; see AFI 36-2502 for additional information).
  - o EPR—135 points max (five years of EPRs rated as "5" earn maximum points; see AFI 36-2502 for additional calculations).

Stripes for Exceptional Performers

STEP is a separate promotion process. This program is designed to accommodate unique circumstances that, in the commander's judgment, clearly warrant promotion. It is intended to provide a means to promote Airmen for compelling—although perhaps nonquantifiable—reasons. Senior commanders (usually wing commander or equivalent) who have been delegated STEP selection authorities by Headquarters USAF establish internal guidelines, procedures, and nomination formats.

Commander Responsibilities

- Appoint a unit WAPS monitor by memorandum and provide a copy to the base WAPS monitor.
- Request training for the WAPS monitor from the military personnel flight (MPF).

Tips for Success

- Ensure your WAPS monitor has a testing notification process in place to guarantee squadron personnel are aware of their test dates and times.
- Emphasize the importance of preparing for testing regardless of whether this is their first or fifth time testing.
- Review the MPF's monthly notification lists of promotees to ensure these Airmen still meet promotion requirements.
- Fully understand the STEP promotion requirements and procedures for your wing.
- Make a big deal of promotions in your unit.
  - o Announce promotions at commander's calls, in the base paper, and through hometown news releases (see PA for assistance).
  - o Consider writing a personal letter to your Airman's spouse or parents recognizing their contribution to your Airman's success.

Enlisted Assignments

Original Author: Maj Tom Smith
42nd Military Personnel Flight Commander

References

Virtual MPF (vMPF)—Additional information is accessible from the main page by selecting the heading "Self-Service Actions," then "Assignments."

AFI 36-2110, *Assignments*, 22 September 2009.

AFPAM 36-2241, *Professional Development Guide*, 1 October 2013.

Personnel Services Delivery Memorandum (PSDM) 11-02, Automated Assignment Notification, 10 January 2011.

Automated Assignment Notification Frequently Asked Questions, AFPC website (MyPers), https://gum-crm.csd.disa.mil.

The majority of the following information is excerpted directly from the above references.

The Air Force assignment process is designed to allocate Airmen to vacant positions worldwide, as equitably as possible, ensuring a high state of military readiness. Given the amount of Airmen serving and the number and diversity of Air Force units and assets worldwide, enlisted assignments are inherently a complex and dynamic process. As a squadron commander, you play a limited but nevertheless important role in the process. Commanders have the ultimate responsibility of ensuring only quality personnel are retained in the Air Force and permitted to be reassigned. Decisions to cancel, reassign, or return Airmen will be based on the overall best interest of the Air Force. Before discussing your specific roles, a little background on the enlisted assignment selection process will be helpful.

Enlisted Quarterly Assignments Listing and EQUAL-Plus

- Enlisted quarterly assignments listings (EQUAL) and EQUAL-Plus listings are a laundry list of all the assignment requirements that need to be filled during the upcoming assignment cycle, compiled quarterly by the Air Force Personnel Center (AFPC).
- EQUAL listings identify what standard assignments are available to SMSgts and below by AFSC and grade at particular locations.
- EQUAL-Plus advertises requirements for special duty (SDA), joint, departmental, and short-notice overseas (OS) assignments, as well as all CMSgt assignments.
- EQUAL-Plus listings typically have a greater level of detail, including any special qualifications, available locations, reporting instructions, and POC for additional information.
- EQUAL and EQUAL-Plus lists are available to Airmen via the AFPC Web page to provide them the opportunity to review the listing and update or otherwise align their personal preferences to actual Air Force needs before assignment consideration begins.
- EQUAL-Plus displays upcoming requirements, any special qualifications a person needs to be eligible for selection, and the available locations, reporting instructions, and POC for additional information.
- EQUAL-Plus advertises MAJCOM/AFPC-controlled special duties (i.e., instructor, recruiting, Thunderbird, postal, and defense attaché duties and Air Staff/MAJCOM positions around the world) and short-notice OS assignments.
- CMSgts (including selects) volunteer for assignments advertised on EQUAL-Plus by notifying their assignment NCOs at the chiefs' group.
- Airmen (SMSgt and below) use the self-service assignment preference application available through the vMPF to record continental United States (CONUS) or OS assignment preferences. Airmen desiring to

update their preferences should log onto the vMPF and select the self-service actions under assignments.

- Enlisted Airmen volunteer for SDAs via the assignment management system (AMS) by update of the SDA job number from the EQUAL-Plus ad. Enlisted Airmen are limited in volunteering for only those SDAs that appear as ads on EQUAL-Plus.
- Each enlisted Airman is individually responsible for the currency and accuracy of his or her assignment preferences in vMPF. When a change in status occurs (marriage, completion of a permanent change of station [PCS], etc.) Airmen should update their preferences accordingly. Outdated preferences or no preferences on file will not be the basis for release of an enlisted Airman from an assignment for which selected.
- The Airman Assignments Branch (DPAA) at AFPC uses the EQUAL and EQUAL-Plus lists in combination with the Airmen-supplied preference data and their personnel records to make assignment decisions.

Commander's Role in Enlisted Assignments

- Update quality force factors.
    - o Ensure appropriate administrative actions—such as a control roster, Article 15, or pending legal or medical action—are taken into account and that the servicing MPF correctly reflects them in the personnel system. Failure to do so may result in an assignment notification for an Airman who can't or shouldn't be reassigned.
    - o Cancelling an assignment after the fact not only can be painful for both you and AFPC but also often forces a short-notice manpower shortage on the gaining unit commander while AFPC makes other arrangements.
- Review assignment notification.
    - o AFPC identifies an Airman for an assignment.
    - o AFPC loads the assignment into the Military Personnel Data System (MilPDS).
    - o The assignment action triggers the vMPF application to send an e-mail to the Airman's e-mail addresses in MilPDS and vMPF.
    - o Airmen will receive an automated email from vMPF notifying them of selection for reassignment.
    - o You review the assignment to ensure the Airman is qualified as specified in the notification.

Tips for Success

- Implement administrative actions resulting from misconduct or otherwise failing to meet standards (i.e., control roster) in a timely fashion, and check that the servicing MPF updates this information.
- Upon notification that an Airman has been selected for assignment:
  - o Cross-check that the Airman meets the basic requirements as outlined in the notification and is otherwise eligible for an assignment.
  - o Ensure suspense actions are tracked and met.
  - o Take any other commander actions directed in the assignment notification (initiate personnel reliability program [PRP] screening).
- Ensure all actions, training, and/or documentation specified in the notification are completed IAW required timelines.

Officer Professional Military Education

Original Authors: Maj Richard J. Parrotte
Commanders Connection Facilitator

Maj Tom Smith
42nd MPF Commander

References

AFI 36-2301, *Developmental Education*, 16 July 2010.

AU-10, *The Air University Catalog, Academic Year 2013–2014.*

The majority of the following information is excerpted directly from the above references.

> *I do not think much of a man who does not know more today than he did yesterday.*
>
> —Abraham Lincoln

Officer PME is a four-level development program that prepares commissioned Airmen for positions of increased responsibility by refining their leadership and management skills while broadening their understanding of our Air Force, its organization, and its many missions. Officer PME also reinforces the values of the Air Force and the officer corps in particular. In addition, it allows attendees to learn about other jobs in the Air Force.

Basic Developmental Education

- **Air and Space Basic Course (ASBC)**—Initial basic developmental education (BDE)
    - o Second and first lieutenants, less than 23 months total active federal commissioned service (TAFCS).
    - o Six-week in-residence course, or 30 training days.
    - o 100 percent resident attendance, usually before first duty assignment.
    - o Areas of focus: guides new officers in realizing their roles as Airmen, understanding and living the Air Force core values, and comprehending the Air Force's unique history, doctrine, and capabilities.
- **Squadron Officer School (SOS)**—Second-level BDE
    - o Captain (must be pinned on), between four and seven years TAFCS.
    - o Five-week in-residence or 18-month distance learning course.
    - o In-residence attendance is competitive (historically around 80 percent of officers attend SOS in residence). Nonresident SOS is available to all eligible officers.
    - o Areas of focus: enhances leadership, followership, and communication skills, as well as broadens officers' knowledge of Air Force history, doctrine, and employment concepts.

Intermediate Developmental Education

- Major or major-select (additional requirements for in-residence program).
- Most common form of intermediate developmental education (IDE) is ACSC; however, other options exist (select Air Force Institute of Technology [AFIT] programs, sister-service IDE courses, internships, fellowships, etc.).
- ACSC is a 10-month in-residence course.
- ACSC via distance learning must be completed within 18 months.
- In-residence attendees earn a master's degree.
- Distance learning now offers a master's degree option.
- In-residence attendance is highly competitive (historically 18–20 percent of officers attend ACSC or other form of IDE in residence).
- Areas of focus

- o Develops skills for higher-level command and staff responsibilities while enhancing officers' abilities to think critically about operational air, space, and cyberspace concepts as well as current and future threats.
- o Emphasizes the joint campaign planning process.

Senior Developmental Education

- Lt colonel–selects through colonels with no more than 23 years of TAFCS by graduation (additional requirements for in-residence program).
- Most common form of senior developmental education (SDE) is Air War College (AWC); however, other options exist (select AFIT programs, sister-service SDE courses, DOD SDE courses, etc.).
- AWC is a 10-month in-residence course.
- AWC distant learning must be completed within 18 months.
- In-residence attendance is extremely competitive.
- Areas of focus
  - o Develops and enhances skills for strategic and institutional leadership, joint and multinational warfighting, multiagency international security operations, air and space force development, and national security planning.
  - o Emphasizes senior leadership roles in joint and coalition operations and environments.

Air Force Form 3849 Process

- Members will see an IDE/SDE button on AFPC secure sites when they are eligible.
- Commanders will get an e-mail once the eligible member sends the Air Force Form 3849, PME/AFIT/RTFB [Return-to-Flying Board] Officer Worksheet, to them for corrections/review.
- Once the commander digitally signs the 3849, it is referred to the senior rater.
- Commanders should review the current year's IDE/SDE message for any other criteria that apply. Ensure the eligible officer understands that the senior rater can nominate only a certain percentage of eligible officers to attend IDE/SDE.

Tips for Success

- Monitor PME status of your officers—know who's not current and why.
- Know each officer's window of opportunity for next level of resident PME.
- Encourage eligible officers to enroll in PME by distance learning at their earliest opportunity.
- Advocate for resident PME attendance for your most qualified officers.
- Meet with each officer selected to attend PME prior to departure, and emphasize the significance and importance of the course.

Additional Resources

- The AFPC website has various resources on current resident PME programs at MyPers, http://gum-cm.csd.disa.mil.

Officer Promotions

Original Author: Maj Serena Armstrong
48th Services Squadron Commander

Reference

AFI 36-2501, *Officer Promotions and Selective Continuation*, 16 July 2004 (incorporating through change 3, 17 August 2009).

The majority of the following information is excerpted directly from the above reference.

AFI 36-2501 states that the fundamental purpose of the officer promotion program is to select officers through a fair and competitive selection process that advances the best qualified officers to positions of increased responsibility and authority. It also provides the necessary career incentive to attract and maintain a quality officer force. Promotion is not a reward for past service. It is advancement to a higher grade based on past performance and future potential.

Promotion Recommendation Form

Squadron commanders generally have an indirect role in the selection of officers for promotion, primarily through the evaluation process. This is particularly true with regard to junior officers. However, it is not uncommon for wing commanders to ask a squadron commander to provide a promotion recommendation on an Air Force Form 709, Promotion Recommendation

Form, on officers competing for major or above. The PRF is essentially a nine-line summary of an officer's career to date. The information in this summary is typically taken from an officer's past OPRs and structured to put as much positive information as possible into the limited space. Wing commanders may have different approaches and philosophies regarding PRFs. The wing commander's executive officer is usually the best source of information for completing PRFs.

Your Responsibilities as Commander

- Notify officer of selection or nonselection for promotion (par. 3.8).
- Generate a "not qualified for promotion" (NQP) for removal, and/or delay actions as appropriate.
- Determine officers' suitability for selective continuation should they not be selected for promotion.

Commander's Role in Enlisted Assignments

- Update of quality force factors.
  - o Ensure appropriate administrative actions—such as control roster, Article 15, or pending legal or medical action—are taken into account and correctly updated in the personnel system by the servicing MPF.
  - o Failure to do so may result in an assignment notification on an Airman who can't or shouldn't be reassigned. Cancelling an assignment after the fact can be painful for both you and the AFPC. Plus, it often forces a short-notice manpower shortage on the unit commander to which the Airman was to have been assigned while AFPC makes other arrangements.
- Notification of assignment.
  - o AFPC identifies an Airman for an assignment.
  - o AFPC loads the assignment into MilPDS.
  - o The assignment action triggers the vMPF application to send an e-mail to the Airman's e-mail addresses in MilPDS and vMPF.
  - o Airmen will receive an automated e-mail from vMPF notifying them of selection for reassignment.
  - o You review the assignment to ensure the Airman is qualified as specified in the notification.

Tips for Success

- Make sure your boss knows who your best and brightest are—you are the prime advocate for your people to those who directly impact officer promotions.
- Familiarize yourself with AFI 36-2501. The selection process and board scoring procedures are a valuable source when mentoring officers on promotion.
- Actively mentor and develop your officers—ensure they get the right experiences and recognition to be competitive for promotion.
- Mentor your officers on writing awards, decorations, evaluations, and PRFs.
- Stratifications are an important part of the PRF process. When PRFs are due, your boss may ask you to rack and stack your officers so they can stratify eligibles among their peers. Ensure you are honest in your rankings. Overinflation or incorrect rankings can damage your credibility and that of your boss.
- When promotions come, make a big deal of them.
- Have a formal promotion ceremony.
- Announce promotions at commander's calls, in the base paper, and through the hometown news releases (see PA for assistance).
- Consider writing a personal letter to your officer's spouse or parents recognizing their contribution to his or her success.

Officer Assignments

Original Author: Maj Tom Smith
42nd MPF Commander

Reference

PSDM 11-02, Automated Assignment Notification, 10 January 2011.

The majority of the following information is excerpted directly from the above reference.

The officer assignment process allocates officers to vacant positions worldwide as equitably as possible to satisfy national security requirements while ensuring a high degree of readiness. Given the number of Airmen serving and the sheer number and diversity of USAF assets worldwide, officer assignment is inherently a complex and dynamic process.

As a commander, you play a central role in this process on two levels:

- You provide strategic career path and assignment counseling to each of your officers.
- You give direct, strategic-level input to each officer's assignment team.

It is vital that you have a basic understanding of the Air Force assignment system (AFAS), the AMS, the Airmen Development Plan (ADP), and the VML. Detailed information is available on the AFPC website.

Assignment Tools

- AFAS/officer assignment selection process overall
    - o Primary goal of the AFAS is to assign the right officer to the right position at the right time to meet Air Force mission requirements.
    - o Other considerations include an officer's professional development and personal preference along with the commander's recommendation.
- Airmen Development Plan
    - o Secure Web-based application accessible on the AFPC website.
    - o The AFAS uses the ADP to ensure timely communication of assignment, command, and developmental education desires/recommendations to individual officers, their commanders, and the AFPC officer assignment team.
- Assignment management system
    - o Uses the personnel requirements display (PRD) to see a snapshot of authorized and required positions across the Air Force.
    - o This tool should be used as a guide only—all open positions may not appear in the AMS.

Vulnerable Movers List

- Tentatively identifies officers as vulnerable for an assignment during a specific window based on career-field-specific criteria (generally the number of years an officer has on his or her current station).
- Compiled three times per year coinciding with the three annual officer assignment cycles (spring, summer, and fall).

- Forwarded for your review and coordination on the timelines outlined below in table 1.

Table 1. Officer assignment cycle

Cycle	Initial VML	ADP Data Due	AFPC Matches Assignments	Assignment Report Dates
Spring	July	Sept	Sept–Oct	Feb–May
Summer	Nov	Jan	Jan–Mar	June–Sept
Fall	Mar	May	May–July	Oct–Jan

Adapted from the Air Force Personnel Center's assignment management website by ACSC.

- Upon receiving the VML (via AMS), you will review the status of your officers and determine if an assignment in this window is in their best interests or those of the Air Force.
- If it is in the best interest of the unit or the officer's professional development for him or her not to be considered during the cycle, request the officer be removed through a reclama process within the VML module of AMS.
- Your MAJCOM and AFPC review your request and subsequently approve or disapprove it based on needs of the Air Force.
- AFPC issues a final VML once all reclamas are processed.
- For each officer you have on the final VML, you have two responsibilities:
  - o Ensure that each has current data in ADP on file at AFPC.
  - o Ensure that a requisition is entered into AMS requesting a replacement for each.

It will take from three to four months for the assignment matching to be complete at AFPC and assignment notifications to reach the base level. However, because an officer was on the final VML and considered for assignment does not guarantee ultimate selection for assignment. It is not uncommon for officers, particularly junior officers, to be on the VML two or more times before being selected for assignment.

Assignment Notification

- AFPC identifies an officer for an assignment. Once AFPC loads the assignment into MilPDS, the assignment action triggers the vMPF to send an e-mail directly to the member.

- The commander may need to assist should the member decide to seven-day opt for separation or retirement. The commander should mentor and counsel the member as needed.

Tips for Success

- Periodically meet with your officers individually to discuss career progression and goals—encourage them to be candid about their career desires.
- Review initial VML as released via AMS in July, November, and March—submit reclama requests as appropriate.
- Review final VML as released via AMS in August, November, and April, and check that each officer on the final VML has current data in the ADP on file at the AFPC.
- ADP data need not be reaccomplished every VML cycle unless you or the officer wishes to make changes.
- Check that your comments in the ADP are clear and accurate and that a requisition is entered into AMS requesting a replacement for each officer remaining on the final VML should reassignment occur.
- Ensure all actions, training, and/or documentation specified in the notification are completed IAW the timelines required.
- Stay updated on the assignment process by reading the MPF memorandums on the AFPC website.

Leading Civilians

2011 Commanders Connection Team

References

AFI 36-1203, *Administrative Grievance System*, 1 May 1996.

AFI 36-601, *Air Force Civilian Career Program Management*, 25 July 1994.

AFI 36-602, *Civilian Intern Programs*, 25 July 1994.

AFI 36-2706, *Equal Opportunity Program Military and Civilian*, 5 October 2010 (incorporating change 1, 5 October 2011).

AFI 36-701, *Labor Management Relations*, 27 July 1994.

AFI 36-1001, *Managing the Civilian Performance Program*, 1 July 1999.

AFI 36-1004, *The Air Force Civilian Recognition Program* (certified current 13 January 2012).

The majority of the following information is excerpted directly from the above references.

> *Coming together is a beginning, staying together is progress, and working together is success.*
>
> —Henry Ford

The federal government is set up with a balance of both military and civilian personnel. The US Air Force was specifically designed with this mix to facilitate institutional memory and continuity and to allow for the deployment of military members in times of conflict. Air Force commanders are increasingly finding themselves leading a mixed military and civilian workforce. The ability to lead civilians is as crucial to your success as a commander as your ability to lead military personnel. While the general philosophies of leadership are the same for both, civilian personnel share unique characteristics since they are often governed by federal law and union and individual contracts. The processes used and tools available to you vary, even with the same type of civilian employees. This overview is designed to identify key similarities and differences between military and civilian personnel, describe differences among the types of civilian employees, and provide a readily available resource listing.

Civilian versus Military

Some of the differences between civilian and military personnel may seem obvious. When overlooked, however, they may cause difficulty for commanders. Military members are on duty 24 hours a day, 7 days a week. Most civilian personnel are paid an hourly wage and are entitled to compensation/overtime if they work beyond the established hours. Generally, civilian employees are limited to the duties and responsibilities identified in their position description or core document. Military members can be tasked to do work outside their assigned lanes and can leave work to go to the doctor or get a haircut on government time. Most civilian employees must request leave for these activities. A military member can be moved to a new desk, office, or building without much planning. Some unions require a two-week notification to make any changes in a civilian's working conditions. These are only a few of the differences. Be aware of the distinctions between your military and civilian staff members, and make decisions accordingly.

Some common ground between military and civilian personnel is their need for mentoring, recognition, awards, feedback, appraisals, leave approval, and discipline. The processes for these vary greatly based upon the type of employee, but these are leadership tools for all of your staff. Just as you will have a senior enlisted advisor, if you are the commander of an organization with a significant percentage of civilian employees, you are likely to have a senior civilian too. If this is so, be grateful because he/she is your right-hand person for civilian issues. Get to know your senior civilian as soon as practical. Rely on him/her for guidance on civilian matters, and give him/her the authority to represent you in civilian matters.

Civil Service

Civil service employees are civilians who work for and are hired by the Air Force directly. Differences exist within the realm of these employees. Some civilian employees are under the General Schedule (GS) pay system while others are under pay-for-performance systems, such as those with the Laboratory Personnel Demonstration Project. Certain categories of civilians are considered salaried exempt (don't get overtime pay) or salaried nonexempt. Some civilians may be part of intern programs or working as nonappropriated fund (NAF) employees. (Contract employees are in a separate category.) Each of these categories comes with its own set of expectations, procedures, and processes and may have different hiring, appraisal, and pay processes and guidelines. Many resources are available to help commanders decipher their civil service employee positions.

Civilian Personnel Office

- Your primary resource for all government civilian employee issues is CPO.
- Know your key points of contact at the CPO for these critical issues (contact the FSS commander if you need help finding them).
  - Employee relations
    - Discipline issues.
    - Administrative grievances.
    - Injury compensation.
    - Leave.
    - Awards and recognition.
    - Appraisals and feedback.
  - Equal employment opportunity (EEO)
    - Discrimination issues.
    - Sexual harassment.

- Hostile working environment.
- Labor relations—union and union contract–related issues.

Civilian Career Field Management

Civil service employees are hired according to a job series that identifies skills and education requirements for a given position (as determined by the Office of Personnel Management [OPM]). The series identifies a career field much like the AFSC identifies enlisted jobs. Civilian careers are managed by a career field management team (CFMT) much like officer careers. Members of the CFMT can assist commanders with career field management issues, the hiring process, developmental education, intern programs, and much more. The same basic concepts used to lead Airmen apply to civilians, and some of the same resources are available.

Nonappropriated Fund Employees

NAF employees are federal civilian employees paid by nonappropriated funds. Civil service positions are paid for by money appropriated by Congress. NAF money is self-generated by Air Force clubs, bowling centers, golf courses, and other activities.

Interns

Although Air Force interns are federal employees, they are under a specific contract and usually on a probationary period the first year. The intern must agree to meet specific criteria, such as being mobile and graduating from college by a certain date. Conversely, an intern has contracted with the Air Force for prescribed benefits, such as tuition assistance, training, certain job rotations, and guaranteed promotions. Know what you are obligated to provide for your intern and what they have agreed to contribute.

Civilian Contract Employees

Civilian contract employees work for a company the Air Force has contracted to provide resources or services and not directly for the Air Force. Since they do not work directly for you, your job in terms of managing these employees is made much easier. While leadership principles apply to contract civilians, the contract company manages their careers, discipline, leave, appraisals, and union issues.

Your role in managing the work of these individuals will be specified in the contract and can vary dramatically. Your focus must be on the work specified in the contract. Is the contractor meeting the terms of the contract? Know your limitations and stay in your lane! You will have limited oversight over your contract employees. Know your contract, and don't overstep your authority. If you have contract employees, you may have a liaison to help you with contract issues.

Your leadership skills are greatly needed to inspire and motivate contract employees. They may be earning a lower salary than their civil service counterparts. Share your vision with them, and use the tools available to you to encourage them. Lead!

Tips for Success

- Know your senior civilian well.
- Know all your civilians—not only what category they fall in but their goals and aspirations.
    - Ensure civilians are mentored and are offered professional development.
    - Recognize superior performers (see AFI 36-1004, *The Air Force Civilian Recognition Program*).
    - Know which of your civilians are members of the Reserve forces—support them and their families, and have a plan to cover their duties if they deploy.
- Know your contacts. Get to know the people at CPO before you need them.
- Know your contracts for contract employees.
- Know your limitations.
    - Attend mandatory training for new commanders on supervising civilians—take it seriously.
    - Ensure civilian employees are never discouraged or prevented from using available grievance channels.
    - Read the union handbook within 30 days of taking command.
    - Document all contact you have with civilian employees and their supervisors related to a formal grievance (within guidelines).
    - Always remain clearly neutral on issues surrounding unionization, union membership, or any similar union representation topic.

Additional Resources

- For help in understanding the civilian personnel system and specific information on leading civilians, visit https://www.nafjobs.org/about.aspx, http://www.opm.gov, and http://www.afpc.af.mil.

Feedback

Original Author: Maj Richard J. Parrotte
Commanders Connection Facilitator

Reference

AFI 36-2406, *Officer and Enlisted Evaluation Systems*, 2 January 2013 (corrective actions applied on 5 April 2013).

The majority of the following information is excerpted directly from the above reference.

> *Champions know that success is inevitable; that there is no such thing as failure, only feedback. They know that the best way to forecast the future is to create it.*
>
> —Michael J. Gelb

Feedback is a type of communication that we give or receive. Unfortunately, feedback is often interpreted as *criticism*, but this significantly limits its meaning. It is a way a leader, commander, supervisor, or peer lets people know how effective they are or how they affect you or others. Feedback can be formal or informal, and it can be positive or negative. Feedback has two parts: giving feedback and receiving it.

The Importance of Feedback

Feedback is a must for people who want to have good relationships, improve performance, and achieve personal growth. A meaningful channel for communication, giving feedback connects us—and our behavior—to the world around us. "If we can understand and use it, this feedback can empower us to communicate more openly and improve many facets of our daily lives."[1]

Giving Feedback

Most of your focus as a commander will be in giving feedback, but understanding both sides of feedback is necessary. Giving feedback requires preparation. How you deliver feedback is as important as how you accept it because how it is received determines its usability. Effective feedback includes the attributes of being attentive, sensitive, supportive, and honest while also being direct, specific, descriptive, and timely. Commanders are required to give formal feedback to subordinates in the form of performance feedback.

Performance feedback is a private, formal communication that a rater uses to tell a subordinate what is expected regarding duty performance and how well he or she is meeting those expectations. Providing this information encourages positive communication, improves performance, and allows for professional growth. Always remember, feedback is the responsibility of the supervisor, not the subordinate. Additionally, informal feedback conducted on an ongoing basis is a powerful supplement to the formal feedback process. A simple "good job" immediately after observing a positive action goes a long way.

Receiving Feedback

Although as a commander your focus will be on giving feedback, you will likely receive feedback too. Commanders get a great deal of feedback directly and indirectly. Your boss will provide feedback, but you may also receive informal feedback from peers, climate surveys, and perhaps unit members. Some people experience feedback as pure criticism and are not open to hear it. Others see it as personally crushing—an attack on them personally. Still others want to hear only positive feedback but nothing that might suggest the need for improvement. Willingness to receive feedback or even seek it out can be an asset for commanders. Believing that feedback will help you grow can benefit you. When preparing to receive feedback, it is wise to prepare mentally and not be defensive or disrespectful. Rationalizing behavior is not a proper response to receiving feedback. Listen actively, thank the person giving feedback, and contemplate the usefulness of the feedback. Make changes as necessary.

Elements of Effective Feedback

- Balanced (positive and negative).
- Specific (provide examples).
- Timely.
- Frequent (less experience equals more frequent feedback).
- Personal.
- Focus on behavior rather than the person.[2]
- Focus on behavior that can be changed.[3]
- Be descriptive rather than evaluative.[4]

Commander Responsibilities

- Provide initial, midterm, and follow-up feedback to your subordinates.
- Document subordinates' feedback on the performance feedback worksheet (PFW) and provide them the form at the conclusion of the session—make a copy of the signed PFW for your personal records.

- Ensure supervisors within your unit are conducting feedback sessions properly and in a timely manner.
- Hold supervisors who fail to conduct appropriate feedback sessions accountable.

Tips for Success

- Put the next feedback appointment with your subordinates on your calendar immediately after completing each evaluation or feedback session.
- When giving feedback to subordinates
  - o Prepare in advance for the session.
  - o Use the PFW as a guide for organizing and conducting feedback.
  - o Clearly outline for subordinates what you expect of them.
  - o Tell them directly and honestly how well they are currently meeting those expectations.
  - o Offer specific suggestions for improvement.
- Consistently and repeatedly communicate the importance of proper feedback to supervisors.
- Remember—these sessions are most productive when supervisors stay abreast of current standards and expectations!

Notes

1. Patti Hathaway, *Giving and Receiving Feedback: Building Constructive Communication* (Menlo Park, CA: Crisp Publications, 1998), 3; and Deborah Jude-York and Susan Wise, *Multipoint Feedback: A 360-Degree Catalyst for Change* (Menlo Park, CA: Crisp Publications, 1997), 3.
2. Ian McGill and Liz Beaty, *Action Learning: A Practitioner's Guide* (London: Kogan Page, 1994), 159–63.
3. Ibid.
4. Ibid.

Officer and Enlisted Evaluations

Original Authors: Maj Serena Armstrong
48th Services Squadron Commander

Maj Tom Smith
42nd MPF Commander

References

AFI 36-2406, *Officer and Enlisted Evaluation Systems*, 2 January 2013 (corrective actions applied on 5 April 2013).

AFPAM 36-2241, *Professional Development Guide*, 1 October 2013.

AFPAM 36-2506, *You and Your Promotions—The Air Force Officer Promotion Program*, 1 September 1997.

MPF Memorandum (MPFM) 07-44, Subject: Implementing Instructions and Processing Procedures for the new AF Form 910, *Enlisted Performance Report (AB thru TSgt)*; the AF Form 911, *Enlisted Performance Report (MSgt thru CMSgt)*; the AF Form 931, *Performance Feedback Worksheet (AB thru TSgt)*; and the AF Form 932, *Performance Feedback Worksheet (MSgt thru CMSgt)*, 11 July 2007.

MPFM 07-45, Subject: Implementing Instructions and Processing Procedures for the new AF Form 707, *Officer Performance Report (Lt thru Col)*, and AF Form 724, *Performance Feedback Worksheet (Lt thru Col)*, 11 July 2007.

The majority of the following information is excerpted directly from the above references.

While officer and enlisted evaluations have obvious differences, they share several similarities. By the time you are a commander, you have seen plenty of OPRs and EPRs to know the difference between a well-written evaluation and a poorly written one. It is safe to say that anyone can write a firewall-5 EPR or referral EPR, but you will find a 3 much tougher to write. The above references offer guidance on the formal process, but here are some key nuggets to help you with the art of writing.

Feedback

The feedback process cannot be stressed enough. It is vital that these are taken seriously and documented well. While documented actions such as a letter of counseling or letter of reprimand make strong cases, continuous feedback helps build the case in the event of a complaint. By offering advice on how to correct an issue, you can help that individual get better. Getting the individual's signature shows that an attempt was made to correct any issues and helps justify a rating.

Referral Evaluations

Referral evaluations (officer or enlisted) are those that contain negative or potentially negative comments. There is a specific referral process that must be followed. Anytime you encounter a referral evaluation, take the time to read the AFI and double-check that each step is correctly followed and that you have the required documentation to support it. Minor mistakes can invalidate the evaluation and require the process to be reaccomplished. Immediately contact the evaluation section of the MPF for assistance in correctly completing the referral report process.

Stratification

Stratification has received a lot of attention over the last few years. It is the numerical ordering of an individual with respect to his/her peers (for example, #2 of 12 field grade officers). While stratification is common in an officer report, it has crept into the SNCO reports as well. Stratification is prohibited on EPRs, with the exception of MSgts and SMSgts who are time-in-grade eligible. If used, the stratification statement must be in quantitative terms, comparing peers in the same grade within the evaluator's rating scope. Stratification statements are not authorized on EPRs for Airmen first class (A1C) through TSgts, CMSgts, or CMSgt selectees. Make sure your stratification is strong and carries weight. Refer to local guidance on the use of stratifications for all ranks.

Letters of Evaluation

As a deployed commander, I was not the rater for anyone in my squadron. I wrote letters of evaluation (LOE) for all SNCOs/officers in my squadron and encouraged flight chiefs to do the same for Airmen whose rater was not deployed with them. I brought each SNCO/officer in for a one-on-one feedback session at the beginning of the deployment and then gave them a final LOE review before they redeployed. I would then send a note to the home-station commander with the LOE. This gave the home-station commander a good idea of how their Airmen performed.

Ratee Acknowledgement

Use this opportunity to mentor your subordinates. If everything is glowing, use this time to encourage and keep them motivated. Showing you care will go a long way. If someone is receiving a mediocre report, explain the reason for this evaluation. If you have been doing feedbacks, the Airman should not be surprised by the ratings. Use this time to motivate your people to do better. Bottom line, be honest and up front.

Commander Responsibilities IAW AFI 36-2406

- Administer and manage the performance feedback program for the organization.
- Monitor raters and ratees to determine whether feedback sessions are conducted properly and in a timely manner.
- Consider disciplining and removing from supervisory positions those raters who fail to conduct documented performance feedback sessions.
- Prepare and maintain the unit's mission description.
- Determine the rating chain for assigned personnel.
- Ensure first-time supervisors receive mandatory training within 60 days of being assigned supervisory duties.
- Ensure the first sergeant (or designated SNCO) conducts a quality force review on all enlisted evaluations.
- Ensure the evaluation accurately describes performance and makes realistic recommendations for advancement.
- Ensure that no member is in the rating chain of his/her spouse or other relative.

Tips for Success

- Be on time. Per AFI, the MPF must receive evaluations no later than 30 calendar days after the last day of the evaluation period; some wings brief late reports at wing staff meeting.
- Be proactive. An evaluation is normally due on each military member annually but can be earlier if supervisors change or the individual is being reassigned.
  - Most of these situations can be forecasted and an initial draft evaluation requested 30 days before it is due.
  - These early versions are draft only. By AFI, an evaluation cannot be completed and signed before the final day of the evaluation period.

Awards and Decorations

Original Author: Maj Serena Armstrong
48th Services Squadron Commander

References

AFI 36-2803, *The Air Force Awards and Decorations Program*, 15 June 2001.

AFI 36-2805, *Special Trophies and Awards*, 14 March 2013.

Department of Defense Manual 1348.33, vol. 1, *Manual of Military Decorations and Awards: General Information, Medal of Honor, and Defense/Joint Decorations and Awards*, 23 November 2010 (incorporating change 2, 7 March 2013).

The majority of the following information is excerpted directly from the above references.

Recognizing the efforts and accomplishments of your Airmen is a critical part of your role as a commander. Along with local quarterly and annual wing-level awards, numerous formal Air Force programs are available to help you in that effort.

Two general programs are (1) the Air Force Awards and Decorations program that awards decorations such as the Air Force Achievement Medal (reference: AFI 36-2803) and (2) the Special Trophies and Awards program that includes recognition such as the 12 Outstanding Airmen and the Lance P. Sijan awards (reference: AFI 36-2805).

Specific eligibility criteria and nomination processes for these awards vary too dramatically to summarize here. However, each is clearly outlined in the references cited above. As a commander you will rarely be the approval authority for such awards. However, you will be the one best able to advocate for your people in your base award programs; take this role seriously. In addition, each functional area normally selects its outstanding enlisted members, officers, and civilians for yearly awards. Various publications cover the details for these awards. Take advantage of available opportunities to recognize your top performers.

Tips for Success

- Be personally familiar with all the functional awards programs that apply to your Airmen—including those outside your specific career field, such as personnel, information management, and training manager.
- Review your unit's awards program or OI.
- Assign a unit awards monitor to do the following:
    - Stay familiar with relevant guidance—local and Air Force level.
    - Track when each of your Airmen last received a decoration.
    - Track the nomination windows for special trophies and awards programs that might apply to one of your Airmen—most run on the same schedule each year.
    - Track award nomination packages in progress within your unit to meet suspenses.
- Be proactive on nominations, especially the special trophies and awards nominations. If you wait until the formal call for nominees to filter down through the MAJCOM and wing, you will be left with little time to put a package together.
- Periodically review the situation surrounding any Airman who hasn't received a decoration in over three years—not everyone deserves a decoration, but you want to make sure it isn't an oversight.
- Don't overlook civilian awards for government civilian employees.
- Maintain the integrity of the awards program by nominating only deserving people for appropriate awards. This affects your credibility not only with your Airmen but also with your boss and wing commander.
- Remember that nominations for decorations for a specific achievement or act of heroism must be generated within 60 days of the act.
- On PCS awards, an award for a single act or achievement during the assignment period (such as a deployment medal) does not preclude an award for meritorious service at the end of an assignment. It means the achievement was already recognized and must be excluded from the second nomination package.
- Always brag on your Airmen. Publicize your award winners at commander's calls, in the base paper, and through hometown news releases (see PA for assistance).
- Check with the CCM to fully understand procedures and requirements for SNCO end-of-tour decorations.

Building Future Leaders

Original Author: Maj Terri Sheppard
Cadet Squadron 17 Commander

Never tell people how to do things. Tell them what to do, and they will surprise you with their ingenuity.

—Gen George C. Patton

Empower Your People

Great leaders never tell people how to do their jobs. Instead, they present the need, establish the playing field, and then allow subordinates to achieve their own successes.

The success of the follower is a success for the leader and the organization. You, as the commander, maintain responsibility for a task, but all share in getting the job done. When you solicit input, you will discover the knowledge, interest, and parameters of support you can expect from others. As one noted author stated, "You want innovation? Just ask for it."[1]

Empowerment involves assigning tasks to subordinates and allowing freedom for creativity. It also means granting subordinates authority to make decisions and then to act upon them. It is not simply fire-and-forget workload distribution but instead requires effective delegation.

To empower subordinates, you must

- Allow subordinates decision-making authority and flexibility.
- Provide direction and support based on individual experience, maturity, and leader and subordinate relationship.
- Maintain responsibility.
- Promote contributions from all members.
- Recognize and reward subordinates for contributions.
- Provide resources and knowledge.
- Establish mutual trust.

Empowered subordinates must

- Take ownership and pride in achieving the vision—you must allow decision making and flexibility.
- Control their own work but keep you informed.
- Become stakeholders in and committed to your squadron's vision.
- Transform into responsible participants through learning and development.

Empowerment *does not*

- Detract from authority.
- Abdicate responsibility.
- Equate to laissez-faire leadership.
- Utilize decision making by consensus.

Grow Future Leaders

You, as the commander, are responsible for getting the job done. Despite the overwhelming demands and challenges of accomplishing the mission, do not forget the primary responsibility of leaders—developing future leaders. It takes extra time and effort, but investing in future leaders is well worth the effort.

Avoid showing favoritism and creating divides within your squadron when assigning "opportunities to excel." Always consider the development and growth of everyone, balancing equity and capabilities. While looking to challenge "fast burners" with leadership potential among your officer, enlisted, and civilian personnel based on their readiness, do not overlook "late bloomers" with experience, maturity, and untapped potential.

Things to consider when growing future leaders include:

- Challenge every individual—all will benefit, and the sharpest will rise to the top.
- Identify leadership potential early, and challenge those individuals appropriately.
- Look for late bloomers, and tap into their maturity and experience.
- Develop an understanding of roles and responsibilities.
- Clarify expectations.
- Strengthen squadron and service identity.
- Advise and mentor, both professionally and personally.
- Encourage subordinates to make decisions, experience leadership, and take risks—they learn from both triumphs and failures.
- Provide opportunities for professional growth and promotion.
- Encourage and facilitate formal education.

To best identify and develop future leaders, you should

- Know your people's strengths, weaknesses, and goals.

- Set a tone that encourages subordinates to take reasonable risks, and treat setbacks as opportunities for improvement.
- When initiatives fail, applaud the attempt; use the experience as a learning opportunity—fight the fear of failure that often prevents capable people from pursuing their visions and achieving their full potential.
- Recognize when subordinates need assistance or encouragement and when they need to be reeled in.

Guidelines for Command

- Empower subordinates to be creative.
- Set standards that give squadron members goals to reach.
- Provide challenging and enlightening tasks.
- Identify and develop people with leadership potential.
- Recognize unit and individual successes.
- Encourage and facilitate formal education.
- Begin developing and training future commanders. Since experience is the best training for commanders, give your officers opportunities to participate in your decision-making process and the overall operation of the squadron.

Note

1. Tom Peters, *Thriving on Chaos: Handbook for a Management Revolution* (New York: Alfred A. Knopf, 1987), 309.

Squadron Mentorship Program

Original Author: Maj Richard J. Parrotte
Commanders Connection Facilitator

References

AFPD 36-26, *Total Force Development*, 27 September 2011.

AFM 36-2643, *Air Force Mentoring Program*, 1 May 2013.

The majority of the following information is excerpted directly from the above references.

The greatest good you can do for another is not just to share your riches but to reveal to him his own.

—Benjamin Disraeli

Mentorship refers to a personal and professional relationship in which a more experienced or knowledgeable person helps a less experienced or knowledgeable person learn. The person in receipt of mentorship may be referred to as a protégé, an apprentice, or, in recent years, a mentee. Mentoring involves the informal communication of knowledge and the introduction of social and professional connections; it is relationship based. Mentoring may be simply the sharing of processes to aid in promotion or assignments or may involve personal advice, encouragement, guidance, and practical support.

Mentoring is a fundamental responsibility of Air Force supervisors. Commanders and supervisors must know their people, accept personal responsibility for them, and be accountable for their professional development. Air Force mentoring covers a wide range of areas including

- Career guidance.
- Professional development.
- Air Force history and heritage.
- Knowledge of air and space power.
- Warrior ethos.
- Air Force core values.

Keep in mind that mentoring goes beyond formal feedback sessions. Required periodic feedback is a part of mentoring, but a good mentoring program addresses the current capabilities and needs of subordinates and looks for creative ways to foster development. You must set the tone for the entire squadron with a solid mentorship program. Subordinate leaders will follow your lead and mentor their subordinates, producing professional Airmen capable of performing the Air Force mission today and in the future.

Tips for Success

- Establish goals for your squadron mentorship program, such as monthly or quarterly mentorship sessions.
- Look for opportunities outside formal feedback sessions to mentor your own subordinates (thoughtful delegation of special projects, involvement in professional organizations, or a lunch at the club).
- Mentor your subordinates about ways to capitalize on strengths and overcome weaknesses.
- Watch for opportunities for group mentoring, such as functional experts visiting your base.
- Remember that your civilians need mentoring too. Their processes are often different, so you may need to call in experts.

Additional Resource

- The AFPC website has various resources on mentoring military and civilians in several career fields and specialties at myPers, https://gum-crm.csd.disa.mil.

Chapter 3

Commanding Expeditionary Forces

Overview of the Air and Space Expeditionary Force

Original Author: Maj Rich Fillman
455th Expeditionary Logistics Readiness Squadron Commander

References

AFPD 10-4, *Operations Planning: Air and Space Expeditionary Force* (*AEF*), 30 April 2009.

Air Force Personnel Center (AFPC), Directorate of AEF and Personnel Operations, *Wing Leadership Guide to the AEF*, version 6, 1 February 2011, https://aef.afpc.randolph.af.mil/education.WLGV6_final.pdf.

The majority of the following information is excerpted directly from the above references.

From its inception, the AEF construct has evolved to provide combatant commanders the capabilities they require as part of the joint team. As a force management tool, the AEF battle rhythm has changed from its original vision to now align with global force management, providing the Air Force agility in adaptive planning. The global AEF provides a level of predictability and stability while being flexible enough to allow AEF operations to meet combatant commander requirements.

Every Airman is "in" the AEF. Some are deployed to an area of responsibility (AOR) while others are employed "in place," perhaps executing 24/7 satellite command and control (C2) to provide instantaneous combat effects halfway around the world. Every Air Force service member—regardless of AFSC, rank, or staff or line duty—is considered an expeditionary Airman and must be trained and ready to fight our nation's wars.

Air and Space Expeditionary Force Key Principles

- **Predictability**
  - o The AEF battle rhythm allows us to maintain a high state of readiness for all of our forces at all times.

- o Most Airmen are aligned with this battle rhythm, and the expectation should be perfectly clear to all: be ready to deploy during your entire window.
- o There is no such thing as a "short notice" deployment during one's designated deployment window.
- o It is the commander's responsibility to ensure all Airmen are correctly aligned and assigned to the proper AEF and are ready to deploy.

- **Equitability**
  - o Are we treating everyone the same?" Yes, at the Air Force level.
  - o Our AEF concept allows us to look across our entire Air Force and deploy Airmen at the same rate within the same skill set.
  - o Expeditionary taskings in a dynamic world are always changing so deployment rates will vary throughout your wing and across our Air Force.
- **Transparency**
  - o As our processes and systems mature, we will see an ever-increasing transparency in the day-to-day operation of the AEF, providing confidence from the ground up.
  - o There should be no mystery to the process: the when, why, and how should be visible to and understandable by every Airman.

Air and Space Expeditionary Force Key Roles and Responsibilities

Original Author: Maj Rich Fillman
455th Expeditionary Logistics Readiness Squadron Commander

Our policy is to posture all funded military manpower authorizations in UTCs [unit type codes] and ensure all uniformed Airmen, regardless of assignment, are trained, ready for mobility, informed on how they are postured, and are prepared to deploy during their assigned deployment window.

—Air Force Chief of Staff Message
6 May 2005

Your understanding of the roles and responsibilities that contribute to the AEF process is critical to its success. This insight leads to highly prepared forces and successful delivery of capabilities to supported combatant commanders.

Commander

- Ensure that each Airman is postured correctly IAW AEF guidance.
- Ensure that each Airman is notified of his or her AEF assignment.
- Ensure that Airmen are personally notified of taskings within 96 hours of receipt of tasking.
- Ensure that personnel are trained and prepared for deployment within reporting timelines.
- Ensure accurate reporting and signing of the AEF reporting tool.
- Know UTC requirements and capabilities for your unit.
- Appoint a UDM for 24 months minimum (per AFI 10-403, *Deployment Planning and Execution*, par. 1.9.1.15).
- Advise the chain of command up to the wing commander of resource changes that may impact unit capabilities.
- Commanders with UTCs in the AEF library will associate all unit members filling positions against a specific AEF tempo band/block in the MilPDS.
- Commanders will not select individuals outside their associated AEF deployment periods to fill UTC taskings without first gaining a MAJCOM vice-commander waiver. If tasked to fill a requirement and resources aren't available, the unit commander identifies the shortfall condition (1 or 5) and initiates a reclama using a reclama processing tool (RPT).
- Ensure minimal shortfalls and reclamas. Reclamas will occur only under the most extenuating circumstances.

Superintendent

- Works with the UDM to ensure proper UTC coding.
- Coordinates weekly with the UDM to ensure the AEF UTC status reporting tool is updated.
- Assesses incoming personnel and assigns to a UTC and AEF.

First Sergeant

- Assists members and advises commander on personal affairs preparation prior to deployment.
- Ensures members know about programs available to them in their deployed status.

- Ensures families are taken care of and know about available support programs.
- During members' deployment, ensures their families are contacted regularly.
- Maintains contact with deployed members, and ensures their needs are being taken care of.
- Prepares for the return of deployed members; spearheads the reintegration process, ensuring families are kept informed.

Unit Deployment Manager

- Works with the installation deployment officer (IDO) and installation personnel readiness to ensure all unit personnel and equipment are ready to deploy.
- Reports unit deployment readiness to the commander.
- Serves as liaison with the unit training manager, squadron superintendent, and wing training functional managers to notify them of required just-in-time training and specific AOR or required functional-area special training IAW line remarks and other guidance.
- Works with squadron leadership to posture members in UTCs and assign them to an AEF.
- Ensures the ART report is updated IAW requirements and is accurate.

Installation Deployment Officer and Installation Deployment Readiness Cell

- Normally assigned to the logistics readiness squadron.
- Accountable to wing commander for all deployment planning and execution operations.
- Responsibilities
    - o Informs the wing commander of all deployment requirements and taskings.
    - o Coordinates with appropriate commanders for deployment preparation and execution issues.
    - o Receives all deployment taskings, including individual personnel taskings in support of the OPLAN, concept plan (CONPLAN), time-phased force deployment data (TPFDD), and/or AEF commitments.
    - o Identifies, validates, and distributes AEF taskings and information.

- o Presents AEF decision-quality information to wing leadership.
- o Compiles unit inputs and presents the AEF UTC reporting tool briefing to wing leadership; normally conducted monthly with all unit commanders present.

Logistics Readiness Flight

- Normally assigned to the LRS.
- Provides logistics planning; war reserve materiel (WRM) management; deployment planning, training, and execution; base or expeditionary support planning; sustainment; redeployment processing; mobility bags; small arms weapons; and logistics command and control.
- Provides logistics-readiness deployment training for all installation personnel.
- Manages air terminal operations and squadron-level contingency support requirements.

Individual Personnel Readiness

- Individual personnel readiness (IPR) is aligned under the FSS.
- Provides personnel deployment planning and execution in matters pertaining to deployment availability information, deployed personnel accountability, and duty status reporting for contingency, exercise, and deployments.
- Conducts war planning for unit personnel, maintains accurate personnel strength and force accountability, and processes personnel for deployment.

Traffic Management Flight

- Traffic management flight (TMF) is assigned to the LRS.
- Coordinates with personnel readiness function to schedule commercial travel to aerial port of embarkation (APOE) and military channel airlift into aerial port of debarkation (APOD) for deploying personnel.
- Checks TPFDD to ensure passengers aren't already scheduled for aggregation airlift.
- Briefs deploying personnel on expected layovers at APOD awaiting intratheater airlift and limitations regarding excess baggage.
- Books commercial tickets for those areas in the AOR without commercial travel offices from the APOE (Baltimore-Washington International Airport) back to home station for redeploying passengers.

Tips for Success

- Know which functions handle which deployment actions.
- Make sure your Airmen are ready to deploy.
- Understand the selection process.
- Assign a mature, competent individual as UDM.
- Assign your Airmen to UTCs with alternates and backups when possible.
- Understand ART reporting.
- Keep your first sergeant and superintendent informed and involved.
- Know where your Airmen are deployed.
- Ensure supervisors and duty sections stay in contact with deployed Airmen.
- Ensure supervisors and duty sections check on family members of deployed Airmen.

Unit Type Code Overview

Original Author: Maj Rich Fillman
455th Expeditionary Logistics Readiness Squadron Commander

References

AFI 10-401, *Air Force Operations Planning and Execution*, 7 December 2006 (incorporating through interim change 4, 13 March 2012).

AFPC, *Force Providers Guide to the AEF*, version 1.0, 1 May 2012, Air Force Portal, https://www.my.af.mil.

The majority of the following information is excerpted directly from the above references.

The Air Force presents its forces to the combatant commander through the development of an air and space expeditionary task force (AETF). The basic building block used in joint force planning and the deployment of an AETF is the unit type code. A UTC is a five-character, alphanumeric code that identifies a potential capability focused on accomplishing a specific mission. UTCs can consist of personnel and/or equipment requirements. Air Force units present their capabilities or make their UTCs available through a process called UTC posturing and coding. To ensure proper posturing and coding of a unit's capabilities, commanders must "know their UTCs" and the capabilities their wings and units are making available.

Commanders can view UTC details in the mission capability (MISCAP) statement that defines the basic mission the UTC is capable of accomplishing. The MISCAP will clearly define all substitution rules, if applicable (e.g., AFSC, skill-level requirement, grade, special experience identifier, equipment), to include thresholds on the maximum number of positions that could be substituted. Aviation UTCs must reference the Air Force War and Mobilization Plan (WMP), volume 5, for sortie and attrition rates and durations. Every MISCAP is required to have the UTC point of contact and date of the last UTC review. This is the last item in the MISCAP.

Tips for Success

- Ensure you are aware of which UTCs you are tasked to support IAW the DOC statement.
- Ensure all positions on your UMD are postured into UTCs.
- Establish a working relationship with your functional area manager (FAM), responsible for changing UTC posturing codes.
- Know your unit's UTC capabilities and requirements.
- Know which UTCs are postured in each AEF library for your unit.

Air and Space Expeditionary Force Reporting Tool Management

Original Author: Maj Rich Fillman
455th Expeditionary Logistics Readiness Squadron Commander

References

AFI 10-244, *Reporting Status of Air and Space Expeditionary Forces*, 15 June 2012.

AFPC, *Force Providers Guide to the AEF*, version 1.0, 1 May 2012, Air Force Portal, https://www.my.af.mil.

AEF Operations, *AEF UTC Reporting Tool (ART) User Manual*, version 3.0.28.

The majority of the following information is excerpted directly from the above references.

Commander Responsibilities

- Ensure assigned personnel meet mission training requirements and plan for deployment IAW AFI 10-401, *Air Force Operations Planning and Execution*, and AFI 10-403, *Deployment Planning and Execution.*
- Advise the wing commander of resource changes that may impact UTC capabilities.
- Associate, track, and manage personnel and equipment in UTCs, and assign them to the proper AEF.
- The squadron/unit commander is the authority for status of the unit's UTC(s) as reported in ART.
- Report your unit's current ability through the next six months to support each allocated UTC.
  - o Submit an out-of-cycle report within 24 hours of any significant event that changes the assessment for the current AEF plus two additional AEF rotations (i.e., AEFs 1 and 2 plus AEFs 3 and 4 and AEFs 5 and 6).
  - o Submit an out-of-cycle report when notified of a UTC change or addition.
  - o Submit a UTC assessment using ART within five days of deployment notification.
- Assess UTC readiness based on your unit's ability to provide the UTC for mission execution at any time.
- Rate each UTC against the unit's current ability to deploy and employ the UTC using the "stoplight" assessment process (green, yellow, or red) to address whether the UTC can perform its MISCAP:
  - o Green—go; all personnel, equipment, and training are available to deploy within 72 hours of notification.
  - o Yellow—caution; missing or deficient capability that does not prevent the UTC from being tasked and accomplishing the mission. Provide detailed explanation of the shortfall, corrective action, and projected get-well date.
  - o Red—no go; missing or deficient capability that prevents the UTC from being tasked and accomplishing its mission. Provide detailed explanation of the shortfall, corrective action, and projected get-well date.

Tips for Success

- Provide UTC assessment using a stoplight assessment process (green, yellow, or red) to address whether the UTC can perform its MISCAP.
- Know your UTC and MISCAP capability.
- Assess the UTC every 30 days even if there is no status change.
- Submit UTC 24-hour status-change updates (current AEF plus two AEF rotations).
- Assess UTC immediately when UTC is tasked to deploy.
- Update ART within five days when UTC is tasked.
- Cover items that affect future health of UTC in remarks.
- Allocate personnel to only one UTC.
- Single UTC assessments are confidential, and two or more are secret.
- Bottom line: if you assess a UTC as green, it had better be ready to deploy.

Status of Resources and Training System

Original Author: Maj Kathy Goforth
898th Munitions Squadron Commander

References

AFPD 10-2, *Readiness*, 6 November 2012.

AFI 10-201, *Status of Resources and Training System*, 19 April 2013.

The majority of the following information is excerpted directly from the above references.

The Status of Resources and Training System is an internal management tool that the CJCS, services, unified commands, and combat support agencies may use. It is the single automated reporting system within the DOD, functioning as the central registry of all operational units of the US armed forces and certain foreign organizations.

Threefold Purpose of SORTS

- Provides data critical to crisis planning.
- Provides for the deliberate or peacetime planning process.

- USAF chief of staff (CSAF) and subordinate commanders use it to assess their effectiveness in meeting Title 10 responsibilities to organize, train, and equip forces for combatant commands.

Frequency of SORTS Reporting

- Monthly at a SORTS brief to the wing commander.
- When changes affect
    - o Unit's overall category level (C-level).
    - o Four measured-area levels (personnel, training, equipment and supplies on hand, and equipment condition).
    - o Associated reason codes (see AFI 10-201).
    - o Get-well or get-worse date.
- When desired by the unit commander.

Category Levels

- C-1—unit can meet the full wartime mission(s); does not require any compensation for any deficiencies.
- C-2—unit can meet most of the wartime mission(s); requires little, if any, compensation for deficiencies.
- C-3—unit can meet many, but not all, portions of the wartime mission(s); requires significant compensation for deficiencies.
- C-4—unit requires additional resources or training to undertake its wartime mission(s); may be tasked with resources on hand.
- C-5—unit is undergoing a service-directed resource action.
    - o Resource actions include aircraft conversion, mission change, change in home station location, or a unit activation, reactivation, or deactivation.
    - o Within the chemical and biological defense reports, units will use C-5 to indicate when they have no nuclear, biological, and chemical (NBC) defense equipment or training requirements.
- C-6—unit is not required to measure assets in a specified area.

Designed Operational Capabilities Statement Purpose

- Summarizes the purpose for the unit's organization or design.

- Describes unit's mission narrative.
- Details SORTS measurement criteria.

Commander Responsibilities

- Designate (in writing) alternates capable of completing SORTS reporting actions in your absence.
- Appoint unit SORTS monitors (two or more), and ensure they are adequately trained to perform SORTS duties.
  - o Units must maintain ability to deploy a SORTS-trained monitor and allow for peacetime leave and TDYs without disrupting normal reporting requirements.
  - o Reports will not be delayed due to unavailability of SORTS monitors.
    - ▪ Ensure report submissions meet established timelines.
    - ▪ Ensure data reflected in the SORTS report adequately reflects the unit's ability to accomplish missions on the DOC statement.
    - ▪ Review remarks monthly for additions, changes, or deletions.
    - ▪ Explain deficiencies in layman's terms, addressing planned corrective actions and a realistic resolution date.
    - ▪ Review and sign applicable SORTS product.
- Review, sign, and date DOC statement(s) as soon as possible after assuming command. A new statement is received upon a change to an existing statement and then annually thereafter.
- Ensure your commander's support staff monitors personnel duty status (e.g., medical, leave, TDY, administrative action) daily.
- Ensure that a process is established for the availability tracking of DOD civilians reported in the unit's SORTS reports.

Unit SORTS Monitor Responsibilities

- Prepares monthly unit SORTS report.
- Advises you regarding DOC statement discrepancies.
- Tracks discrepancies in subsequent reports to ensure they have been corrected.
- Ensures remarks contain all appropriate details such as AFSCs, part numbers, projected improvement or degradation dates, and defined acronyms.

- Verifies personnel duty status accuracy with the commander's support squadron (CSS).
- Briefs you prior to obtaining your signature on the unit SORTS report for release authority, advising of any discrepancies noted in previous reports and actions being taken to correct them.

Tips for Success

- Ensure accurate and timely reporting is accomplished.
- Assign overall C-level in SORTS.
- Provide clear, concise comments as needed or required.
- Ensure SORTS is reported at least every 30 days.
- Ensure SORTS report is submitted within 24 hours of a change in C-level, reason code, or measured area.
- Ensure two units do not report the same resources.
- Ensure UTCs and their status are accurately reflected in the ART.
- Remember that DOC statements are directive in nature and that SORTS reporting must continue even when resolving DOC statement issues.

Air and Space Expeditionary Force Training and Exercises

Original Author: Maj Rich Fillman
455th Expeditionary Logistics Readiness Squadron Commander

References

AFI 10-250, *Individual Medical Readiness*, 9 March 2007 (incorporating through change 2, 28 November 2011; certified current 8 March 2012).

AFI 10-403, *Deployment Planning and Execution*, 20 September 2012 (incorporating change 1, 29 April 2013).

AFPC, *Force Providers Guide to the AEF*, version 1.0, 1 May 2012, Air Force Portal, https://www.my.af.mil.

The majority of the following information is excerpted directly from the above references.

In no other profession are the penalties for employing untrained personnel so appalling or so irrevocable as in the military.

—Gen Douglas MacArthur

Training and exercises are the keys to ensuring our Airmen are prepared for current and unexpected operations in the world. They are an important investment to the safety of our members and the successful execution of our mission. Training requirements must be identified accurately and conducted consistently and in a timely manner and Airmen given opportunities to increase their skill and confidence levels. Additionally, all Airmen must be medically cleared to deploy. Your unit mobility manager works closely with base medical personnel to ensure all preventive health assessment and individual medical readiness (PIMR) requirements are completed. Your unit's PIMR report requires a monthly review.

Predeployment Training

- Readiness and ancillary training requirements
  - o Information assurance (IA) awareness.
  - o Law of armed conflict (LOAC).
  - o Self-aid and buddy care (SABC).
  - o Air Force level I antiterrorism (AT).
  - o Explosive ordnance recognition (EOR).
  - o Small arms.
  - o Chemical, biological, radiological, nuclear, and high-yield explosive (CBRNE).
  - o AOR-specific update.
  - o Language and cultural familiarization.
  - o Personal legal and finance readiness briefings.
- Special training
  - o Based on function and/or the assigned deployment location.
    - ▪ Request for forces (RFF).
    - ▪ In-lieu-of sourcing.
    - ▪ Individual mobilization augmentee (IMA) taskings.
  - o Conducted "just in time" to provide deploying Airmen expeditionary combat skills.
  - o Curriculum consists of 19 hours of training.
    - ▪ Weapons issue (.5 hours).

    - Load-bearing equipment and body armor (1 hour).
    - Use of force (2 hours).
    - Combat skills (4 hours).
    - Rifle fighting (.5 hours).
    - Fighting position (.5 hours).
    - Air base defense (1 hour).
    - M-16 maintenance (1.5 hours).
    - Field exercise (8 hours).
  - Taught by wing-level subject matter experts (typically SFS); the AEFC provides standardized lesson plans (available on the AEFC website).
  - Designed to make Airmen proficient and comfortable with handling a weapon and working within a team to defend themselves, their team, and their mission.

Preventive Health Assessment and Individual Medical Readiness Requirements

- Preventive health assessment (PHA)
  - Conducted annually; some bases conduct PHAs during member's birth month.
  - 90-day grace period; member remains "medically ready."
  - One day after 90-day grace period member is "not medically ready."
  - Exceptions to this policy are explained in AFI 10-250, *Individual Medical Readiness.*
- Dental readiness
  - Annual dental exam (every 365 days; some bases conduct these exams during member's birth month).
  - Grace period extends through the end of the month following the month dental exam was due; member remains medically ready.
  - First day of the month following the grace period, member will receive a dental classification of "4" and be determined not medically ready.
- Immunization status
  - All recommended vaccinations are current.

  - Grace periods vary by shot.
  - When shot is due but not overdue (for most immunizations), member remains medically ready.
- Individual medical equipment
  - One pair of gas mask inserts, if required.
  - 30-day grace period when the inserts are on order and being shipped; member remains medically ready.
  - After 30-day grace period, member becomes not medically ready.
- Medical readiness laboratory studies
  - Screening tests required upon accession.
    - Blood type and Rh factor.
    - DNA specimen collection.
    - Human immunodeficiency virus (HIV), required every two years.
    - Any other requirements from other policies.
- Deployment-limiting conditions
  - Members on a 4T profile recommending "not worldwide qualified" or "not deployable."
  - Assignment limitation code (ALC) C (1, 2, or 3).
  - Assignment availability code (AAC) 31, 37, or 81.

Air Force–Level Exercises

- AEF center nominates sourcing for approximately 38 joint exercises each year for Airmen to exercise mission capabilities before deploying.
- Units not tasked to fill operational combatant command (COCOM) requirements are considered "residual" capabilities for that AEF and can be utilized to support joint CONUS and outside the continental United States (OCONUS) exercises.
- Expeditionary combat support (ECS) Airmen may be tasked to attend exercise Eagle Flag.
  - What Red Flag is to the fighter community.
  - Focus is on the application of skills associated with establishing an air base at an austere location.

- o Opportunity to practice expeditionary combat skills in a mock environment based on challenges faced during Operations Enduring Freedom and Iraqi Freedom.
- o Current concept involves deploying a combat support team to open and establish an expeditionary operating location within nine days of deploying to the training site at Fort Dix, New Jersey.

Tips for Success

- Ensure Airmen are fully qualified with predeployment training.
- Ensure Airmen are medically cleared to deploy.
- Review theater reporting instructions for required special training such as convoy drivers, security forces, civil engineers (CE), or EOD.
- Remain postured to support deployments and exercises during your AEF deployment window.
- Ensure unit remains postured and ready to support exercises during your AEF training window.

Online Air and Space Expeditionary Force Resources

Original Author: Maj Rich Fillman
455th Expeditionary Logistics Readiness Squadron Commander

References

AEF Online, https://aef.afpc.randolph.af.mil.

USAF Lessons Learned, https://www.jllis.mil/USAF.

The majority of the following information is excerpted directly from the above references.

A multitude of websites offer AEF information at your disposal. The following are two that you as a commander should be familiar with.

AEF Online

Welcome to AEF Online
Click to learn more about the Directorate of AEF & Personnel Operations
AIR FORCE PERSONNEL CENTER

AEF Online is an excellent website to get you started on a plethora of topics, including the following. Below each topic is the type of information available.

- Deployment information
  - Deployment preparation.
  - Personal preparation.
  - Civilian deployment guidance.
  - Airman and family preparation.
- Force providers
  - Deployment preparation.
  - MAJCOM AEF debriefs.
  - AEF metrics.
  - Passenger travel.
- Air Reserve Component (ARC)
  - Air Force Reserve.
  - Air National Guard.
  - Reserve component guidance.
- Education and training
  - AEF courseware.
  - Guides to the AEF.
  - AEF articles.
- Indeterminate TDYs
  - AFIs, policy, and guidance.
  - Provincial reconstruction team (PRT).
  - Volunteer information (active duty).

- Volunteer information (ARC).
- Other information.

- Personnel readiness operations
    - Personnel support for contingency operations (PERSCO).
    - Links.
    - Briefings and training.
    - PRF/IPR.
    - Casualty.
    - Policy/guidance.

Action Items

- Deliberate Crisis Action Planning and Execution System reconciliation reports
- Commander's Toolkit (CCTK)
    - Provides detailed information on the deployment readiness of your squadron.
    - A Nonsecure Internet Protocol Router Network (NIPRNET)-based application designed for commanders to review their unit's state of AEF readiness.
    - Caution: The CCTK is *not* an authoritative source for deployment readiness status; it serves only as a snapshot for planning purposes. Actual readiness status is determined by the entities who own/control the readiness data.
    - The CCTK allows you to
        - View general statistical data about your unit.
        - View level 2 or line-item details of statistical data.
        - View outstanding health assessment items.
        - Filter data by AEF.
        - View general deployment criteria.

The *Commander's Toolkit User Manual* includes instructions on how to request access (https://aef.afpc.randolph.af.mil/UserManuals/CTK/CTK_User_Manual.pdf).

USAF Lessons Learned

- Contains after action reports (AAR) from previous AEFs; familiarizes you with issues at deployed locations.
- Provides additional lessons learned websites including Marine Corps, Army, and Air Force MAJCOMs.
- The Air Force Joint Lessons Learned Information System (JLLIS) training module gives instructions on how to access the reports and upload your own AARs if needed (https://www.jllis.mil).

Shortfalls, Waivers, and Reclamas

Original Author: Maj Glenn Basso
380th Expeditionary Contracting Squadron Commander

References

AFI 10-401, *Air Force Operations Planning and Execution*, 7 December 2006 (incorporating through change 4, 13 March 2012).

AFI 10-403, *Deployment Planning and Execution*, 20 September 2012 (incorporating change 1, 29 April 2013).

AFPC, *Force Providers Guide to the AEF*, version 1.0, 1 May 2012, Air Force Portal, https://www.my.af.mil.

The majority of the following information is excerpted directly from the above references.

Shortfall and Reclama Procedures

Air Force active duty, the AFRC, the ANG, MAJCOMs, wings, groups, and units will make every effort to meet all taskings (IAW AFI 10-401, par. 9.16; see also par. 10.21 for definitions of *shortfall* and *reclama*). Generally, relief should only be sought when (1) a wing or tasked unit does not possess sufficient or qualified personnel to support a crisis tasking, (2) the deployed commander is unable to waive the requirement, or (3) the tasking is impossible to meet or will shut down critical elements of the home-station mission, as determined by the wing commander or equivalent. Filling shortfalls in one UTC may mean moving a person from another UTC as long as the UTC and associated person are in the on-call AEF being sourced by the AEFC. Units will immediately update ART to reflect the status of the UTC(s).

When your unit is unable to meet its AEF tasking due to personnel or equipment or both, you must take immediate action to inform your chain of command. Once you've identified the shortfall, you have two options: submit either a waiver request or a reclama. You'll work closely with your UDM and the IDO during the waiver or reclama process. If you deploy a troop who is unqualified or does not meet the tasking specifications, he or she will be returned home at your unit's expense, and you will still be required to fill the deployment tasking.

Units will submit reclamas only after exhausting all other options. Reclamas will occur only under the most extenuating circumstances and require MAJCOM vice-commander approval (category 5) unless the unit does not have the capability (categories 1–4). All reclamas must comply with the tasking and sourcing processes and priorities described in AFI 10-401, chapter 5 (see section 10C in the AFI for more information on the shortfall and reclama change process). Reclamas are minimized when unit type code availability (UTA) and ART are properly maintained. Units must ensure UTA and ART are accurate and up to date.

Commanders should not view the AOR's requirement criteria as an "all or nothing" demand when their judgment tells them an exception should be made. Extenuating circumstances often prevent the tasked commander from delivering the "perfect Airman."

Shortfall Conditions

- Condition 1—insufficient authorized, assigned, eligible, qualified, or trained personnel within tasked unit.
- Condition 2—insufficient on-hand or serviceable equipment within tasked unit.
- Condition 3—no capability available in the on-call AEF pair within tasked unit.
- Condition 4—desired capability not inherent within tasked unit.
- Condition 5—deployment of personnel would cause severe adverse impact on the wing and unit mission.

Waiver Request

- Submitted before requesting a reclama.
- Submitted whenever your unit has the ability to meet the requirement under substitution rules (see AFI 10-403, chap. 5).
- Submitted to deployed group commander to waive tasking or permit substitution.

  - AFSC—person can meet the functional requirements of the originally tasked AFSC.
  - Enlisted grade—person must have the tasked grade or one grade higher.
  - Enlisted skill level—person with two skill levels higher or one skill level lower, unless prohibited.
  - Officer grade—person with one grade higher or one grade lower than the required grade, unless prohibited.

Reclama Request

- When the wing or tasked unit does not possess sufficient or qualified personnel to support a crisis tasking.
- When deployed commander is unable to waive requirement.
- When the wing or unit tasking is impossible to meet without shutting down critical elements of the home station's mission.
- Request relief via IDO to the wing commander.
  - If the wing commander concurs with a condition 1, 2, 3, or 4 reclama, IDO forwards to AEFC via reclama reporting tool (RRT).
  - If the wing commander concurs with a condition 5 reclama, IDO forwards to MAJCOM.
  - If the wing commander nonconcurs, IDO informs the tasked unit.
- Will occur only under the most extenuating circumstances.
- Minimized when the UTA and ART are properly maintained.

Reclama Processing Tool

- A Web-based process used to submit reclamas or unit identification code (UIC) changes.
  - NIPRNET—used for training and local and higher headquarters exercises, and
  - Secret Internet Protocol Router Network (SIPRNET)—used to initiate, review, and approve or disapprove reclamas for AEF taskings.
- Provides total visibility of reclamas from unit initiation to AEFC resourcing.
- Communicates unit's inability to meet a combatant commander's requirements for personnel and/or equipment in a timely, effective manner.

- RPT user manual is at https://aef.afpc.randolph.af.mil/UserManuals/RPT/RPT_User_Manual.pdf.

Tips for Success

- Report ART status accurately.
- Fully understand the waiver and reclama processes.
- Avoid a reclama if possible.
- Work closely with your UDM and IDO as you work through the waiver or reclama process.
- Look at current assets, and determine if you need a waiver.
- Make the decision to submit a waiver or reclama as early as possible.

First Seven Days of Deployed Command

Original Author: Maj Rich Fillman
455th Expeditionary Logistics Readiness Squadron Commander

Volumes of articles and guidance have been written on what to do during your first 90 days as an "in-garrison" squadron commander. However, little has been written on what to do at a deployed location, especially in a combat zone. Many of the same basic concepts of command apply, but there are some added deployment-related requirements. Not only is your time for "what to do" compressed significantly, but quite often you'll have no transition time with the previous commander. Some key areas for your attention during your first seven days of command in a deployed environment are addressed below.

Tips for Success

- Meet your group and wing commander to identify expectations, priorities, concerns, written or unwritten guidance, and decoration policy on day one.
- Know your unit's mission and capabilities and how they fit into the overall combat picture.
- Meet with squadron officer and SNCO leadership and set the tone for them. Quickly find out lessons learned and what issues they have worked since they arrived in country.
- Know where emergency medical facilities are located—ensure your squadron knows.

- Ensure you and the squadron understand the local rules on attack-response procedures, wear of body armor, weapons procedures, and off-base travel (if allowed).
- Update recall rosters and ensure accuracy in the event you have to conduct accountability procedures.
- Know where all of your facilities are located and visit them.
- Visit all shifts and ensure proper supervision is spread throughout all shifts.
- Establish a work/rest schedule (e.g., six days on, one day off).
- Know General Order Number 1 (GO-1) (alcohol use in deployed locations), and become familiar with discipline standards and procedures at the base.
- Find the locations and POCs for all of the "external contact points" to your squadron (e.g., supply, fuels, air terminal operations center [ATOC], command post, weather, contracting, security forces, and CE).
- Identify joint and coalition partnerships you may be supporting or are supported by.
- Assume nothing—the culture of "assumption" will bite you—be hesitant with the statement "this is the way the last rotation did it."
- Meet your RA to learn how purchases are processed and whether you have a budget.
- Meet with fellow squadron commanders, SJA, medical, command post, chaplain, CCM, and wing safety.
- Read contracts and know what workload requirements the contractor is responsible for.
- Validate status of equipment accounts—check for open reports of survey.
- Safety! Meet and appoint a squadron safety representative, and conduct a squadron safety walk-around.
- Know where your unit is in the rotation of forces, and track to completion.
- Ensure your unit personnel have all required deployment gear.
- Contact home-station commanders and first sergeants and give them contact info for you and your first sergeant.

- Know who is eligible for promotion, and ensure you and the first sergeant have all required paperwork for PERSCO. Make sure the home station has initiated waivers for PME if required.
- Find out what open projects the previous commander left for you to continue or complete.
- Conduct a self-inspection every rotation. Fresh eyes will identify deficiencies in work centers and help everyone understand that operations will be conducted just like at home. Getting everyone out of the "deployed operations" mentality will go a long way.
- Hold a commander's call; present your vision and expectations for the rotation.
- Take care of you; get enough rest and exercise. It is easy to burn yourself out very quickly.

Postdeployment Issues and Concerns

Original Author: Maj Glenn Basso
380th Expeditionary Contracting Squadron Commander

References

American Red Cross, *Coming Home from Deployment: The New "Normal,"* http://www.redcross.org.

The National Military Family Association has resources for assistance before, during, and after deployment at http://www.militaryfamily.org/get-info/deployment.

The majority of the following information is excerpted directly from the above references.

Many commanders emphasize preparation and training for deploying Airmen. However, postdeployment requires the same diligence from squadron commanders. Reintegration brings its own stressors and complications. You need to prepare your unit for postdeployment just as you prepared it for the deployment. This also includes the transition of members back into their families.

Commander Responsibilities

- Know your people.
- Accept personal responsibility for them.

- Be accountable for their smooth transition from the AOR back to their CONUS or OCONUS assignments.
- Ensure your Airmen attend mandatory reintegration briefings upon return.
- Ensure your Airmen are aware of the following areas of concern:
    - Reuniting with a spouse
        - It's normal to feel anxious about homecoming.
        - Plan for homecoming day—after homecoming, spouses should make time for each other on their schedules for the next few days or weeks.
        - Spouses may not have slept much and may be worn out from preparations—returning service members shouldn't be surprised if their spouses are a bit resentful of their mobilization and deployments.
        - Take time to get used to each other again.
    - Communicating
        - Encourage your Airmen to tell their spouses how they feel.
        - Advise Airmen to listen to their spouses in return: the best way to get through the reacquaintance jitters, regain closeness, and renegotiate their roles in the family is by talking and actively listening.
    - Being flexible
        - Advise Airmen to be prepared to be flexible: Airmen and/or their spouses may be facing a change in job assignment or a move; readjustment and job transition cause stress.
        - Especially true for demobilizing Guard members and Reservists transitioning back to civilian life.
    - Budgeting
        - Advise Airmen to resist the temptation to go on a spending spree celebrating their return.
        - Extra money saved during deployment may be needed later for unexpected household expenses—encourage them to stick to a budget.
    - Reuniting with children
        - Children may feel the same confusion Airmen and their spouses feel.
            - Depending on age, they may not understand how the Airman could leave them if he or she really loved them.

- They may be unsure of what to expect from their returning parent.
- They may feel uncomfortable around or think of the Airman as a stranger.
- Children's reactions to the Airman's return will differ according to their ages.

- Some normal reactions you can expect
  - Infants may cry, fuss, pull away, or cling to the spouse or caregiver they know.
  - Toddlers may be shy or clingy, not recognize the returning Airman, cry, have temper tantrums, or return to behaviors they had outgrown (e.g., no longer toilet trained). Give them space and warm-up time.
  - Preschoolers may feel guilty for making the Airman go away; they may need time to warm up to the returning Airman, have intense anger, act out to get attention, or become demanding; need to reinforce that they are loved unconditionally.
  - School-age children may show excitement or joy, talk constantly to bring the Airman up to date, boast about the returning Airman, or feel guilt about not doing enough or being good enough. Review pictures, schoolwork, family scrapbook; give praise for what children did during the Airman's deployment; do not criticize.
  - Teenagers may show excitement or guilt about not living up to standards, have concerns about rules and responsibilities, or feel too old or be unwilling to change plans to meet or spend extended time with the returning Airman.

o Single Airmen or single parents reuniting with parents, extended family members, and friends

- Your Airmen have certainly missed their family and friends, and they have missed them—advise your Airmen to let them be a part of the reunion but balance their needs with those they love and care about and expect a period of readjustment when they return home.
- If your Airmen are single or live with their parent(s), family, or a friend, many of the above tips for reuniting with spouses and children may apply. A change in the house or routine may be stressful.
- Advise your Airmen to go slowly in trying to make the adjustment to being home again. Some things will have changed at home while they were gone.

    - Married friends will be involved with their families. Others may return to their old friends, and your Airmen may feel left out.
    - Your Airmen's parents and families have been very worried about them over the past months. Advise your Airmen to give them time and special attention.
    - Your Airmen may be facing a change in job assignment or a move, trying to meet new people, or looking for a new relationship. All of these things cause additional stress.
  - Take time for yourself.
    - You may have seen or experienced some things that were very upsetting—talking with others who were there and/or counselors trained in crisis stress reactions is extremely important.
    - Look into ways to manage stress (e.g., diet, exercise, recreation).
    - Make time to rest.
    - Limit alcohol! Remember that alcohol was restricted during your deployment, and your tolerance is lower.
    - Depend on your family, unit, and friends for support.

What Returning Airmen Need to Remember

- Go slowly—don't try to make up for lost time.
- Accept that your partner and loved ones may be different.
- Take time to get reacquainted.
- Seek help if needed.

Tips for Success

- Meet the members when they return from deployment.
- Ensure leave and compensatory time off are sufficient for members to reintegrate into their everyday life.
- Ensure Airmen complete the necessary redeployment checklist (e.g., medical appointments, equipment turn-in).
- Keep an eye on your Airmen when they return to duty; there may be difficulties reintegrating into the day-to-day work routine.
- Ensure Airmen attend mandatory briefings when they return from deployment.

Additional Resource

- The Airman and family readiness center offers a return and reunion briefing.

Chapter 4

Commander's Programs

This chapter presents a wide range of topics encompassing many facets of a commander's duties. Formal programs—such as safety, security, environmental management, and squadron fitness—that require following specific guidance are discussed. Other topics—such as unit budget, informal recognition, and commander's calls—are areas necessary for an effective and healthy squadron. The following outlines key points for these programs to help commanders maximize squadron effectiveness.

Safety Programs

Original Author: Maj Kathy Goforth
898th Munitions Squadron Commander

References

AFI 91-202, *The US Air Force Mishap Prevention Program,* 5 August 2011 (incorporating change 2, 20 August 2013).

AFI 36-2833, *Safety Awards,* 31 October 2012.

The majority of the following information is excerpted directly from the above references.

> *Safety is a personal program. . . . When something goes wrong, inevitably there is a person somewhere that either made a decision or refused to make a decision that affected the outcome.*
>
> —Gen Ronald E. Keys, USAF, Retired

While safety is everybody's responsibility, a commander is required to provide a safe work environment for all assigned personnel and to encourage them to integrate mishap prevention and safety awareness on and off duty. Ensure your Airmen evaluate the work environment and job tasks in day-to-day squadron operations to identify hazards, prevent mishaps, and minimize property damage and severity of personnel injuries. Your appointed unit safety representative (USR) will serve as your "eyes and ears" in the unit, ensuring mishaps are properly reported and your unit personnel are appropriately trained. Your unit will undergo an annual safety inspection—the USR will complete the safety checklist and should provide you regular feedback on the health of *your* safety program.

Commander Responsibilities

- Implement a unit safety and health program.
- Provide a safe and healthy work environment.
- Ensure all unit members receive necessary job safety training.
- Ensure all applicable Airmen complete off-duty safety training associated with high-risk activities prior to participating in them. Typical high-risk activities are listed below, but consult with your MAJCOM or wing supplement to AFI 91-202 to verify current high-risk activities.
    - o Motorcycle riding.
    - o Dirt biking.
    - o Skydiving.
    - o Kayaking.
    - o Snow skiing and snowboarding.
- Ensure all appropriate hazard abatement actions needed to resolve identified hazards are implemented and followed up until all actions are complete.
- Ensure ORM principles are utilized at all levels of your unit.
- Implement a proactive mishap prevention program to include the procurement and proper use of appropriate personal protective equipment (PPE) and facility compliance with applicable Occupational Safety and

Health Administration (OSHA) and Air Force Occupational Safety and Health (AFOSH) standards.

- Ensure mission-specific and unique safety standards are addressed, including confined spaces, weapons safety, explosives safety, and lock-out/tagout procedures.
- Appoint a USR.

Unit Safety Representative Responsibilities

- Advises the commander, functional managers, and supervisors on safety and health matters.
- Must begin base safety office training within 30 days of appointment.
- Ensures assigned personnel are aware of the requirement to immediately report both on- and off-duty mishaps.
- Maintains unit safety bulletin board (minimum items: Air Force Form 457, USAF Hazard Report, with directions for its completion; Air Force Visual Aid (AFVA) 91-307, AFOSH Program; and wing commander's safety policy).
- Serves as your focal point for all unit safety items, such as unit mishaps, inspections, and crosstells.
- Implements special holiday safety projects or programs as needed, such as for three-day weekends, winter holidays, and the 101 Critical Days of Summer.
- Analyzes HHQ reports (e.g., inspection reports, crosstells, and lessons learned) to identify problems or potential problem areas, and initiates actions to resolve them.
- Assists supervisors in establishing an aggressive AFOSH training program for assigned personnel; ensures all training is documented.
- Attends wing safety office quarterly USR meetings.
- Conducts periodic safety inspections, briefs you on findings, and tracks corrective actions.
    - Monthly spot inspections and scheduled and no-notice inspections.
    - Semiannual self-inspections.

Tips for Success

- Ensure your Airmen understand your safety policy.
- Appoint a USR, preferably an aggressive NCO (TSgt or senior SSgt).
- Understand risk assessment codes (RAC):
  - o Have qualified safety, fire protection, and health personnel evaluate and assign RACs to potential hazards.
  - o RACs rated 1, 2, and 3 normally get the wing commander's attention and are funded when money is available.
- Review unit safety inspections and crosstell information.
- Take corrective actions to resolve current or potential safety problems.

If warranted, submit USR or other unit member for safety awards (see AFI 36-2833 and MAJCOM guidance).

Traffic Safety Program

Original Author: Maj Kathy Goforth
898th Munitions Squadron Commander

References

DOD Instruction (DODI) 6055.04, *DOD Traffic Safety Program*, 20 April 2009 (incorporating change 2, 23 January 2013).

AFI 91-207, *The US Air Force Traffic Safety Program*, 27 October 2011.

The majority of the following information is excerpted directly from the above references.

The best car safety device is a rearview mirror with a cop in it.

—Dudley Moore

The DOD Traffic Safety Program's goal is to prevent and reduce the frequency and severity of vehicle mishaps involving USAF personnel and equipment.

DOD Traffic Safety Standards

- Operator duty time—establish and enforce duty-hour limits for motor vehicle operators based on a careful operational risk assessment.
- Occupant protection.

- o Occupants must use vehicle's installed protective devices.
- o Number of passengers must be limited to designed seating capacity.
- o All military personnel under age 26 with a driver's license will receive at least four hours of traffic safety training.
- o Stresses individual responsibility and the correct response to routine and emergency driving situations.
- o Should be given shortly after initial entry into the military.
- o No cost to the individual.
- o Training is available from the wing safety office.

Cell Phone Use

- DOD personnel are prohibited from text messaging or using any cell phone or other handheld electronic devices while driving any vehicle on installations.
- Exceptions are if the vehicle is safely parked or personnel are using a hands-free device.
- Applies to personal and government-supplied electronic equipment.

DOD Impaired Driving Prevention Program

- Impaired driving is incompatible with the military's high standards of performance, military discipline, DOD personnel reliability, and readiness of military units.
- While driving on any DOD installation, operators and passengers of motor vehicles are prohibited from having open containers of alcoholic beverages in their ready possession.
    - o Open container—any receptacle having any alcoholic beverage that has been opened or had the seal broken.
    - o Ready possession—alcohol is located in the passenger compartment or is accessible to the driver or passenger(s) from the passenger compartment.

Motorcycle Rider Requirements

- PPE requirements.
    - o Helmets—Department of Transportation certified and properly fastened under the chin.
    - o Goggles and face shields—impact- or shatter-resistant goggles or full-face shield properly attached to helmet.

  - o Sturdy footwear.
  - o Clothing—includes long-sleeved shirt or jacket, long trousers, and full-fingered gloves or mittens designed for use on a motorcycle.
  - o Garment visibility—brightly colored outer upper garment during the day and a reflective upper garment at night.
- Must complete safety course.
  - o Includes initial and refresher training.
    - ▪ Course IVA, initial training, such as the Basic Riders Course (BRC) or the Motorcycle Rider Course: Riding and Street Skills (MRC:RSS).
    - ▪ Course IVB, refresher training, such as the BRC 2, Military Sport-bike Rider Course (MSRC), and Advanced Riders Course (ARC).
  - o If member has a state motorcycle license that requires a Motorcycle Safety Foundation (MSF)-approved training course, he or she is not required to complete Course IVA or IVB.
  - o Air Force military and civilian personnel do not pay for and are not charged leave for training and education mandated or implied by DOD and Air Force directives.
- Failure to wear the proper PPE or meet training requirements may be considered during line-of-duty (LOD) determinations if an injury is a result of member's noncompliance.

Privately Owned Vehicles

- Privately owned vehicle license requirements—abide by state issuing authority.
- Use of headphones or earphones is prohibited while operating a vehicle on DOD installations.
- Use of cell phone without a hands-free device is prohibited while operating a vehicle on Air Force bases.

Tips for Success

- Commanders must develop a DUI prevention program.
  - o Educate unit members concerning drinking and driving and potential punishments if convicted of DUI.

- o Institute a strong Wingman Program.
- o Set a goal for days without a DUI arrest; if your unit's members reach that goal, reward them.
- o Create designated driver (DD) cards, and distribute them to your Airmen.
  - Include unit members who voluntarily perform DD duties.
  - Include base Airmen against Drunk Driving phone numbers.
  - Include first sergeant's and your phone numbers.
- Revoke driving privileges of Airmen who don't comply with the DOD Traffic Safety Program requirements.
- Maintain a robust safety program; brief traffic safety compliance.
- Check with wing safety, and find out who pays for mandated motorcycle safety courses.
  - o If you're responsible for funding, ensure you budget for it.
  - o If the wing pays, find out how to schedule your Airmen

Additional Resources

- For more information, visit the Air Force Safety Center Web page, http://www.afsec.af.mil.
- Review your MAJCOM supplement to AFI 91-207.

Security Programs

Original Author: Maj Kathy Goforth
898th Munitions Squadron Commander

References

DOD Manual 5200.1, *DOD Information Security Program*, vols. 1–4, 24 February 2012.

DOD 5200.2-R, *DOD Personnel Security Program*, January 1987 (incorporating through change 3, 23 February 1996).

AFPD 31-4, *Information Security*, 1 September 1998.

AFPD 31-5, *Personnel Security Program Policy*, 1 August 1995.

AFI 31-401, *Information Security Program Management*, 1 November 2005 (incorporating change 1, 19 August 2009).

AFI 31-501, *Personnel Security Program Management*, 27 January 2005 (incorporating through change 2, 29 November 2012).

The majority of the following information is excerpted directly from the above references.

Security programs vary among units, but as a minimum, your unit security program will include information security and personnel security. Protecting sensitive information is critical to mission accomplishment.

The goal of the DOD Information Security Program is to protect DOD unclassified, sensitive, and classified information. The Air Force Information Security Program does this by ensuring everyone understands his or her roles and responsibilities and by integrating security procedures into our processes so they become transparent.

The purpose of the DOD Personnel Security Program is to ensure classified information is disclosed only to authorized DOD members, DOD contractors, and other affiliated persons consistent with the interests of national security.

Commander Responsibilities

- Appoint unit security manager (USM).
- Ensure assigned personnel complete security training IAW AFI 31-401, chapter 8.
- Budget for security awareness training products and materials.
- Review UIFs on Airmen under your jurisdiction.
- Establish a security information file (SIF) when an Airman's activity, conduct, or behavior is inconsistent with security criteria.
- Actively support and monitor security training.
- Ensure self-inspections are completed.
- Take appropriate actions when a security breach or violation occurs.

Unit Security Manager Responsibilities

- Provides guidance and assistance to supervisors and managers in the areas of physical, information, and personnel industrial security.

- Develops and monitors organizational-level implementing instructions, policies, and procedures to support host-installation security plans.
- Monitors the classification management program; supports program managers in developing classification guidance and decisions.
- Provides guidance on classification marking, accountability, control, storage, safeguarding, downgrading, declassifying, and destruction procedures for classified material.
- Conducts and documents security education and training.
- Maintains training documentation, on a calendar-year basis, for initial, refresher, and specialized security training.
- Prepares requests for the issuance and control of restricted area badges, processing of security clearances, and other functions within the security area.
- Provides guidance and assistance to the commander on establishing SIFs when derogatory information is discovered on a unit member with a security clearance.

Tips for Success

- Review the installation security plan available from the wing plans office.
- Appoint a USM.
    - o Must complete required security manager training from the installation security office within 90 days of appointment.
    - o Develops and updates unit security OIs.
    - o Advises you on unit security issues.
    - o Attends base security manager meetings.
    - o Reports security breaches and violations to the installation security office.
- Appoint a unit member, other than USM, to conduct the security program self-inspection.
- Ensure security training is completed and documented as directed.
- Act immediately in the event of a classified message incident (CMI).
    - o A CMI occurs when someone transmits classified information over an unclassified system.

- Notify your work group manager (WGM) when a CMI occurs.
  - Isolate and sanitize affected computers.
  - Inform network control center of CMI; it is responsible for isolating and sanitizing any servers affected by the CMI.
- Be knowledgeable of other security programs and their POCs or program managers.
  - Computer security (COMPUSEC) work group manager.
  - Communications security (COMSEC) monitor.
  - Operations security (OPSEC) monitor.

Additional Resources

- For more information on computer vulnerabilities and incidents, see AFI 33-138, *Enterprise Network Operations Notification and Tracking*, 28 November 2005.
- For help with your COMSEC program, see AFI 33-201, vol. 1, *Communications Security (COMSEC)*, 1 May 2005.
- For more information on the OPSEC program, see AFI 10-701, *Operations Security (OPSEC)*, 8 June 2011.

Antiterrorism and Force Protection Program

Original Author: Maj Kathy Goforth
898th Munitions Squadron Commander

References

DODI 2000.12, DOD *Antiterrorism (AT) Program*, 1 March 2012 (incorporating change 1, 9 September 2013).

DODI 2000.16, DOD *Antiterrorism (AT) Standards,* 2 October 2006 (incorporating through change 2, 8 December 2006).

AFI 10-245, *Antiterrorism* (*AT*), 21 September 2012.

The majority of the following information is excerpted directly from the above references.

IAW DODI 2000.12, commanders at all levels will enforce appropriate security measures to ensure protection of DOD personnel under their control and shall ensure AT awareness and readiness of all DOD personnel (including dependent family members). IAW AFI 10-245, the AT program seeks to deter terrorist acts against the Air Force by providing guidance on collecting and disseminating timely threat information, providing training to members, developing comprehensive plans to deter and counter terrorist incidents, allocating funds and personnel, and implementing AT measures. AT also requires every individual's participation to maintain awareness, practice personal security measures, and report suspicious activity.

Antiterrorism Program Components

- Antiterrorism—defensive measures used to reduce vulnerability of individuals and property to terrorist acts.
- Force protection (FP)—actions taken to prevent or mitigate hostile actions against DOD personnel (including family members), resources, facilities, and critical information.

Unit Antiterrorism Officer

- The unit antiterrorism officer (UATO) is the unit AT program expert.
- Designated by unit commander; provide names to wing ATO in writing.
- Officer or NCO (E-5 or above) or civilian equivalent.
- Must be AT level 2 certified.
- Documents commander's annual review of unit AT program and plan.
- Unit-level liaison with wing ATO on installation AT matters.
- Disseminates and conducts random antiterrorism measures (RAM) as required.

Commander Responsibilities

- Thoroughly integrate AT into unit mission.
- Continually review AT posture to keep current with changing policies and threat levels.
- Determine potential vulnerabilities and resource prioritization.
- Forward any threat and potential vulnerability that cannot be controlled to senior leadership.
- Review installation's or higher level's unit supplement to AFI 10-245 implementing unit-specific FP standards.
- Ensure unit members receive level 1 AT awareness training.

  - o Annually for CONUS-based DOD personnel eligible for OCONUS deployment.
  - o Annually for active uniformed CONUS-based members of combatant commands and services.
  - o Annually for CONUS-based DOD personnel, regardless of duty status, if CONUS terrorism threat level is promulgated above "moderate."
  - o Document training IAW AFI 10-245.
- Ensure UATO develops unit AT plan (OI, checklist, or annex to installation AT plan).
- Annually exercise unit AT plan.

Tips for Success

- Appoint a UATO.
- Review unit AT program and plans annually and as threat level changes.
- Develop a process to raise and lower force protection condition (FPCON) based on current terrorism threat information and/or guidance from HHQ.
- Develop and implement an AT plan addressing the following key elements:
  - o Terrorism threat assessment.
  - o Vulnerability assessment.
  - o Risk assessment.
  - o AT physical security measures.
  - o Terrorist incident response measures.
  - o Terrorist consequence management measures.
- Prepare an annual terrorism threat assessment concerning unit personnel, assets, and mission-critical infrastructure.
- Develop procedures to ensure terrorism threat advisories, terrorism warning reports, terrorism threat-level changes, and FPCON changes are immediately disseminated to all unit personnel.
- Ensure personnel deploying, PCSing, or traveling on leave outside CONUS receive predeployment AT with special emphasis on AOR-specific terrorist and medical threats.

Environmental Management

Original Author: Maj Arlen Hammock
Detachment 2, 22nd Space Operations Squadron Commander

Reference

AFI 32-7086, *Hazardous Materials Management*, 1 November 2004, certified current 29 December 2009.

The majority of the following information is excerpted directly from the above reference.

The Air Force is committed to complying with environmental laws and regulations. Because fiscal and manpower costs associated with environmental programs are staggering, you must be familiar with the multiple operational constraints and be sensitive to any interface between the mission and environmental restrictions. Delay in responding to environmental problems may cost thousands of dollars and hamper a base's ability to perform its mission. Not only must you be concerned due to mission impacts, but you also must be aware of the precedent for personal criminal liability.

While understanding the environmental laws and regulations that restrict or affect Air Force activities may appear to be a daunting task, environmental experts are available within the Air Force to guide and assist you through this process. Engineering and legal experts are available at all levels—MAJCOM, regional, and base—to provide support in the environmental arena (e.g., the environmental lawyer in your SJA office and the civil engineering [CE] environmental flight).

All pollution-abatement statutes (i.e., pertaining to the pollution of air and water as well as the handling of hazardous waste) carry civil and criminal penalties. Federal or state agencies may enforce these statutes. Additionally, foreign host-nation agencies may enforce statutes in overseas locations. Under normal circumstances, military members and civilian employees are exempt from civil or administrative penalties. But regulators may seek civil or criminal penalties from the Air Force and its personnel.

Your best defense against being charged for active, knowledgeable, participation in illegal activities is quite simple: obey the law. If you are in violation, work with your federal and state environmental regulators or host nation (if applicable) to become compliant with the law. In your role as commander, vigilance is your defense against being charged for a violation of the law. Stay informed about what is going on environmentally on the base; consult with CE and the SJA on matters of environmental compliance.

Tips for Success

- Be familiar with the environmental hazards in your squadron.
- Ensure your unit maintains a robust hazardous material (HAZMAT) program—know the requirements and follow them thoroughly.
- Appoint a knowledgeable unit HAZMAT program manager.
- Determine the HAZMAT items used or handled by your personnel.
- Consult the installation ground safety staff and the CE staff for assistance if required.
- Establish and implement hazard reporting and abatement programs.
- Brief all personnel on the findings and recommendations contained in annual and baseline industrial hygiene surveys and reports.
- Ensure compliance with the Air Force Hazardous Communication Program.
- Ensure hazardous waste is properly characterized, segregated, marked, labeled, weighed, stored, packaged, and transferred for disposal.
- Consult with CE, bioenvironmental engineering services, and the HAZMAT planning team before any hazardous waste disposal process or activity is modified or any new process or activity is planned.
- Contact the CE environmental flight to determine if any endangered species exist on or near your facilities.
- Contact the bioenvironmental engineering flight (base medical) to determine if there are any concerns (radon gas levels, lead paints, asbestos, noise levels) within your facilities.
- Attend the base Environmental, Safety, and Occupational Health Council meetings.

Additional Resources

- Check out the additional 32-7000 series AFIs for more detailed information concerning individual environmental protection programs.
- Each base should have a HAZMAT disposal plan, a pollution prevention plan, or other environmental plans; contact your wing plans office or CE to get a copy and review it.

Air Force Emergency Management Program

Original Author: Maj Arlen Hammock
Detachment 2, 22nd Space Operations Squadron Commander

References

AFPD 10-25, *Emergency Management*, 26 September 2007 (certified current 23 June 2010).

AFI 10-2501, *Air Force Emergency Management (EM) Program Planning and Operations,* 24 January 2007 (incorporating through change 3, 29 April 2013; corrective actions applied on 10 May 2013).

The majority of the following information is excerpted directly from the above references.

Protection of Air Force personnel and operational resources is essential to successful Air Force operations. The primary missions of the Air Force emergency management (EM) program—previously known as full-spectrum threat response—are to save lives; minimize the loss or degradation of resources; and continue, sustain, and restore operational capability in an all-hazards physical threat environment at Air Force installations worldwide.

The ancillary missions of the Air Force EM program are to support homeland defense and civil support operations and to provide support to civil and host-nation authorities IAW DOD directives and through the appropriate COCOM. Major program elements of the EM program include warning and reporting, commanding and controlling, planning, equipping, organizing, training, exercising, evaluating, conducting response operations, and implementing incident management.

Full Spectrum of Physical Threats

- Terrorist use of weapons of mass destruction (WMD) involving chemical, biological, radiological, nuclear, and explosive material.
- Enemy attacks in a nuclear, biological, chemical, and conventional (NBCC) environment.
- Major accidents.
- Hazardous materials.
- Natural disasters.
- Humanitarian actions.

Commander Responsibilities

- Appoint unit EM representatives to manage and coordinate unit EM program.
- Ensure your unit EM representative completes semiannual self-inspections.
- Request CE readiness flight leadership provide you a briefing on EM policies and responsibilities.
- Appoint emergency operations center (EOC) members required by the installation Comprehensive Emergency Management Plan (CEMP) 10-2.
- Establish a unit control center, EOC, and specialized team requirements, such as managing shelters and leading contamination control teams (CCT).
- Provide the CE readiness flight a written reply to EM program SAV observations or findings; include corrective actions and estimated completion dates (ECD).
- Participate in installation EM planning and exercises.
- Ensure unit personnel are trained IAW AFI 10-2501, chapter 6; units are responsible for scheduling, tracking, and documenting all training.
- Appoint members to the base exercise evaluation team.
- Identify requirements and budget for, obtain, store, and maintain unit passive defense operational and training equipment.
- Identify and equip augmentees to support the EM program (see AFPAM 10-243, *Augmentation Duty*, 1 August 2002).
- Ensure EOC and UCC members participate in at least one exercise per year; document training IAW AFI 10-2501, chapter 6.
- Ensure personnel who are inherently deployable to CBRNE defense threat areas can perform mission-essential tasks in a contaminated environment.
- Ensure all unit military personnel and emergency-essential civilians and contractors maintain and use AFPAM 10-100, *Airman's Manual*, during exercises and real-world contingencies.

Tips for Success

- Appoint unit EM representatives to manage and coordinate unit requirements of the unit EM program.
  - Attends training IAW AFI 10-2501, chapter 6.
  - Conducts semiannual self-inspections IAW AFI 10-2501.

- o Creates and maintains a unit EM program folder, either hard copy or electronic. Contents must include
  - A copy of the unit quarterly EM report; update the report at least quarterly, or when you appoint a new primary or alternate unit EM representative.
  - Current and previous year SAV and self-inspection reports.
  - Copies of correspondence concerning EM SAV and self-inspection reports.
  - Observations and corrective actions; deficiencies should be tracked until closed.
  - Other items as required by MAJCOM or local guidance.
- Appoint EOC members required by the installation CEMP 10-2 from within your unit to support the installation EM program.
  - o Upon selection, team members must have at least two-thirds of their time on station left to serve for OCONUS and CONUS-isolated locations.
  - o Upon selection, team members must have at least 18 months retainability at CONUS nonisolated assignments
- Appoint team members required by the installation CEMP 10-2.
  - o Readiness support team (RST) members must possess a valid driver's license, have at least a secret security clearance, and meet any local qualifications designated by the CE commander.
  - o Team members must have normal color vision, a minimum physical profile of "two" under "P," "U," "L," "H," and "E" and a "one" under "S," and the ability to lift at least 50 pounds.
  - o RST members must not be assigned to other additional duties that conflict with RST duties; when the RST is recalled, it becomes every RST member's primary duty.
  - o Notify the CE commander when approving the release of a trained team member for reasons other than PCS, retirement, discharge, or medical disqualification; the replacement must be trained before releasing the incumbent.
- Establish a UCC and ensure it is staffed with competent Airmen.
- Appoint your most qualified managers, leaders, or technicians who can provide an effective evaluation of EM objectives as EET members.

- Ensure dissemination of EM training material throughout the unit to support the installation EM information program.
- Identify and equip augmentees to support the EM program.
- Ensure interoperable communications and visual information services are available for incident response.
- Ensure pre-positioned material is stored and maintained for additive forces IAW theater, installation, and joint support plans.
- Ensure that all unit Airmen and emergency-essential civilians and contractors maintain and use the *Airman's Manual* during exercises and real-world contingencies.

Risk Management

Original Author: Maj Arlen Hammock
Detachment 2, 22nd Space Operations Squadron Commander

References

DODI 6055.1, *DOD Safety and Occupational Health (SOH) Program*, 19 August 1998.

AFI 90-802, *Risk Management*, 11 February 2013.

AFPAM 90-803, *Risk Management (RM) Guidelines and Tools*, 11 February 2013, is the process guide for the RM Program as prescribed by AFPD 90-8, *Environment, Safety and Occupational Health Management and Risk Management*, 2 February 2012. The "how-to book" for RM, it provides definitions, guidelines, procedures, and tools for the integration and execution of RM.

The majority of the following information is excerpted directly from the above references.

By direction of the secretary of the Air Force, all Air Force personnel will apply RM principles, concepts, and techniques to assess the risks associated with their daily missions and duty-related activities. RM is a decision-making process to systematically evaluate possible courses of action, identify risks and benefits, and determine the best course of action for any given situation. RM enables Airmen to maximize operational capabilities while limiting all dimensions of risk by applying a simple, systematic process appropriate for all personnel and functions both on and off duty.

RM Program Goals

- Enhance mission effectiveness at all levels while preserving assets and safeguarding health and welfare.
- Integrate RM into mission processes, ensuring decisions are based upon assessments of risk integral to the activity and mission.
- Create an Air Force in which every Airman is trained and motivated to manage risk in both on- and off-duty activities.
- Identify opportunities to increase Air Force war-fighting effectiveness, helping to ensure decisive victory in any future conflict at the least possible cost.

RM Principles

- Accept no unnecessary risk.
- Make risk decisions at the appropriate level.
- Accept risk when benefits outweigh the costs.
- Integrate RM into all levels of operations and planning.

RM Six-Step Process

- Identify the hazards.
- Assess the risk.
- Analyze risk-control measures.
- Make control decisions.
- Implement risk controls.
- Supervise and review.

Levels of Risk Management

- Time critical
  - On the run—mental or verbal review.
  - Used during execution phase of training or operations.
  - Most easily applied level of risk management in off-duty situations.
  - Helpful for choosing the appropriate course of action when an unplanned event occurs during execution of a planned operation or daily routine.
- Deliberate
  - Complete RM process is applied.

  - o Experience and brainstorming are used to identify hazards and develop controls.
  - o Most effective when done in a group.
  - o Useful when preparing for upcoming operations, reviewing maintenance procedures, and planning disaster response.
- Strategic
  - o Used to study hazards and associated risks in a complex operation or system.
  - o Involves research of available data, use of diagram, and analysis tools, formal testing, or long-term tracking of hazards associated with a system or operation (normally assisted by technical experts).
  - o Useful on high-priority or high-visibility risks.

Commander Responsibilities

- Serves as unit advocate for RM.
- Appoints an RM manager.
- Ensures all assigned Airmen complete RM training.
- Tailors RM application and techniques to accommodate unique mission needs.
- Directs RM integration into all operational decision-making processes.
- Ensures all supervisors and leaders support and implement basic RM principles on a continuing basis.

Managing High-Risk Activities

- High-risk activities are those with an inherent increased risk of personal injury.
- With the proper training and adequate safety measures, high-risk activities can be performed safely.
- Examples of this category include flying civil aircraft, skydiving, white-water rafting, motorcycle and auto racing, scuba diving, dirt-bike riding, hunting, mountain climbing, participating in rodeo events, kayaking, and other exciting activities that can result in injury when not properly executed.
- Each squadron USR should ensure participants are aware of risks associated with their activities and are properly trained to participate in them.
- Document and maintain all safety briefings and training within the squadron.

Tips for Success

- Constantly apply RM to enhance mission effectiveness at all levels—to preserve assets, safeguard health, and ensure personnel welfare.
- Integrate RM into mission processes; ensure decisions are based on assessments of risk integral to the activity and mission.
- Ensure every member is trained and motivated to manage risk in his or her on- and off-duty activities.
- Identify opportunities to increase Air Force war-fighting effectiveness on the battlefield and in the operational aerospace environment in any future conflict at the least possible cost.
- Emphasize RM at commander's calls.
- Some MAJCOMs and wings require that an extreme sports and high-risk activity form be completed for participating Airmen.
  - o Identify individuals in high-risk activities, and ensure they maintain proof of required training.
  - o Complete an activity brief (usually one on one), document the briefing, and approve or disapprove the Airman's participation in a high-risk activity.
  - o Ensure USR maintains brief as required by local guidance.
  - o Critical since this information may be used in a LOD determination.

Additional Resource

- The Air Force Safety Center provides online resources; see http://www.afsec.af.mil.

Equal Opportunity and Treatment Program

Original Author: Maj Jonathan Bland
80th Maintenance Squadron Commander

Additional Contributions: 2011 Commanders Connection Team

References

AFI 36-2706, *Equal Opportunity Program, Military and Civilian*, 5 October 2010 (incorporating change 1, 5 October 2011).

US Air Force Judge Advocate General's (JAG) School, *The Military Commander and the Law*, 2012.

The majority of the following information is excerpted directly from the above references.

The primary objective of the Equal Opportunity and Treatment Program for military and civilian members is to improve mission effectiveness. It promotes an environment free from personal, social, or institutional barriers that prevent Air Force members from achieving their highest possible levels of responsibility based on individual merit and capability. Commanders must not tolerate any form of discrimination and must take action to correct the cause of any discriminatory practice. The base equal opportunity office can assist the commander in resolving problems and offers both sexual-harassment and human-relations training.

The EO office is the subject matter expert for commanders and organizations conducting investigations related to unlawful discrimination or sexual harassment. Organizations may include, but are not limited to, inspector general, security forces, Office of Special Investigations, sexual assault response coordinator, chaplain, SJA, and personnel. The function of providing SMEs is to ensure EO issues are handled correctly and efficiently. Processes differ for handling military and civilian complaints of discrimination or harassment.

For military personnel, the EO office can assist commanders with requirements for unlawful discrimination complaints based on race, color, religion, national origin, or sex (including sexual harassment); unit climate assessments; human relations education; use of alternative dispute resolution procedures; equal opportunity and treatment incidents; dissident and protest activities; affirmative action planning and assessment; accommodation of religious practices; and appeals procedures.

For civilian personnel, the EO office can address the requirements for implementation of federal law and the regulations of the Equal Employment Opportunity Commission (EEOC) that prohibit unlawful discrimination based on race, color, religion, sex, national origin, age (40 or older), disability, genetic information, or reprisal for participating in the EEO process or opposing discriminatory practices. Although Air Force policy prohibits unlawful discrimination based on sexual orientation for civilians, complaints are not handled through the EO office but may be raised under other appropriate grievance or appeal procedures. Unit climate assessments and human relations education also apply to civilian personnel. EO personnel will assist commanders by conducting SAVs.

The Air Force, US government, and DOD support a zero-tolerance policy for discrimination. They do not condone or tolerate unlawful discrimination—to include sexual harassment—of any kind. This zero-tolerance policy ensures that once unlawful discrimination or sexual harassment is alleged, immediate and appropriate action will be taken to investigate/resolve the allegations and ensure any proven unlawful behavior stops. Further, the Air Force will take appropriate disciplinary action against any military or civilian member who engages in unlawful discriminatory practices. Air Force EO policy compliance is a function of commanders/leadership.

Tips for Success

- Communicate that no form of discrimination is tolerated in the organization.
- Correct the cause of any discrimination practice.
- Contact your EO office when an allegation is made to receive subject matter expertise in how to handle the process; procedures vary for informal and formal complaints as well as for military and civilian allegations.
- Contact your EO office when handling allegations against civilian personnel.
- Brief unit members on their right to file an EO complaint without fear of reprisal. Encourage members to use the chain of command, but ensure that all members are aware of the independent EO complaint process.
- Protect the complainant's identity when a formal EO complaint is filed.
- Inform alleged military offenders that they are the subject of a formal EO complaint.
    - o Provide only the general nature of the EO-related allegation filed against them.
    - o Warn them against taking any reprisal measure against the complainant.
    - o Brief them on the outcome of the EO case when it is closed.
    - o Advise them of their right to appeal the outcome of the case.
- Do not iSnvestigate allegations of unlawful discrimination or sexual harassment when the complainant files a formal EO complaint. However, investigate the allegations when the complainant elected not to file a formal complaint, and inform the EO office of the results.
- Ensure supervisors evaluate compliance with EO directives and/or federal law, and document repeated or serious violations.
- Contact EO and request a UCA to determine the human-relations climate within your squadron.

Military Drug Demand Reduction Program

2011 Commanders Connection Team

The drug demand reduction program utilizes state-of-the-art technology to detect and deter drug use by members. An effective program requires coordination with legal and law-enforcement agencies.

References

DOD, *Manual for Courts-Martial, United States*, 2012.

USAF JAG School, *The Military Commander and the Law*, 2012.

DODI 1010.1, *Military Personnel Drug Abuse Testing Program*, 13 September 2012.

AFI 44-120, *Military Drug Demand Reduction Program*, 3 January 2011 (incorporating change 1, 6 June 2012).

AFI 44-107, *Air Force Civilian Drug Demand Reduction Program*, 7 April 2010 (incorporating change 1, 6 May 2013).

AFI 44-121, *Alcohol and Drug Abuse Prevention and Treatment (ADAPT) Program*, 11 April 2011.

The majority of the following information is excerpted directly from the above references.

Purpose of Drug Demand Reduction Program

- Assist commanders in ensuring their Airmen are mission ready.
- Deter military members from abusing illegal drugs or illicit substances.
- Detect and identify those individuals who use or abuse illegal drugs or other illicit substances.
- Provide a basis for action, adverse or otherwise, against a member based on a positive test result.

Close command coordination with legal, law enforcement, and other agencies is required for an effective drug demand reduction program.

Predominant Types of Testing

Besides unit-administered random drug testing, five common situations may require urinalysis testing. Each of these has its own legal considerations for when it can be done and how it can be used. These include consent, probable cause, commander-directed, inspection, and medical care.

- **Consent (Also Known as Voluntary Consent)** (Military Rules of Evidence [MRE] 314[e], *Manual for Courts-Martial*)
  - o Coordinate with SJA.
  - o Used prior to probable cause or command-directed testing.
  - o Reading Article 31 rights not required prior to asking for consent.
  - o Consent is not valid if it is mere acquiescence to authority.
  - o Results may be used for *UCMJ* and administrative action.
- **Probable Cause** (MRE 315[i])
  - o Search and seizure, ordered by you, when you believe member has ingested drugs.
  - o Reasonable belief illegal drugs are present or will be found in individual's urine.
  - o Must consult with SJA before taking this action.
  - o Results may be used for *UCMJ* and administrative action.
- **Commander Directed**
  - o Used when there is reasonable suspicion of drug abuse but does not amount to probable cause.
  - o To determine member's competency for duty, need for counseling, rehabilitation, and so forth.
  - o Seek SJA advice before ordering such tests.
  - o Results may be used for administrative action.
- **Inspection** (MRE 313[b])
  - o Defined as the "examination conducted as an incident of command the primary purpose of which is to determine and to ensure the security, military fitness, or good order and discipline of the unit."
  - o Primary function of an inspection is ensuring mission readiness.
  - o Conducted as unit sweep or randomly on segments of unit, duty section, or dorm.
  - o Used to determine proper command function; standards of readiness; and presence, fitness, and readiness of personnel.
  - o Does not have to encompass entire squadron, unit, duty section, or dorm; may not single out specific individuals or small group.
  - o Results may be used for *UCMJ* and administrative action.

- **Medical Care (Valid Medical Purpose)** (MRE 312[f])
    - o Urine specimens obtained from valid medical exams such as emergency treatment or periodic physical exams may be used for any purpose.
    - o Urinalysis tests of individuals following entry into the Alcohol and Drug Abuse Prevention and Treatment (ADAPT) program may not be used for disciplinary purposes if member self-identified.
    - o Results may be used for *UCMJ* and administrative action.

Other Types of Testing

- **Self-Identification**
    - o Member may self-identify as drug user prior to being selected for urinalysis.
    - o Member may not be disciplined under *UCMJ* when legitimately self-identifying for drug abuse and entering the ADAPT program.
    - o Results may be used for nonadverse administrative action.
- **Safety Mishap**
    - o Urine specimen may be collected from any individual directly or indirectly involved in a safety-related incident. Results may be used for any lawful purpose.
    - o Urine specimens collected as part of formally convened Air Force mishap investigation will be handled IAW DODI 6055.7 and applicable Air Force instructions. Results may be protected and have limited use as determined by Air Force directives.
- **New Entrant**
    - o Conducted during preaccession physical or initial period of military service.
    - o Refer to DODI 1010.1.

Tips for Success

- Brief the consequences of drug abuse at commander's calls—preferably have a judge advocate speak at the commander's call.
- Consult with SJA before implementing drug-abuse testing.
- Order commander-directed drug testing as required.
- Be familiar with provisions of AFI 44-120.

- Ensure military members and applicable civilian employees are subject to inspection testing.
- Personally sign the written order directing each selected member to report for urinalysis testing.
  - o Notify the member not earlier than two hours prior to scheduled collection time.
  - o Member must acknowledge receipt, including date, time, and signature.
  - o If member is a shift worker, TDY, flying, on crew rest, or on leave, notify the member to report for testing on his or her next duty day. Note: Do not notify earlier than two hours prior to scheduled collection time.
- Ensure members selected for testing report to collection site within the designated time.
- Take disciplinary action on any member who fails to report for testing without valid reason.
- Provide credible observers (personnel without UIFs, Article 15s, letters of reprimand, or similar administrative actions for misconduct).

Dormitory Management Program

Original Author: Maj Serena A. Armstrong
48th Services Squadron Commander

Reference

AFI 32-6005, *Unaccompanied Housing Management,* 9 October 2008, certified current 1 December 2010 (incorporating through change 2, 7 May 2013).

The majority of the following information is excerpted directly from the above reference.

Housing is a quality-of-life issue for all Airmen. This is true for your single and junior Airmen just as it is for anyone else in the squadron. Its impact on readiness and retention has driven new DOD standards and priorities. The purpose of unaccompanied housing (dormitories) is to create a residential community promoting pride, professionalism, and personal dignity. As the commander, you will be the best advocate for your people on this issue. But you will also be the one charged to hold them accountable for maintaining these areas in a safe and orderly manner. Below are a few tips to help you in that effort.

Tips for Success

- Be an active member of the quarters improvement committee (QIC).
- Establish specific guidance on dormitory standards in the form of policy letters, directives, or OIs.
- Ensure dormitory occupants are aware of required standards—use newcomer's briefings and commander's calls to spread the word.
- Personally meet with the dormitory manager to ensure open dialogue.
- Show you care about the quality of life within your dormitory—walk through and check out the facilities periodically with the manager.
- Involve supervisors and flight commanders in the inspection process so they are aware of living conditions.
- Keep a balance between group welfare and individual privacy when scheduling inspections.
- Ensure furniture is in good repair in the rooms.
- Reward and recognize positive behavior—implement programs such as a "room of the month" competition.

Fitness Program

2011 Commanders Connection Team

Reference

AFI 36-2905, *Fitness Program,* 12 January 2010, effective 1 July 2010.

The majority of the following information is excerpted directly from the above reference.

FIT TO FIGHT
Airmen embracing fitness culture

Regular Air Force, AFRC, and ANG (Title 10) members are mandated to complete an official fitness assessment (FA) at a minimum of twice yearly. Members must test by the last day of the month, six calendar months following the previous passing test (e.g., if member tested on 15 April, then member must retest on or before 31 October of the same year). ANG (Title 32) members are mandated to complete an official FA at least yearly. Members must be tested by the last day of the month, 12 calendar months following the previous test (e.g., if a member tested on 15 April, the member must retest on or before 30 April of the following year).

Regular Air Force, AFRC, and ANG (Title 10) Airmen who test in all four components (cardio—1.5-mile run or one-mile walk, abdominal circumference measurement, push-ups, and sit-ups) of the new fitness program on or after 1 July 2010 and who score an "excellent" (90 or above) are only required to test yearly. These Airmen will retest by the last day of the month, 12 calendar months following the previous "excellent" test date.

Commander Responsibilities

- Execute and enforce the unit fitness program (FP), and ensure appropriate administrative action is taken in cases of noncompliance.
- Provide a work environment that supports healthy lifestyle choices.
- Implement and maintain a unit/squadron physical training (PT) program IAW AFI guidelines. Commanders will consult with the exercise physiologist/fitness program manager (EP/FPM) to assist unit physical training leaders (PTL) in developing safe and effective PT programs.
- While not mandatory, commanders are encouraged to provide written guidance to Airmen describing fitness expectations. This policy can include
    - o Expectations for remaining current and meeting standards.
    - o PT program requirements. Unit PT programs can encourage members to participate in physical fitness training up to 90 minutes three to five times per week.
- Appoint PTLs in writing to conduct and lead unit PT programs.

  - o PTLs should be available a minimum of one year from the time of appointment.
  - o PTLs must attend the initial and annual PTL certification courses provided by the EP/FPM prior to overseeing and conducting the unit FP.

- Appoint a unit fitness program manager (UFPM) in writing.
- For units not supported by a fitness assessment cell (FAC), appoint PTLs in writing to conduct FAs; appointed PTLs must receive training from the EP/FPM prior to conducting FAs.
- Administer personnel actions of the program. See AFI 36-2905 for commander's actions available for members who fail PT assessment(s).
- Ensure assigned or attached unit personnel are in compliance with all FP requirements, to include unit PT; scheduled FAs; health and wellness center (HAWC) classes and follow-up; and participation in a fitness improvement program (FIP) / self-paced fitness improvement program (SFIP) or healthy living program (HLP) / healthy living program reserves (HLPR), if applicable.
- Air Reserve Component (ARC) members in the unsatisfactory fitness category will complete HLPR online when HAWC education and HLPR are not available or accessible. Pay and points may be authorized to accomplish mandatory HLP/HLPR.
- Document command response to unsatisfactory fitness scores on FAs IAW AFI 36-2905, par. 7.2. Elevate matters to higher command where appropriate.
- Ensure closed fitness case file is placed in the MPS outprocessing package for members departing for PCS or PCA and hand-carried to the gaining unit. The losing UFPM will retain a copy for 90 days.
- Provide open fitness case files to the MPS for members departing for PCS/PCA. Open case files will be sealed and mailed to member's gaining commander for review and handoff to UFPM.
- Ensure prior exempted members returning from deployment are assessed after the period of acclimatization (42 days from return to home station for regular Air Force and Active Guard and Reserve [AGR]; 90 days for other ARC members) unless member requests to assess earlier.
- Ensure member's fitness score is current prior to deployment.
- Direct unofficial unit-run practice tests as needed.

- o Practice FAs are not reported as official scores in the Air Force Fitness Management System (AFFMS) but may be used as a commander's tool to evaluate things such as fitness/readiness and dress and appearance.
- o Commanders may refer and track members not meeting standards for FIP and/or HLP/HLPR.

Note: Installation or unit commanders may appoint trained PTLs to augment FACs during periods where there are gaps in FAC manning. PTLs will be appointed in writing and must be trained IAW AFI 36-2905 requirements. They will conduct fitness assessments in the FAC and will not test members from their own units. PTLs will be used sparingly to minimize the additional duty burden placed on Airmen.

Deployed Commander Responsibilities

- Provide an environment that supports, encourages, and motivates a healthy lifestyle.
- Appoint a deployed unit PTL to facilitate the unit PT program if required or feasible.
- Ensure personnel enrolled in a FIP continue to meet program requirements if feasible.
- If determined reasonable and safe, may conduct official FAs but must have the necessary elements required supporting the fitness program standards (i.e., trained PTL[s], 1.5-mile and 1.0-mile commander-approved course, screening process, appropriate medical support, and access to the AFFMS).

Individual Responsibilities

- Know the block of time within which his/her FA is required to remain current.
- Ensure the FA is scheduled (this is ultimately the member's responsibility).
- Remain current as defined in AFI 36-2905, par. 2.12.
- Monitor FA exemptions, schedule necessary medical examinations, and initiate FA test arrangements in a timely manner.

Tips for Success

- Set the example with regards to fitness.
- Be a regular part of unit PT activities.
- Take appropriate administrative action when a member fails to participate in the unit FP or meet fitness standards.
- Request that the HAWC staff conduct a periodic fitness program review.
- Refer deploying members enrolled in FIP to the HAWC for consultation prior to deployment.
- Post the current PT standards for squadron members to see and work toward.

Human Immunodeficiency Virus Program

2011 Commanders Connection Team

References

DODD 6485.02E, *Human Immunodeficiency Virus (HIV) / Acquired Immune Deficiency Syndrome (AIDS) Prevention: Support to Foreign Militaries*, 7 November 2006.

AFI 48-135, *Human Immunodeficiency Virus Program*, 12 May 2004 (incorporating change 1, 7 August 2006, certified current 13 May 2010).

AFI 36-3212, *Physical Evaluation for Retention, Retirement, and Separation*, 2 February 2006 (incorporating through change 2, 27 November 2009).

AFI 44-102, *Medical Care Management*, 20 January 2012.

The majority of the following information is excerpted directly from the above references.

> *Health is the greatest gift, contentment the greatest wealth, faithfulness the best relationship.*
>
> —Buddha

AIDS and Military Members

The Air Force tests all members for antibodies to HIV, medically evaluates all infected members, and educates members on means of prevention.

- All applicants for the Air Force are screened for the HIV infection. Applicants infected with HIV are ineligible to join the Air Force, with no waiver authorized.

- All active duty, ANG, and ARC personnel are screened for the HIV infection whenever they have periodic physical examinations, for clinically indicated reasons, before an overseas assignment, during pregnancy, when diagnosed with a sexually transmitted disease, or upon entry to drug or alcohol rehabilitation programs.
- All active duty personnel must have a routine HIV test at no more than two-year intervals.
- ARC personnel must have a current HIV test within two years of the date they are called to active duty for 30 days or more.
- Medical personnel are tested annually.
- An active duty member testing positive for HIV is referred to Wilford Hall Medical Center (WHMC) at Lackland AFB, Texas, for definitive diagnosis, treatment, and disposition. A medical evaluation board (MEB) is convened at WHMC after the initial exam.
- HIV-infected active duty members retained on active duty must be
    - medically evaluated semiannually;
    - assigned within the United States, including Alaska, Hawaii, and Puerto Rico;
    - assigned to nonmobility positions;
    - placed on DNIF status pending medical evaluation if on flying status; and
    - considered for waivers using normal procedures established for chronic diseases.
- Testing Confidentiality: Air Force policy strictly safeguards results of positive HIV testing.
    - No release to persons outside the Air Force without the member's consent.
    - The Air Force will neither confirm nor deny testing results of specific service members.
    - Very limited release within the Air Force on a need-to-know basis only; unit commanders should NOT inform first sergeants and/or supervisors unless a determination is made that those individuals truly need to know. The commander should consult the director of base medical services (DBMS).

Adverse Administrative Actions

Information the DOD obtains as a result of epidemiological assessment (EA) with a member identified as having been exposed to a virus associated with AIDS may not be used to support any adverse personnel action against a member (see AFI 48-135, attach. 11).

- Adverse personnel actions include court-martial, nonjudicial punishment, LOD determination, demotion, involuntary separation for other than medical reasons, denial of promotion or reenlistment, and unfavorable entry in a personnel record.
- Nonadverse personnel actions in which limits on use of epidemiological assessment results do not apply include reassignment; disqualification (temporary or permanent) from the PRP; denial, suspension, or revocation of security clearance; suspension or termination of access to classified information; transfer between Reserve components; removal (temporary or permanent) from flight status or other duties requiring high degree of stability or alertness; and removal of AFSC.
- These nonadverse actions cannot be accompanied by unfavorable entries in service member's records.
- Safe-sex orders: "order to follow preventive medicine requirements" is issued to all HIV-positive personnel who remain on active duty.
    - Health care provider will notify member that he or she has tested positive.
    - DBMS notifies unit commander.
    - Unit commander issues order to follow preventive medicine requirements.
    - Commander and member sign and date the order.
    - Unit commander is responsible for safeguarding the order. To protect the member's privacy, the commander should do the following:
        - Seal the envelope and mark it "FOR THE EYES OF THE COMMANDER ONLY."
        - Sign across the envelope seal.
        - File with unit PIF or in a classified safe.
    - Upon member's reassignment, the unit commander forwards the order to the gaining commander in a sealed envelope marked "TO BE OPENED BY ADDRESSEE ONLY."

Disability Evaluation and Medical Separation

Military members may not be separated merely because they are HIV positive. HIV-positive members who show no evidence of illness or impairment shall not be separated solely on the basis of being infected with the AIDS virus. Medical retirement is, however, a strong possibility once a member develops AIDS.

- A member subject to separation first undergoes an MEB and then an informal physical evaluation board (PEB) to determine whether the member should be retained on active duty or separated from the service due to being "unfit" for continued service. The member has appeal rights to appear personally before a formal PEB and also to appeal to AFPC.
    - o The member may be simply separated with a medical severance lump sum payment or temporarily or permanently medically retired with monthly medical retirement pay depending on the board's recommendations and the final action by the secretary of the Air Force (SECAF).
    - o Placement on the temporary disability retired list (TDRL) is termed a temporary retirement because the member is reevaluated every 18 months to determine if fit for return to active duty or unfit and separated or retired. Maximum time on the TDRL is five years.
- The member may voluntarily separate upon request.

Military Justice / Policy Issues

A service member who knows he or she is HIV positive but engages in sexual intercourse can be punished under the *UCMJ* for

- Having unprotected sexual intercourse.
- Violating a "safe-sex" order.
- Failing to warn sexual partner about HIV status, despite wearing a condom (merely taking safe-sex precautions won't remove the duty to warn).
- Having unprotected sexual intercourse even though the partner is aware of the member's HIV status and consents.

AIDS and Air Force Civilian Employees

The Air Force does not test Air Force civilian employees for AIDS. An exception is that those civilian employees (appropriated or nonappropriated) selected for assignment overseas will be screened for HIV infection pursuant to host country requirements. This screening does not apply to contractor personnel, family members, or foreign nationals.

AIDS is a disability under federal civil rights laws; discrimination is prohibited on the basis of physical or mental disability. Under these laws, disabled employees could recover back pay, compensatory damages, attorney fees, costs, and expert fees against liable employers.

Tips for Success

- Applicants infected with HIV are ineligible for enlistment or appointment to the active duty Air Force and ARC.
- Active duty Air Force members found fit for duty are not separated solely for HIV.
- Use AFI 36-3212 to separate or retire active duty members who are HIV-infected and whom a medical evaluation has determined to be physically unfit for further duty.
- Initiate transfer of HIV-infected Reservists not on extended active duty or full-time ANG to the Standby Reserve if they cannot be used in the Selected Reserve.
- Ensure HIV-infected active duty members are medically evaluated semiannually; assigned only within the United States or Alaska, Hawaii, or Puerto Rico; appointed to something other than a mobility position; placed on DNIF status; and removed from security-sensitive positions pending medical evaluation.
- Ensure HIV-infected healthcare workers are relieved from patient care responsibilities until counsel from expert review panel is sought.
- Give HIV-infected member an "order to follow preventive medicine requirements" (see AFI 48-135, attach. 14).
- Allow HIV-infected members to continue working as long as they maintain acceptable performance and pose no health hazard.

Military Leave, Passes, and Permissive TDY Programs

Original Author: Maj Kathy Goforth
898th Munitions Squadron Commander

References

DODI 1327.06, *Leave and Liberty Policy and Procedures*, 16 June 2009 (incorporating change 2, effective 13 August 2013).

AFI 36-3003, *Military Leave Program*, 26 October 2009.

The majority of the following information is excerpted directly from the above references.

Experience shows that vacations and short periods of rest from duty as well as authorized absences to attend to emergency situations provide benefits to morale and motivation, essential to maintaining maximum effectiveness. Therefore, a leave program is a necessary military requirement. As a commander, you should maintain an environment that permits and encourages time away from work.

Types of Leave

There are various types of leave. As a commander, you need to be knowledgeable of leave options available for your Airmen. Below are several of those options.

Annual (Ordinary) Leave

- Members earn 2.5 days of ordinary leave each month.
- Typically approved by the first-line supervisor.

Advance Leave

- Chargeable leave that exceeds a member's current leave balance but doesn't exceed the amount of leave the member will earn during the remaining period of active duty.
- May be granted to resolve emergency or urgent personal problems when members have little or no accrued leave.
- Limited to 30 days or number of leave days that could be accrued during current enlistment—whichever is less.
- AFPC/DPSIMC (Special Programs Branch) must approve requests for over 30 days.
- Is a leave loan and must be paid back.
- The unit commander, deputy, or equivalent is the approval authority.

Emergency Leave

- Chargeable leave granted for personal or family emergencies involving the member's immediate family.
- Since most family emergencies are time sensitive, swift action is essential.
- Advise members to apply for humanitarian reassignment or separation for hardship reasons if leave period is for more than 60 days.

- Commanders can approve up to 30 days of emergency leave with authority for an additional 30-day extension.
- Commanders may delegate approval authority to no lower than the first sergeant.
- AFPC/DPSIMC must approve emergency leave requests that exceed 60 days.

Excess Leave

- Granted over and beyond the amount that may be accrued before discharge or separation.
- Members are not entitled to receive pay and allowances or to accrue leave while in excess leave status.
- Approved only for emergencies or in unusual circumstances (e.g., member pending administrative discharge or awaiting execution of a punitive discharge imposed by a court-martial).
- Refer to AFI 36-3003, table 6, for detailed rules on excess leave.

Convalescent Leave

- Authorized absence not chargeable as leave when member is under medical care and when part of treatment prescribed is for recuperation and convalescence.
- Approval based on written recommendation of military physician most familiar with patient's condition; however, unit commander is approval authority.
- Allow 42 days of convalescent leave for pregnancies.
- Other reasons are limited to 30-day (or less) increments.
- Additional medical review is required to extend convalescent leave beyond 30 days.
- Charge ordinary leave for convalescent time when members use civilian medical care at their own expense.

Terminal Leave

- Ordinary leave is limited to member's leave balance at time of separation or retirement.
- Member's last day of leave coincides with the last day of active duty.

- Ensure members complete all required separation or retirement processing and have orders in hand before starting leave.
- Members should not return to duty after this leave begins.
- Unit commander must approve.
- Disapprove terminal leave for military necessity or in best interest of Air Force.

Accrued Leave in Excess of 60 Days

- Prevents members from losing accrued leave if they are unable to take normal leave due to significant and unforeseen operational mission requirements.
- Unit commanders must send requests and full justification for excess leave through command channels to MAJCOM for approval.

Environmental and Morale Leave

- Environmental and morale leave (EML) is ordinary leave granted to members and their dependents from designated overseas austere, isolated, or environmentally depressed areas for the purpose of priority use of space-required or space-available air transportation to EML destinations.
- Destination locations offer closest environmental relief, recreation facilities, and suitable accommodations.
- Travel time counts as leave for unfunded EML program; for funded EML program, leave is not charged for travel time to specially designated locations.

Passes

- Afford time off without charge of leave for unusual reasons such as special recognition or observance of major religious events.
- Cannot use to extend leave, in place of leave, or in conjunction with leave.
- May not exceed four days (96 hours).
- Commander may not impose mileage limits during pass period but can require members to be able to return to duty within certain time limits (based on potential mission requirements).

Permissive TDY

- Authorized absence without charge of leave; granted so that member may participate in official or semiofficial programs that do not qualify as funded TDYs.
- Do not grant for reasons listed in AFI 36-3003, par. 12.8.
- Grant if no expense to government and if program in which member desires to participate enhances individual's value to or increases his or her understanding of the Air Force.
- Commanders who have approval authority must exercise care in evaluating requests to ensure the best interest of Air Force is served.
- Authorized situations are outlined in AFI 36-3003, table 7.

Commander Responsibilities

- Ensure maximum use of earned leave and minimize the loss of leave.
- Enforce Air Force and command-approved leave guidelines.
- Document all leaves.
- Ensure members who refuse to take leave understand their obligation to comply with the unit leave program and that refusal to take leave may result in loss of earned leave.
- Encourage members to take one leave of at least 14 continuous days every fiscal year (FY) and to use leave accrued each FY.
- Ensure members schedule leave annually at the beginning of the FY and update their leave schedule periodically.
- Advise members who schedule "use or lose" leave in August or September that they risk losing leave on 1 October if military requirements and personal circumstances prevent them from taking leave.
- Seek American Red Cross verification when members request emergency leave.
- Charge leave for leave periods, such as those taken by members waiting for family members' passports or visas or for the outcomes of humanitarian reassignment requests.
- Combine ordinary leave with other kinds of leave, unless specifically prohibited, and treat a combination of leave types as one leave period.

- Make sure members taking ordinary instead of terminal leave return to duty 15 days before their scheduled separation or retirement date to prevent pay problems.

Tips for Success

- Ensure unit members project leave at start of FY; update as needed.
- Know guidelines for granting advance leave.
- Understand emergency leave procedures.
- Grant emergency leave (usually 30 days or less) for a personal emergency requiring member's presence.
- Terminal leave is not mandatory; Air Force mission will dictate.
- Limit passes to four days (96 hours).
  - o You cannot impose mileage restrictions.
  - o You can require members to be able to return to duty within a certain time.
- Do not grant permissive TDY for reasons listed in AFI 36-3003, par.12.8.

Unit Budget

Original Author: Maj Kathy Goforth
898th Munitions Squadron Commander

References

DOD 7000.14-R, *Department of Defense Financial Management Regulation*, vols. 1–15, dates vary by volume.

AFI 65-601, vol. 1, *Budget Guidance and Procedures*, 16 August 2012.

AFI 65-601, vol. 2, *Budget Management for Operations*, 18 May 2012.

The majority of the following information is excerpted directly from the above references.

Financial management is inherent to command, and your squadron will need a budget to survive. However, your budget will never be large enough to buy everything you want. To be a successful money manager, get to know your CPTS commander, talk to your RA, and learn such budget processes as the budget execution review (BER), initial funds distribution, productivity enhancement, financial management board (FMB), financial working group (FWG), and important budget timelines.

Authorized Operations and Maintenance Expenditures

- TDY expenses.
- Supplies.
- Equipment under $250K (K=thousand).
- Trophies and plaques for authorized recurring recognition programs.
- Furnishings.
- Contracts.
- Computers.

Unauthorized O&M Expenditures

- Entertainment (except for official representation funds).
- Entry fees for contests.
- Coins (except for approved award programs).
- Gifts (going away and retirement).
- Food and serving supplies.

Possible Authorized O&M Expenditures (check with your RA)

- Organizational clothing.
- Memberships in professional and community organizations.
- Equipment lease versus buy (comptroller and contracting must validate first).
- Portable buildings and temporary structures.
- Purchases for LANs.

Commander Responsibilities

- Legally responsible for unit funds.
- Set tone for resource use.
- Decision authority for allocation of unit's resources.
- Establish funding priorities.

- Appoint unit RA.
- Know your budget baseline and what it buys.
- Plan early for FY closeout.

Tips for Success

- Appoint a unit RA who will
  - o Keep you informed on status of funds.
  - o Monitor financial obligations via GPC program.
  - o Prepare financial plan, BER inputs, and distribute funding per your instruction.
- Establish funding priorities.
- Determine how you'll distribute unit funds:
  - o Will RA make and approve all purchases?
  - o Will you provide each flight or section its own budget to spend?
  - o Will you consolidate all funds into one budget and approve all purchases?
- Develop a plan to live within the budget given.
- Review, validate, and balance financial plan to ensure successful financial management.
- Review financial programs for each of your responsibility centers.
- Improve resource management by inquiring about program conditions, reviewing causes, weighing alternatives, and directing actions.
- Know what you can and cannot purchase; contact the budget office when in doubt.
- Be postured to spend effectively if end-of-year closeout dollars are made available; if there's money left, those best prepared to spend usually receive it.
  - o Have a prioritized purchase list.
  - o Have Air Force Form 9s filled out and ready to execute.
  - o Have GPC cardholders ready to purchase.

Government Purchase Card Program

2011 Commanders Connection Team

References

Federal Acquisition Regulation (*FAR*).

Defense Federal Acquisition Regulation Supplement (*DFARS*).

AFI 64-117, *Air Force Government-Wide Purchase Card (GPC) Program*, 20 September 2011.

AFI 65-601, vol. 1, *Budget Guidance and Procedures*, 16 August 2012.

The majority of the following information is excerpted directly from the above references.

Although core AFIs are referenced here, they are not intended to substitute for contacting your local CONS, CPTS, or JA as required. Consult your RA or finance for further information and guidance. Be sure to check for currency of AFIs for updates and final authority.

The General Services Administration (GSA) provides commercial GPC and associated services to military members and federal civilian employees to make official purchases. Use of a GPC constitutes expenditure of appropriated funds and is limited to official authorized transactions only. Some organizations have both appropriated and nonappropriated funds available for use.

Spending Guidelines

- Distribute micropurchases equitably among qualified suppliers, with special consideration paid to local and small businesses.
- Overseas cardholders (CH) may be authorized to make commercial purchases up to $25K, if purchase is made outside of the United States from vendors outside of the United States for use outside of the United States.
- Warranted contingency contracting officers are authorized to support contingency and exercise operations.

Authorized Expenditures

See AFI 64-117, pars. 4.1 and 4.2, for complete list; expenditures over $3K require specific actions.

- Supplies.
- Equipment.
- Nonpersonal services.

Authorized Expenditures over 3K (up to a maximum of 25K)

- Only obtained from prepriced contracts and agreements including
  - Federal supply schedules.
  - Blanket purchase agreements (BPA).
  - Indefinite delivery and indefinite quantity contracts.
  - GSA schedules.
- Must be approved by the approving official (AO) and coordinated with the agency or organization program coordinator (A/OPC).
- DD Form 1057 reporting required.

Purchases Requiring Authorization

- Listed in AFI 64-117, chapter 4.
- Except where specifically noted in AFI 64-117, chapter 4, documented verbal approval—including date and identity of AO—is sufficient.

Purchases Requiring Coordination and Review

- Nonexpendable (budget code 9) equipment over micropurchase threshold purchased on existing contracts must have accountability records established through base supply.
- Repair services for general equipment.
- Books, periodicals, and manuals.
- Professional services.
- Payment for domestic express (next business day) delivery.
- Service contract payment for domestic express (next business day) small package delivery.

Unauthorized Expenditures

- See AFI 64-117, par. 4. 5, for complete list; see also AFI 65-601, vol. 1.
- Cash advances.
- Travel-related purchases.
- Rental or leases of land or buildings.
- Repair of GSA-leased vehicles.

- Gifts (exemption is mission accomplishment awards).
- Entertainment.
- Safety-of-flight items.
- Utility services.

Tips for Success

- Consider requesting a brief from the GPC program office to familiarize yourself with the program.
- Appoint AO and CH in writing to base contracting.
    - o Base contracting must annually review accounts exceeding the 7:1 ratio.
    - o CH is responsible for documenting all transactions in Web-based program.
- Ensure AO and CHs receive training and sign statement of training prior to assuming duties.
- Ensure AO and CHs receive annual refresher training.
- Take appropriate actions when notified of the AO incorrectly approving purchases or CH misuse of GPC.
- If CH repeatedly violates GPC procedures, remove GPC privileges.
- Ensure GPC accounts are closed and transferred when CH PCSs, PCAs, or retires.

Government Travel Card Program

2011 Commander's Connection Team

I have enough money to last me the rest of my life, unless I buy something.

—Jackie Mason

References

Deputy Assistant Secretary for Financial Operations (SAF/FMP), Air Force Accounting and Finance Office (AFAFO), *Air Force Government Travel Card Guide*, May 2013, https://www.my.af.mil/gcss-af/USAF/AFP40/d/sA4057E1F290AE3E80129376B0C590555/Files/AF_GTC_Guide_21May2013.pdf.

Travel and Transportation Reform Act of 1998, Public Law 105-264.

Government Charge Card Abuse Prevention Act of 2012.

DOD Financial Management Regulation (DODFMR) 7000.14-R, vol. 9, *Travel Policy*, chap. 3, "Department of Defense Government Travel Charge Card (GTCC)," July 2013.

Air Force Portal/Life and Career/Money—Welcome to Virtual Finance.

Defense Travel Management Office, http://www.defensetravel.dod.mil.

The majority of the following information is excerpted directly from the above references.

The Travel and Transportation Act of 1998 stipulates that the government-sponsored, contractor-issued government travel card (GTC) shall be used by all US government personnel (civilian or military) to pay for costs incurred due to official business travel. Its use improves DOD cash management, reduces DOD and traveler administrative workloads, and facilitates better service to DOD travelers.

Commanders/supervisors are responsible for effective administration and management of the GTCC Program in their organizations. They must ensure individual(s) appointed as agency program coordinators (APC) comply with DODFMR 7000.14-R, volume 9, chapter 3, and that all APCs possess the knowledge, skill, and ability required to perform their duties. Due to PCS and deployments, it is highly recommended that commanders use civilian personnel in this position whenever possible.

Commander Responsibilities

- Ensure effective administration and management of the GTCC Program in your organization. Some questions to check the program include:
  - o Have APCs been designated in writing by an appointment letter and completed mandatory training courses before assuming their role?
  - o When APCs are no longer performing duties as an APC, is access/permission revoked?
  - o Are policies in place to ensure cardholders pay their outstanding balance prior to retirement, separation, or transfer?
  - o Are APCs included on all deployment, PCS, or separation checklists?
  - o Are disciplinary actions consistent with DOD guidelines for military and civilian employees for improper travel card use?

- o Are APCs providing cardholder training on proper use of the travel card?
- o Does the APC perform monthly spot checks of account activity and identify delinquent accounts, infrequent users, nonusers, and inappropriate/unauthorized charges?

- Act as an intermediary.
- Monitor accounts.
- Take disciplinary action when members misuse GTC.

Personnel Exempted from GTC Use

- Employees who have a GTC application pending approval.
- Individuals traveling on invitational travel orders.
- New appointees/recruits.
- Infrequent travelers (no more than two times per year). However, commanders may require infrequent travelers to obtain a travel card for mission readiness.
- For a complete list, see DODFMR 7000.14-R, vol. 9, chap. 3.

Examples of Misuse

- Expenses related to personal, family, or household purposes.
- Cash withdrawals from ATM or banks not related to official travel.
- Intentional failure to pay undisputed charges in timely manner.

Tips for Success

- Appoint an APO and ensure the individual accomplishes the following actions:
    - o Completes mandatory training.
    - o Obtains and maintains applicants' signatures on DOD Statement of Understanding for Travel Cardholders.
    - o Monitors GPC accounts of unit members and informs you of any delinquent accounts or incidents of possible misuse.
- Ensure all cardholders receive initial and biennial refresher GTC training, which includes the following information:
    - o Use of the GTC is mandatory for all DOD employees for official government travel (some exemptions apply).

- o The GTC may only be used for official travel purposes when on official government orders, never for personal use.
- o It is the member's responsibility to ensure the full balance of the GTC is paid no later than the due date on the statement.
- o Members are required to split-disburse all outstanding charges against the GTC when filing the travel voucher.
- o ATM withdrawals are not authorized until three days before scheduled travel.

- When unit members PCA or PCS, ensure GTC accounts are transferred to the members' new units.
- When unit members separate or retire, terminate their GTC accounts.
- Take disciplinary action for members who misuse their GTCs.

Individualized Newcomer Treatment and Orientation Program

Original Author: Maj Serena Armstrong
48th Services Squadron Commander

Reference

AFI 36-2103, *Individualized Newcomer Treatment and Orientation (INTRO) Program*, 30 April 2012.

The majority of the following information is excerpted directly from the above reference.

First impressions are lasting ones, especially to new members entering your unit. The Air Force has a standardized three-phase INTRO program—sponsorship, orientation, and consolidated newcomer scheduling. The INTRO program creates a welcoming atmosphere, allowing newcomers and their families to adapt rapidly and effectively to their new location. The base provides a monthly newcomers' orientation and will take care of scheduling activities for that program. Additionally, Airmen (E-1 and E-2) arriving from basic training or technical school must attend the 10-day first-term Airmen orientation course.

The main program to help welcome newcomers takes place at the unit level. The most important aspect begins with the commander as you select the sponsors for new members. Sponsors should be in the same rank, or grade, and family status as the new member and should attend the A&FRC's sponsorship-training program. The program teaches what sponsorship packages are, how sponsorship letters are written, and what is required of sponsors. Even if this sponsor assignment is delegated, it is important that you keep track of incoming personnel and avail yourself to help in any way possible as they transition into your unit.

Sponsorship is more than just meeting new members at the airport or base gate. It means getting involved with them and their families. Some members require little help in orienting themselves and their families to a new location while others, especially overseas, may take 30 days or more. There is no magic time limit for when sponsorship duties end. Allow sponsors time away from their duty sections—sponsorship takes time. Be sure you schedule appointments to meet with new arrivals during their first few weeks in the unit. How new members and their families are treated directly affects their performance during the time they are in your squadron.

Commander Responsibilities

- Establish a unit INTRO program.
- Appoint an INTRO manager.
- Select individuals for sponsorship duties.
- Send a personalized welcome letter.

Tips for Success

- Sponsorship
    - o Try to use sponsors who are volunteers, and look for similarities in lifestyle when matching sponsors with newcomers.
    - o Make sure the new member receives a list of contact numbers.
    - o Ensure your sponsor letter is current.
    - o Ensure the package from the A&FRC contains current information on housing, schools, local employment, and recreational activities as well as maps and base, unit, and work center information.
    - o Use follow-up surveys or personal interviews (one month later) to assess how well your sponsorship program is really working.
    - o Ensure sponsors bring individuals (and possibly their family members) to their duty sections.

- Orientation program
  - o Conduct personal meetings with new individuals in your unit, and explain your unit's mission and your expectations.
  - o The first sergeant and other key personnel should brief applicable topics. This can be accomplished individually or through a monthly group meeting.
  - o If you have a large squadron with numerous facilities, consider ending the group orientation session with a bus tour of the squadron.

Informal Recognition

Original Author: Maj Tom Smith
42nd MPF Commander

> *Don't worry when you are not recognized, but strive to be worthy of recognition.*
>
> —Abraham Lincoln

Several formal awards programs exist within the Air Force to recognize the exceptional achievements of Airmen. Functional awards, quarterly awards, and decorations are a few examples. However, nominating Airmen for such awards are only one of the options you have to recognize superior performance within the unit. You should also have processes in place to recognize achievements, accomplishments, or career milestones within your squadron. Squadron-level commander's awards, letters of appreciation and congratulations, and time-off awards are some commonly used options. Forwarding a letter to a parent or spouse in conjunction with one of these options extends the recognition outside the workplace as well. Informal recognition can be used every day to acknowledge contributions of individuals, teams, and work groups. As with all recognition, it should be tied to a specific behavior or activity that you want to reinforce. Giving a day off or presenting a civilian with a time-off award is a simple yet meaningful way to recognize an exceptional performance informally.

Squadron-Level Commander's Awards

Many types of squadron-specific commander's awards exist. Perhaps the most universal is the commander's coin. The name, purpose, and frequency of awards vary by unit, career field, and mission. Common examples include a "sharp troop" award you may present for sustained professional appearance or a "hard charger" award for exceptional performance in a challenging task, awarded at each commander's call. The potential variations are almost limitless. As such, you need to consider your unit, mission, and leadership style and then determine what type of commander's award programs are appropriate for your squadron.

Letters of Appreciation

Letters of appreciation are an effective way to recognize accomplishments or exceptional effort that may not rise to the level of a decoration nomination or other formal recognition. They not only can be given to Airmen in your own unit but also may be an appropriate way to recognize efforts of Airmen outside your unit who make a significant positive impact on your unit, mission, or personnel.

Congratulatory Letters

Like letters of appreciation, congratulatory letters are an effective way of offering recognition for personal or professional accomplishments, career milestones, or other significant life events. Possible reasons for a congratulatory letter include selection for promotion, completion of upgrade training, marriage, completion of PME or an educational degree, receipt of an award or decoration, birth of a child, reenlistment, retirement, or any other noteworthy events.

Letters to Parents and Spouses

When recognizing Airmen in any of the ways outlined above, an additional letter sent to parents or a spouse explaining the nature of the recognition and acknowledging the role family members make in an Airman's success may extend the recognition and sense of accomplishment outside the workplace and into an Airman's family life. Be mindful that some Airmen have estranged or difficult relationships with close family members; therefore, do not do this without the Airman's knowledge and consent.

Time Off

A simple, cost-effective, and much appreciated way to acknowledge exceptional performers is by giving them a day off. Coordinate time off with the Airman's immediate supervisor and present the time-off award in a public forum. Civilian employees can be given a time-off award to acknowledge superior or sustained peak performance. Contact the base CPO for more information on civilian time-off awards.

Tips for Success

- Determine what types of unit-level recognition programs are appropriate for your squadron. Some examples may include awards for outstanding CDC or fitness test scores.
- Put processes into place within your CSS to ensure you have the data and support needed.
- Put processes into place within your flights to ensure you have the leadership support needed.
- Remember that your Airmen include your civilian employees too.

Commander's Call

2011 Commanders Connection Team

Reference

AFI 35-113, *Internal Information*, 11 March 2010.

The majority of the following information is excerpted directly from the above reference.

Commander's Call Program

The Air Force considers no leadership function more important than keeping people informed through direct personal contact. A commander's call—a meeting of unit personnel with their commander—provides this contact in a face-to-face forum.

Commander Responsibilities

- Sound leadership, morale, and retention all require consistent communication between leaders and their subordinates. Commanders must help "carry the mail to the lowest levels of the Air Force" on a regular basis. The commander of every unit will personally conduct commander's calls at least quarterly. PA representatives will help commanders develop effective programs and topics of general interest to unit personnel. Overall program content and format will vary according to unit requirements.
- Suitable areas to cover in commander's calls include unit activities, achievements, and goals; recognition of newcomers and persons receiving awards or other honors; and discussion of current issues affecting the Air Force and the unit.

- The program should be used for two-way communication between commanders and their people. Question and answer (Q&A) sessions, group discussions, and other similar methods help establish two-way communication.
- Attendance is highly recommended for all military personnel assigned to the unit and present for duty. Members should not be required to attend during their off-duty hours, and programs should be tailored to accommodate personnel schedules. Encourage civilian employees to attend. Attendance by family members is at the commander's discretion for all or parts of some commander's calls but can be especially effective during individual or unit award presentations.
- *Commander's Call Topics* is a topical publication that the Defense Media Activity in San Antonio produces for use in commander's call. It provides current information on key Air Force–wide items of interest or importance to Air Force military personnel, civilian employees, and their family members. An electronic subscription is available on the Air Force Link, http://www.af.mil ("About Us" drop-down tab). Other useful sources for topics include
    - o PA for assistance with subjects of general interest.
    - o CSAF's "Vector" and "Letter to Airmen," available on the Air Force Link, http://www.af.mil.
    - o Wing and group staff meetings.

Tips for Success

- Hold it the same time each quarter, for example, the third Wednesday of January, April, July, and October at 1500.
- Appoint a POC.
- Rotate responsibility for readers, proffers, and pictures among your unit.
- Ensure a camera is available for pictures of award presentations.
- Create a balanced agenda.
    - o Awards and decorations.
    - o Hails and farewells.
    - o Topics and announcements.
    - o Allot time to the first sergeant.
    - o Allot time to the chief or superintendent.
    - o Allow time for Q&A sessions and/or rumor control.
    - o You finish it off.

- Invite your squadron chaplain to attend.
- If your group commander has letters of appreciation or other tokens (e.g., coins) to present, add this to the agenda.
- Discuss unit activities, achievements, and goals reached since last commander's call.
- Discuss how your unit's mission relates to the Air Force's and wing's missions (periodically).
- If necessary, cover mandatory training items (e.g., sexual harassment prevention), but do not use commander's call as an opportunity to meet ancillary training requirements.
- Conduct any short mandatory briefings.
- Invite guest speakers (e.g., ADC, chaplain, and other squadron commanders) to discuss their missions.
- Discuss current Air Force, base, squadron, and local issues.
- Keep the emphasis upbeat, creative, and tailored to your unit.
- Schedule times and frequency according to unit needs (do not make members attend during their off-duty hours). For round-the-clock operations, you may need to have two or three different times to allow everyone to attend during their duty hours.
- Occasionally, schedule in conjunction with unit sports or picnics.

Health Insurance Portability and Accountability Act

2011 Commanders Connection Team

References

Health Insurance Portability and Accountability Act of 1996, Public Law No. 104-191, 110 Stat. 1936, 21 August 1996.

DOD 6025.18-R, *DOD Health Information Privacy Regulation*, 24 January 2003.

The majority of the following information is excerpted directly from the above references.

The Health Insurance Portability and Accountability Act (HIPAA) made significant changes to the US health care industry. It is more stringent than the Privacy Act and limits the information that can be shared with nonmedical personnel. As a commander, you have access to information covered under this act and the corresponding responsibility to protect it under stringent guidelines.

Tips for Success

- Commanders or their designees may get information from a medical treatment facility (MTF) as it relates to a member's fitness for duty or to ensure proper execution of the mission.
- Appoint in writing members authorized to receive HIPAA information.
- Notify the MTF in writing of HIPAA-trained personnel.
- Ensure members complete HIPAA training prior to accessing personal medical data.
- Ensure all personal information covered by HIPAA is accessed only on a need-to-know basis.
- If you have questions regarding potential personal information covered by HIPAA, contact your SJA and local MPF.

Interactive Customer Evaluation

2011 Commanders Connection Team

References

DODI 8910.01, *Information Collection and Reporting*, 6 March 2007, certified current through 6 March 2014.

Interactive Customer Evaluation (ICE) website, http://ice.disa.mil.

The majority of the following information is excerpted directly from the above references.

> *Honest criticism is hard to take, particularly from a relative, a friend, an acquaintance, or a stranger.*
>
> —Franklin P. Jones

Many support organizations on your base strive daily to provide a consistent, efficient service to their customers and rely on feedback to ensure quality and improve processes. Your unit may be one that relies on this information, but if not, as a commander you must be aware of these programs so you can help encourage feedback and promote timely interaction with base agencies.

One system that most Air Force bases have is the ICE program. The ICE system is a Web-based tool that collects feedback on services organizations provide throughout the base. It allows customers to submit online comment cards to rate the service providers they have encountered at military installations. Designed to improve customer service, it allows managers to monitor the satisfaction levels of services provided through reports and customer comments.

The turnaround time for an ICE comment card is usually 48 hours. As the commander, you can see every ICE comment card that comes into the squadron, and the bigger your squadron is, the more comment cards that will come in. One suggestion to help prioritize your efforts is to gain access to activities that have numerous ICE cards coming in during a given week or any getting a lot of unwanted attention.

Get ICE for Your Unit

If you are interested in using ICE for your unit, visit http://ice.disa.mil/index.cfm?fa=becoming_ice_site&dep=DoD.

Benefits

ICE provides the following benefits for your unit:

- Allows DOD customers to quickly and easily provide feedback to service provider managers.
- Gives leadership timely data on service quality.
- Allows managers to benchmark the performance of their service providers against other DOD organizations.
- Encourages communication across organizations by comparing best practices to increase performance results.
- Saves money.

Additional Resources

Please see the following websites for the ICE program nearest you.

- CONUS—http://ice.disa.mil/index.cfm?fa=geo_branch_site_list&branch_groupings_id=4&geographical_category_id=1.
- Europe—http://ice.disa.mil/index.cfm?fa=geo_branch_site_list&branch_groupings_id=4&geographical_category_id=2.
- Pacific—http://ice.disa.mil/index.cfm?fa=geo_branch_site_list&branch_groupings_id=4&geographical_category_id=3.
- Other—http://ice.disa.mil/index.cfm?fa=geo_branch_site_list&branch_groupings_id=4&geographical_category_id=74.

Chapter 5

Maintaining Standards and Administering Discipline

Often, the tasks associated with maintaining standards and administering discipline are some of the most unpleasant that a commander has to perform. They frequently involve considerations far beyond a simple determination of right and wrong, although that too can sometimes be a complex undertaking. Decisions regarding standards and discipline affect members who are the focus of the action, the unit, the members' friends and families, and even attitudes across a given base or station.

Adding to this is the fact that disciplinary actions are governed by a host of regulatory guidance, all requiring careful adherence to protect members' rights, the service, and even the officer imposing the action. You are not alone in sorting out the complexities of taking disciplinary actions. The SJA is available to assist you in ensuring that requirements are met and that every aspect of the action is given adequate consideration. Just as the SJA assists you, the area defense counsel works with members to ensure their rights are protected. Together the SJA and ADC ensure everyone involved is protected and all regulatory requirements are met.

The information in this chapter is a valuable addition to your commander's toolkit. Coupled with a copy of *The Military Commander and the Law* desk book and the *Manual for Courts-Martial* (*MCM*), it will help you to be well armed to work with your SJA in this critical area. But remember, nothing in this chapter can or should serve as a substitute for advice from your servicing legal office.

Nonjudicial Disciplinary Options

Original Author: Maj Jonathan Bland
8th Maintenance Squadron Commander

Additional Contributions: 2011 Commanders Connection Team

References

AFI 36-2502, *Airman Promotion/Demotion Programs*, 31 December 2009.

AFI 36-2907, *Unfavorable Information File (UIF) Program*, 17 June 2005.

AFI 36-3206, *Administrative Discharge Procedures for Commissioned Officers*, 9 June 2004 (incorporating through change 7, 2 July 2013).

AFI 36-3208, *Administrative Separation of Airmen*, 9 July 2004 (incorporating through change 7, 2 July 2013).

AFI 51-202, *Nonjudicial Punishment*, 7 November 2003 (incorporating through change 3, 11 August 2011).

USAF JAG School, *The Military Commander and the Law*, 2012.

The majority of the following information is excerpted directly from the above references.

When disciplining Airmen, commanders have a wide range of options. Each option impacts the individual's career differently, so the commander must carefully weigh the circumstances against the effects of the discipline he or she wants to impose. Before making a final decision in a disciplinary case, you should gather all the facts and discuss options with supervisors and the first sergeant and, if necessary, the SJA and other involved base agencies. The following describes the basic disciplinary options available to commanders and gives references to applicable Air Force guidance.

Disciplinary Counseling by Letter

Counseling is the first—and simplest—corrective action. All supervisors should conduct basic counseling, documented or undocumented, to keep Airmen on the right path. Disciplinary counseling is documented in one of three increasingly severe forms: a letter of counseling (LOC), a letter of admonishment (LOA), or a letter of reprimand (LOR). All disciplinary counseling letters must contain the following information:

- A description of what the member did, or failed to do, citing specific incidents and their dates.
- A statement of what improvement is expected.
- A warning that further deviation may result in more severe action.
- A statement telling the member to respond and provide rebuttal matters within three duty days (30 days for nonextended active duty Reservists).
- A statement that all supporting documents become part of the record.
- A statement that the person who initiates the LOC, LOA, or LOR has three duty days to advise the individual of a decision regarding any comments that the individual submits.
- A Privacy Act statement.

Unfavorable Information File

The UIF provides commanders with an official and single means of filing derogatory data concerning an Air Force member's personal conduct and duty performance. With some exceptions, the commander has wide discretion as to what should be placed in a UIF and what should be removed.

- Mandatory UIF entries.
    - A record of nonjudicial punishment under Article 15 of the *Uniform Code of Military Justice* (*UCMJ*) when punishment is suspended or when the punishment period is in excess of one month. Commanders may remove the record early only if the punishment is complete.
    - A record of conviction by a civilian court or an action equivalent to a finding of guilty for an offense that resulted in or could have resulted in a penalty of confinement for more than one year or death.
    - Records of court-martial convictions.
    - Control roster actions.
    - LORs (officers only).
- Optional entries.
    - A record of nonjudicial punishment under Article 15 of the *UCMJ* when punishment is not suspended or does not exceed one month. Commanders may remove the record early only if the punishment is complete.
    - A record of conviction by a civilian court or an action equivalent to a finding of guilty for an offense where the maximum confinement penalty authorized for the offense is one year or less.
    - Written LOCs, LOAs, or LORs (enlisted only).
- The unit commander must review all UIFs
    - Within 90 days of assuming or being appointed to command;
    - Annually, with the assistance of the SJA; or
    - Whenever individuals are being considered for, among other things, promotion, reenlistment, PCS, PRP duties, retraining, EPRs, or OPRs.

Control Rosters

Commanders at all levels are authorized to use a control roster for individuals whose duty performance is substandard or who fail to meet or maintain Air Force standards of conduct, bearing, or integrity, on or off duty.

- The control roster is a rehabilitative tool.
- A single incident of substandard duty performance or an isolated breach of standards not likely to be repeated should not ordinarily be a basis for a control roster action. Other actions should be considered first.
- Placing an individual on the control roster is not a substitute for more appropriate administrative, judicial, or nonjudicial action.
- The control roster observation period may last for up to six months for active duty personnel.
- Commanders may direct an OPR or EPR before entering an individual on and/or removing someone from the control roster.
- Placing a member on a control roster affects numerous personnel actions, including the following:
  - o PCS/PCA reassignment is limited.
  - o All formal training must be canceled.
  - o Member is ineligible for promotions and reenlistments.

Nonjudicial Punishment under Article 15

Nonjudicial punishment (NJP) under Article 15 of the *UCMJ* provides commanders with an essential and prompt means of maintaining good order and discipline and also promotes positive behavior changes in service members without the stigma of a court-martial conviction. While no specific standard of proof is applicable to NJP proceedings, commanders should recognize that a member is entitled to demand trial by court-martial, where proof beyond a reasonable doubt by competent evidence is required for conviction. Commanders should consider whether such proof is available before initiating actions under Article 15. If not, NJP is not usually warranted.

- Commanders must confer with the SJA, or a designee, before initiating NJP proceedings or imposing punishment.
- Acceptance of NJP is not an admission of guilt. It is simply a member's choice not to assert the right to a trial by court-martial, instead allowing the commander to determine whether the member is guilty or innocent of the alleged offense and the punishment, if any, to be imposed.
- Commanders should tailor the punishment to the offense and the member. Punishment limitations based upon both the commander's and the member's grade is summarized in AFI 51-202, tables 3.1 and 3.2, and on page 3 of Air Force Form 3070, Record of Nonjudicial Punishment Proceedings.

- Members are entitled to appeal nonjudical punishment to the next superior authority in the commander's chain of command.

Administrative Demotions

An administrative demotion is another force management tool commanders have available to help ensure a quality enlisted force. In cases where demotion actions may be appropriate, members should be given the opportunity to overcome their deficiencies prior to initiation of the action.

- The demotion authority is the group commander (or equivalent level commander) for master sergeants (E-7) and below. For senior master sergeants (E-8) and chief master sergeants (E-9), the MAJCOM/CC, field operating agency (FOA)/CC, or direct reporting unit (DRU)/CC is the demotion authority (unless delegated to the vice-commander, chief of staff, manpower and personnel, director of personnel, or the NAF/CC).
- The appellate authority is the next-level commander.
- Reasons for demotion include
  - o Elimination from training (e.g., officer trainees, or pipeline students).
  - o Termination of student status of members attending TDY Air Force schools.
  - o Failure to maintain or attain the appropriate skill/grade level.
  - o Failure to fulfill NCO responsibilities.
  - o Failure to keep fit.
  - o Failure to perform.

Involuntary Administrative Discharge

Commanders and supervisors must identify enlisted members who show likelihood for early separation and make reasonable efforts to help these members meet Air Force standards. Members who do not show potential for further service should be discharged. Commanders must consult the servicing SJA and military personnel flight before initiating the involuntary separation of a member. Some of the reasons to initiate discharge include

- Failure of drug- or alcohol-abuse treatment (mandatory).
- Fraudulent or erroneous enlistments (mandatory).
- Convenience of the government.

- Entry-level performance and conduct.
- Unsatisfactory performance.
- Misconduct.
- Failure in the Air Force fitness program.

Generally, the acts or conditions on which the discharge is based must have occurred in the current enlistment except for cases involving fraudulent or erroneous enlistment, the interest of national security, or a commander being unaware of the facts warranting discharge until after the member reenlisted, with no break in service.

Mistakes Commanders Make When Executing Discipline

As a commander, the proper use of discipline can be an effective tool for maintaining good order within a unit. Disciplinary actions should achieve three basic objectives: (1) accurately address and document the offense, (2) correct the individual's behavior, and (3) discourage others in the unit from repeating that action in the future. Below are some missteps commanders make when executing discipline.

Not Progressive. For repeat offenses, discipline should correspondingly escalate. If the individual received an LOC the first time, giving an LOA or LOR is the next step, or a letter should come from a higher level (e.g., LOR from the flight chief, then LOR from commander). Bouncing up and down the range of options doesn't send a clear message to the violator or your unit. That doesn't mean that the first step in every disciplinary action is an LOC. The level of discipline should be relative to the nature of offense. Some offenses may start with an LOR or Article 15 from the commander.

Doesn't Allow for Rehabilitation. Unless you are issuing a second Article 15 to someone with the intent to discharge, most of the time the expectation is that the NJP action has a rehabilitative aspect to it. However, if you take every option away from the member in the NJP action, you are only delaying the inevitable. For example, you give someone a stiff financial penalty for failing to pay their bills because they are in too much debt. If you add to the problems they already have, you are only putting them in a situation where they'll be in front of your desk for another Article 15 in the future.

Making It Personal. When a situation becomes personal, you lose objectivity and possibly overreact in the discipline you hand out. Perhaps you have dealt with an individual several times on the subject, and he or she is still having problems following your directions. If you are following a logical flow and using progressive discipline, the problem will take care of itself. Either individuals will see the light as the level of punishment goes up, or they will work themselves out of the Air Force. Although the process doesn't always happen fast, the issue will come to a close with time if you stay the course.

Inconsistent. Nobody in the unit should be surprised by the discipline administered. If you have been consistent with discipline in your unit, most people in your unit will know the consequences for a specific offense. If you are all over the map with your discipline, that could be construed as either you are playing favorites or out to get someone.

Not Considering the Next Step. Although we all want to think that NJP action will resolve a situation, you always have to consider what you'll do next if individuals repeat an offense. If you give them an LOR, are you prepared to give them an Article 15 if they repeat it (progressive)? Also, what happens if the next person who commits this offense happens to be one of your best personnel? Are you willing to give that individual the same level of discipline (consistent)?

Too Slow. Discipline should be administered quickly without rushing to judgment. Waiting only adds stress to the accused and delays the rehabilitation process. Discipline should be administered as soon as possible so the member can start working on being a positive influence in the unit. Although individuals may do great things the day after an event for which they are being disciplined, the "clock" on their good behavior doesn't start until all administrative actions have been completed.

Too Soft. The discipline should encourage others in the unit to not do the same thing in the future. That is not to say that you should "drop the hammer" for every offense. However, you must realize that the discipline you administer will show the unit members what you feel is important and may make someone think twice about duplicating the act.

Courts-Martial Charges

Original Author: Maj Jonathan Bland
8th Maintenance Squadron Commander

References

DOD, *Manual for Courts-Martial, United States*, 2012 edition.

AFI 51-201, *Administration of Military Justice*, 6 June 2013.

USAF JAG School, *The Military Commander and the Law*, 2012.

The majority of the following information is excerpted directly from the above references.

Commanders prefer court-martial charges against Airmen accused of major crimes or who refuse to accept punishment under Article 15. Trial by court-martial is appropriate only if lesser types of disciplinary or administrative actions are inadequate.

There are three types of courts-martial: general, special, and summary.

- General court-martial (GCM)—A GCM is used for the most serious offenses. Maximum punishment is determined by the offense as set forth in the *MCM*. A GCM is the only type of court-martial that may sentence officers to confinement.
- Special court-martial (SPCM)—An SPCM is used for lesser offenses. Maximum punishment is a bad conduct discharge, confinement for one year, forfeiture of two-thirds pay per month for one year, and reduction to E-1.
- Summary court-martial (SCM)—An SCM is a simple procedure used to dispose of minor offenses. As for an Article 15, the member must consent to the forum. SCMs are not authorized for officers or cadets, and punishment is more limited than in an SPCM.

Tips for Success

- If you have information that a military member under your command may have committed an offense in violation of the *UCMJ*, immediately contact your legal office. The SJA will help you determine what response is appropriate and, if necessary, draft the court-martial paperwork.
- Since you normally prefer the charges and sign as the "accuser," you must first familiarize yourself with the AFOSI report of investigation (or statements) to ensure administration of the required sworn oath before preferring charges.
- After preferring charges, you must personally read the charges to the accused and complete block 12 of DOD Form 458, Charge Sheet.
- Once charges are preferred, you may be required to testify or take other administrative actions.
- Upon conviction of the accused, you may be asked to make a clemency evaluation. The SJA will guide you through this process.

Pretrial Confinement

Original Author: Maj Jonathan Bland
8th Maintenance Operations Squadron Commander

References

DOD, *Manual for Courts-Martial, United States*, 2012 edition.

AFI 51-201, *Administration of Military Justice*, 6 June 2013.

USAF JAG School, *The Military Commander and the Law*, 2012.

The majority of the following information is excerpted directly from the above references.

Pretrial confinement is physical restraint imposed by order of a competent authority that deprives a person of freedom pending disposition of court-martial charges. Only a person who is subject to trial by court-martial may be confined. *Never* confine someone without first consulting the SJA.

You may order a subordinate member into pretrial confinement when

- There is probable cause to believe that the member committed an offense punishable by military court-martial.
- It is foreseeable that the member will not appear for trial or will engage in further serious criminal misconduct.
- Less severe forms of restraint (e.g., restriction to base) are inadequate.

Imposing pretrial confinement starts the trial clock, regardless of whether charges have been preferred. This means the government must bring the accused to trial within 120 days or risk having the case dismissed. Premature or inappropriate confinement can adversely affect the government's case. The *UCMJ* has no provisions for bail.

Tips for Success

- Always consult the SJA before ordering a member into confinement. Restraint can consist of restriction to the dorm, base, or physical jail. If the member is convicted in a court-martial, then this time can be considered time served.
- Order a member into confinement only when less severe forms of restraint have not been successful or are not feasible.

- Promptly advise the accused of
  - o The nature of the offense.
  - o His or her rights under Article 31, *UCMJ*.
  - o Procedures for reviewing pretrial confinement.
- Within 48 hours of confinement, determine whether confinement should continue. Consider the nature of the offense, the accused's ties to the local community, the character of the accused, the likelihood of further misconduct, and the effectiveness of lesser restraints. The legal office will assist you with this process.
- Put your confinement decision in writing; provide a copy to the prisoner and to a military magistrate for review within seven days of the member's entry into confinement.

Arrest by Civilian Authorities

Original Author: Maj Jonathan Bland
8th Maintenance Operations Squadron Commander

References

USAF JAG School, *The Military Commander and the Law*, 2012.

AFI 36-3208, *Administrative Separation of Airmen*, 9 July 2004 (incorporating through change 7, 2 July 2013).

AFI 51-1001, *Delivery of Personnel to United States Civilian Authorities for Trial*, 20 October 2006 (incorporating through change 2, 17 December 2012).

AFPD 51-10, *Making Military Personnel, Employees, and Dependents Available to Civilian Authorities*, 19 October 2006 (certified current 2 December 2012).

The majority of the following information is excerpted directly from the above references.

When a commander receives notice from any source (e.g., a unit member, security forces, or the AFOSI) that a member of his or her command is being held by civilian authorities and is charged with a criminal offense, Air Force directives require certain actions:

- The commander or representative of the unit should contact civilian authorities, inform them the person is a military member, and gather the following information:

  - o Charges against the member.
  - o Facts and circumstances surrounding the charged offense.
  - o Maximum punishment the member faces.
- If possible, make arrangements for the member's return to military control.
  - o Do not state or imply the Air Force will guarantee the member's presence at subsequent hearings.
  - o Do not post bond for the member or personally guarantee any action by the member (unless you are willing to accept personal responsibility and liability).
- The commander may make a statement as to the member's character and prior record of reliability, but do not make slanderous statements concerning the member.
- Off-base offenses committed by a military member on active duty may be tried by court-martial. The question of personal military jurisdiction turns on the status of the offender at the time of the offense, not where the offense occurred.
  - o The court-martial convening authority may request that the civilian authorities waive jurisdiction and permit the Air Force to prosecute the offender.
  - o The SJA will assist in coordinating with the local authorities.
- As a general rule, military status will not be used to avoid civilian court jurisdiction or court orders.
  - o Air Force policy is to deliver a member to federal authorities upon request if the request is accompanied by a warrant.
  - o Air Force policy is to deliver a member to state authorities upon request if the member is physically present in the state and state procedural rules have been followed.
  - o The Air Force will not transfer a member from one base to another to make the member present in the jurisdiction. The state seeking the member must proceed through normal civilian extradition channels.
  - o The Air Force will return a member from an overseas assignment upon request if the member is charged with a felony (an offense that carries a potential punishment of confinement for one year or more) or if the offense involves taking a child out of the jurisdiction of a court or from the lawful custody of another person.

    - The JAG can approve a request to return a member from overseas, and the under secretary of defense for personnel and readiness can deny such a request. The Air Force Legal Operations Agency, Military Justice Division, processes requests for return from overseas.
    - A commander can subject a member to restraint pending delivery to civilian authorities provided there is probable cause to believe the member committed an offense and is a flight risk.
- An AF Form 2098, Duty Status Change, must be prepared and forwarded to the MPF when a member is in civilian custody.
- If the member is convicted of an offense that would, if tried by court-martial, subject the member to a punitive discharge, the member is subject to involuntary administrative separation from the Air Force with a less-than-honorable-service characterization (general or other-than-honorable discharge).
- If the member is convicted of an offense (or one closely related to an offense under the *UCMJ*) that would, if tried by court-martial, subject the member to a punitive discharge and confinement for one year or more, the commander must recommend involuntary separation or waive discharge processing. In either case, the decision should be made promptly. An extended period of inaction may waive the right to process the member for separation.
  - It is the maximum allowable punishment—not the actual sentence imposed—that determines if separation is an option.
  - The member's absence due to confinement in a civilian facility does not bar processing the member for separation.
  - The commander must obtain information from civilian authorities concerning the final disposition of the case. The SJA, with security forces or the AFOSI, will assist.
  - If a member is charged with or convicted of a less serious offense (one that would not warrant separation), various disciplinary actions may be appropriate (consult with the SJA), for instance
    - Putting documents concerning the incident into a UIF.
    - Placing the member on the control roster.
    - Issuing an administrative reprimand to the member.

STANDARDS AND DISCIPLINE

Rights of Suspects

Original Author: Maj Jonathan Bland
8th Maintenance Operations Squadron Commander

References

Article 31, *UCMJ*, Military Rules of Evidence 304 and 306.

DOD, *Manual for Courts-Martial, United States*, 2012 edition.

Air Force Visual Aid 31-231, Advisement of Rights, 1 January 1999.

AF Form 1168, Statement of Suspect/Witness/Complainant, 1 August 2012.

USAF JAG School, *The Military Commander and the Law*, 2012.

The majority of the following information is excerpted directly from the above references.

Advising Suspects of Rights

It is important that a commander understands when and how to advise members of their Article 31 rights.

- The moment a commander or supervisor suspects someone of an offense under the *UCMJ* and starts asking questions or taking any action in which an incriminating response is either sought or is a reasonable consequence of such questioning, the individual must advise the suspect of his or her rights.
- Proper rights advisement enables the government to preserve any admissions or confessions for later use as evidence for any purpose.
- Unadvised admissions and confessions cannot normally be admitted as evidence at trial. Additionally, other evidence—both physical and testimonial—that may have been discovered or obtained as a result of the unadvised confession is usually inadmissible at trial.

When Must Article 31 Rights Be Given?

- Whenever there is formal or informal questioning in which an incriminating response is either sought or is a reasonable consequence of such questioning. This is an interrogation.
- An interrogation does not have to involve actual questions. Sometimes actions, if they are intended to elicit responses, are deemed to be interrogation. For example, a commander declares, "I don't know what you were thinking, but I'm assuming the worst," while shrugging his shoulders

and shaking his head. Even though the commander has not asked a question, his statement and actions could be deemed an interrogation because they were likely to elicit a response.

Advisement for Military Suspect

I am __________ (commander of the) __________, __________ AFB. I am investigating the alleged offense(s) of __________, of which you are suspected. Before proceeding with this investigation, I want to advise you of your rights under Article 31 of the *Uniform Code of Military Justice*. You have the right to remain silent; that is, to say nothing at all. Any statement you do make, either oral or written, may be used against you in a trial by court-martial or in other judicial, nonjudicial, or administrative proceedings. You have the right to consult with a lawyer prior to any questioning and to have a lawyer present during this interview. You have the right to military counsel free of charge. In addition to military counsel, you are entitled to civilian counsel of your own choosing at your own expense. You may request a lawyer at any time during this interview.

Advisement for Civilian Suspect

I am __________ (grade, if any, and name), (a member of the Air Force Security Forces/AFOSI). I am investigating the alleged offense(s) of __________, of which you are suspected. I advise you that under the Fifth Amendment to the Constitution, you have the right to remain silent, that is, to say nothing at all. Any statement you make, oral or written, may be used as evidence against you in a trial or in other judicial or administrative proceedings. You have the right to consult with a lawyer and to have a lawyer present during this interview. You may obtain a civilian lawyer of your own choosing, at your own expense. If you cannot afford a lawyer and want one, one will be appointed for you by civilian authorities before any questioning. You may request a lawyer at any time during the interview. If you decide to answer questions, you may stop the questioning at any time.

Follow-Up Questions

After advising an individual of his or her rights, ask the following questions:

- Have you previously requested counsel after advisement of rights? (If the answer is yes, stop. Contact your SJA before proceeding.)

- If you decide to answer questions during this interview, you may stop the questioning at any time. Do you understand your rights?
- Do you want a lawyer? (If the answer is yes, stop all questioning.)
- Have you already consulted an attorney about this matter? (If the answer is yes, stop questioning and contact the SJA.)
- Are you willing to answer questions?
- Do you understand that you are free to end this interview at any time?

Tips for Success

- Consult with the SJA before questioning a suspect.
- If you suspect someone of an offense, give a rights advisement before proceeding with any questioning.
- Ensure that rights of the accused are protected and that no person is forced to make a statement without first being informed of the right to remain silent, the right to counsel, and the fact that statements can be used as evidence.
- Be cautious when advising intoxicated persons of their rights. If significantly drunk, they may be legally incapable of knowing they are voluntarily waiving their rights.
- Obtain a current rights-advisement card from the SFS, AFOSI, or the SJA.
- If an individual waives his or her rights, obtain the waiver in writing, using an AF Form 1168, and have a witness available.
- If the suspect requests counsel, stop all questioning. Inform the SJA, and get advice before questioning resumes.
- If the suspect, after electing to talk, changes his or her mind, stop the questioning and prepare a memorandum containing the time of the session, what you advised the suspect of, what took place, the suspect's attitude, and the duration of the session.

Investigations and Inquiries

Original Author: Maj Jonathan Bland
8th Maintenance Operations Squadron Commander

References

AFI 90-301, *Inspector General Complaints Resolution*, 23 August 2011 (incorporating change 1, 6 June 2012).

AFI 51-503, *Aerospace Accident Investigations*, 26 May 2010.

AFI 91-204, *Safety Investigations and Reports*, 24 September 2008.

AFI 71-101, *Special Investigations*, vol. 1, *Criminal Investigations Program*, 8 April 2011 (incorporating change 1, 16 May 2013).

AFI 31-206, *Security Forces Investigations Program*, 16 September 2009.

AFI 36-2910, *Line of Duty (Misconduct) Determination*, 4 October 2002 (incorporating through change 2, 5 April 2010).

AFI 36-1203, *Administrative Grievance System*, 1 May 1996.

AFI 36-2706, *Equal Opportunity Program, Military and Civilian*, 5 October 2010 (incorporating change 1, 5 October 2011).

DOD, *Manual for Courts-Martial, United States*, 2012 edition.

USAF JAG School, *The Military Commander and the Law*, 2012.

The majority of the following information is excerpted directly from the above references.

Commanders possess inherent authority to investigate matters or incidents under their jurisdiction. This authority is incident to command. You are responsible under the *MCM* and *UCMJ* for making thorough and impartial investigations for minor offenses committed by members under your command. The SFS or AFOSI will investigate crimes and most major violations of the *UCMJ*.

Key Definitions

- Inquiry—A determination of facts on matters not usually complex or serious and handled through routine channels.
- Investigation—Looks into serious, complex matters requiring a determination of extensive facts.

Guidance for Different Types of Investigations and Inquiries and the Role of the Squadron Commander

Conduct investigations and inquiries pursuant to specific regulations. The squadron commander's responsibilities are summarized below.

- Commander-directed investigations (CDI).
  - o All commanders possess the authority to investigate matters or incidents under their command. The primary purpose of a CDI is to gather, analyze, and record relevant information about the incident(s).
  - o Commanders should first consult with the SJA prior to initiating a CDI.
  - o Refer to the *Commander-Directed Investigation Guide* available at https://www.my.af.mil/gcss-af/USAF/AFP40/d/s6925EC134F1C0FB5E044080020E329A9/Files/editorial/CDI%20Guide_Apr%2010.pdf.
- AFI 51-503, *Aerospace Accident Investigations.*
  - o An accident investigation board (AIB) conducts a legal investigation to determine the facts surrounding an Air Force aircraft accident or mishap.
  - o The wing legal office is the office of primary responsibility (OPR) for an AIB.
  - o The squadron commander will be required and directed to provide any necessary support, information, or personnel for the AIB.
- AFI 91-204, *Safety Investigations and Reports.*
  - o Safety investigations and reports are conducted solely to prevent future mishaps.
  - o The MAJCOM commander will convene the safety investigation board (SIB); the wing safety office is the OPR for SIBs.
  - o The squadron commander will provide logistical and investigative support as required.
- AFI 71-101, vol. 1, *Criminal Investigations Program.*
  - o OSI initiates and conducts independent criminal investigations under its jurisdiction.
  - o When a service member's squadron commander receives an allegation of illegal activity, the commander shall review the allegation and may request the AFOSI to conduct a criminal investigation.
- AFI 31-206, *Security Forces Investigations Program.*

  - o Security forces will investigate all crimes, offenses, or incidents falling within their investigative jurisdiction.
  - o Following interviews with DOD personnel who are the subject of an investigation, security forces will release the individual to his or her first sergeant, commander, or supervisor or their designee.
- AFI 36-2910, *Line of Duty (Misconduct) Determination.*
  - o Line-of-duty determination is a finding made after an investigation into the circumstances of a member's illness, injury, disease, or death.
  - o The LOD determination concludes whether or not the illness, injury, disease, or death occurred while the member was absent from duty and whether the result was due to the member's own misconduct.
  - o The squadron commander has four days to complete the LOD determination and submit it to the SJA for legal review.
  - o The administrative grievance system applies to US citizen employees of the Air Force who are paid from appropriated funds.
  - o Each base's civilian personnel section is the OPR for the administrative grievance system.
  - o See AFI 36-2706, *Equal Opportunity Program, Military and Civilian.* The military and the civilian equal employment opportunity programs apply to all military and civilian personnel.

Squadron commanders will

- Provide an environment free from unlawful discrimination and sexual harassment.
- Ensure all allegations of unlawful discrimination and sexual harassment are thoroughly investigated.
- Inform unit members of their right to file EO complaints without fear of reprisal.
- Investigate allegations of unlawful discrimination or sexual harassment when the military complainant has elected not to file a complaint with the EO office.

Tips for Success

- Consult with SJA before conducting an investigation.
- Investigate minor matters and incidents under your jurisdiction when presented with credible (not hearsay) evidence.
- Notify SFS or AFOSI for investigations involving crimes or major violations of the *UCMJ*.
- Consult with the SJA to ensure you know when to advise military members of their rights.
- Prepare a written report for any investigations conducted under your inherent authority.

Searches and Inspections

Original Author: Maj Jonathan Bland
8th Maintenance Operations Squadron Commander

References

AFI 51-201, *Administration of Military Justice,* 6 June 2013.

AFI 31-121, *Military Working Dog Program*, 17 October 2012.

AF Manual (AFMAN) 31-116, *Air Force Motor Vehicle Traffic Supervision*, 9 May 2012.

USAF JAG School, *The Military Commander and the Law*, 2012.

The majority of the following information is excerpted directly from the above references.

As a commander, military law allows you to direct inspections of persons and property under your command and to authorize probable cause searches and seizures of persons and property under your command. However, a commander who authorizes a search or seizure must be neutral and detached from the case and facts. Therefore, the command functions of gathering facts and maintaining overall military discipline must remain separate from the legal decision to grant search authorization.

Most bases have centralized the search authorization role in the installation commander, who is also often the special court-martial convening authority. The installation commander has discretion to appoint, in writing, up to two military magistrates who may also authorize search and seizure (including apprehension) requests. Each magistrate must receive training provided by the SJA on search and seizure issues.

A commander should also know the differences between inspections/inventories and search/seizures. Understanding this distinction will help ensure crucial evidence can be introduced at trial.

Key Definitions

- Inspections—Examinations of persons, property, or premises for the primary purpose of determining and ensuring the security, military fitness, good order, and discipline of your command.
- Inventories—Administrative actions that account for property entrusted to military control.
- Searches—Examinations of a person, property, or premise for the purpose of finding criminal evidence.
- Seizures—Meaningful interference with an individual's possessory interest in a property.

Commanders are authorized to conduct routine safety and health inspections of their areas, including dormitories, but may not use these inspections as a pretense for investigating suspect individuals. If, during inspections or otherwise, information arises that may result in a legal search and seizure issue, the commander should not personally investigate but should

- Freeze the situation.
- Notify the AFOSI or SFS to request a legal search.
- Note any evidence or incriminating statements.
- Coordinate with the SJA.

The law on search and inspection is complex. It also changes frequently due to court decisions. It is imperative that you consult the SJA prior to conducting any unusual examinations.

Tips for Success

- Conduct routine inspections of persons and property under your command.
- Inspections can be "announced" or "unannounced" and may be authorized without probable cause.
  - o Inspections are authorized unless conducted for the purpose of obtaining evidence to use in disciplinary proceedings.

- Inspections must be reasonable (see SJA for clarification).
- If you authorize an inspection based on information that contraband or other items are within a particular room or premise, it will be a "sham inspection," and the evidence seized will be inadmissible.

- Searches are generally authorized by the installation commander or magistrate and may be approved only
  - When the suspect has been lawfully apprehended.
  - When the person who owns the area to be searched gives voluntary consent.
  - When based on probable cause.

Line-of-Duty Determination

Original Author: Maj Jonathan Bland
8th Maintenance Operations Squadron Commander

References

AFI 36-2910, *Line of Duty (Misconduct) Determination*, 4 October 2002 (incorporating through change 2, 5 April 2010).

USAF JAG School, *The Military Commander and the Law*, 2012.

The majority of the following information is excerpted directly from the above references.

As a commander, military law authorizes you to direct inspections of persons, and a line-of-duty determination is an administrative tool for determining a member's duty status at the time of injury, illness, disability, or death. On the basis of the LOD determination, the member may be entitled to benefits administered by the Air Force or exposed to liabilities. The key is the nexus between the injury, illness, disability, or death and the member's duty status.

Limits on Use of LOD Determination

- An LOD determination shall not be used as disciplinary action against a member.
- An active duty member cannot be denied medical treatment based on an LOD determination. Moreover, an LOD determination does not

authorize the United States to recoup the cost of medical care from the active duty member.

- An LOD determination may impact
  - o Disability retirement and severance pay.
  - o Forfeiture of pay.
  - o Extension of enlistment.
  - o Veteran benefits.
  - o Survivor Benefit Plan.
  - o Medical benefits and incapacitation pay for members of the ARC.
  - o Basic educational assistance death benefit.

When LOD Determinations Are Required

The LOD process must be initiated when a member, whether hospitalized or not, has an illness, injury, or disease that results in

- Inability to perform military duties for more than 24 hours.
- Likelihood of permanent disability.
- Death of a member. In every case where a member dies on active duty, at a minimum an Air Force Form 348, Line of Duty Determination, must be completed. An administrative determination is not sufficient in a case of death.
- Medical treatment of an ARC member regardless of the member's ability to perform military duties.
- The likelihood of an ARC member applying for incapacitation pay.

Possible LOD Determinations

- In line of duty: Presumed unless disease, death, illness, or injury occurred while member was absent without authority (AWOA) or as a result of member's misconduct.
- Existed prior to service (EPTS), LOD not applicable: Medical diagnosis determined that the death, illness, injury, or disease, or the underlying condition causing it, existed before the member's entry into military service or between periods of service and was not aggravated by service.

- Not in line of duty, not due to own misconduct: A formal investigation determined that the member's illness, injury, disease, or death occurred while the member was absent from duty.
- Not in line of duty, due to own misconduct: A formal investigation determined that the member's illness, disease, injury, or death was proximately caused by the member's own misconduct (regardless of whether member was AWOA).

Presumption of LOD Status

An illness, injury, disease, or death sustained by a member in an active duty status or in inactive duty training (IDT) status is presumed to have occurred in the line of duty. However, the presumption can be rebutted.

Types of LOD Determinations

- Administrative determinations are made by a medical officer. If the medical officer determines that the condition existed prior to service, the medical officer simply annotates the member's medical record with an entry of "EPTS, LOD Not Applicable." If the illness, injury, disease, or death falls into one of the following conditions—incurred as a passenger in a common carrier or military aircraft, characterized as a hostile casualty, an illness or disease clearly not involving misconduct or caused by abuse of drugs or alcohol, or a simple injury that is not likely to result in permanent disability—the medical officer makes an administrative determination by finding the member's condition to be "in the line of duty."
- Informal determinations are processed on an AF Form 348 and initiated when an administrative determination is not appropriate. The commander investigates the circumstances of the case to determine if the member's illness, injury, disease, or death occurred while the member was AWOA or is due to the member's own misconduct.
- Formal determinations are initiated with an AF Form 348 but also include an investigation report and DD Form 261, Report of Investigation—Line of Duty and Misconduct Status.
  - o Required to support a determination of "not in line of duty."
  - o Immediate commander will recommend a formal determination of the conditions under which the member's illness, injury, disease, or death occurred.

- Under strange or doubtful circumstances or due to member's misconduct or willful negligence.
- While the member was absent without authority.
- Under circumstances the commander believes should be fully investigated.

o The commander forwards AF Form 348 to the SJA for review for legal sufficiency.

LOD and Misconduct Determinations for Various Situations

See AFI 36-2910, attach. 5, for appropriate guidance and rules. Some of these rules are based on historic precedents. For more in-depth research, check the *Digest of Opinions of the Judge Advocate General of the Armed Forces*.

Report of Survey

Original Author: Maj Kathy Goforth
898th Munitions Squadron Commander

References

AFMAN 23-220, *Reports of Survey for Air Force Property*, 1 July 1996.

AFI 51-502, *Personnel and Government Recovery Claims*, 1 March 1997 (incorporating change 2, 10 November 2008).

Title 18, *United States Code*, section 1361, "Government Property or Contracts," http://www.law.cornell.edu/uscode/text/18/1361.

DOD 7000.14-R, *DOD Financial Management Regulation*, vol. 12, *Special Accounts Funds and Programs*, chap. 7, "Financial Liability for Government Property Lost, Damaged, Destroyed, or Stolen," June 2012, http://comptroller.defense.gov/fmr/current/12/Volume12.pdf.

The majority of the following information is excerpted directly from the above references.

All Air Force personnel (military, civilian, ANG, and Air Force Reserve) are responsible for the proper care and safekeeping of Air Force property. Nonappropriated fund activities are not typically covered in these instructions. Commanders are responsible for government real and personal property under their control and can hold Airmen liable for loss, damage, or destruction of government property caused by their negligence, willful misconduct, or deliberate unauthorized use.

As stated in AFMAN 23-220, a report of survey (ROS) is an official report of facts and circumstances supporting financial liability assessment for loss, damage, or destruction of government-controlled property. It serves as the basis for restitution for loss or damage against a person, state, territory, or activity and ensures that justice is served for all parties. Many items used in the Air Force are no longer on accountable records; however, commanders are still responsible for assuring that equipment is properly maintained.

Purpose of a Report of Survey

- Research and investigate cause of loss, damage, or destruction of property; determine if it is attributable to an individual's negligence or abuse. At a minimum, the ROS will identify
  - What happened.
  - How it happened (is there evidence of negligence).
  - Where it happened.
  - Who was involved.
  - When it happened.
  - Any evidence of negligence, willful misconduct, or deliberate unauthorized use or disposition of the property.
- Assess monetary liability against individuals who have lost, damaged, or destroyed government property or relieve them from liability if there is no evidence of negligence, willful misconduct, or deliberate unauthorized use.
- Provide documentation that can be used to support adjustment of accountable records.
- Provide commanders with case histories, enabling them to address and correct materiel management weaknesses to prevent recurrence of the incident(s).

Disciplinary Action

- Commanders must decide if the case warrants *UCMJ* action or a separate action (not related to assessment or nonassessment of financial liability).

- Commanders are encouraged to use administrative actions when assessment of financial liability by ROS is not practical or desirable.

Tips for Success

- Ensure all personnel under your command are thoroughly instructed in government property responsibilities and are constantly alert to guard against loss, damage, or destruction of the property.
- Ensure assessment of financial liability against an individual is not used instead of, or as a form of, disciplinary action.
- Develop inspection procedures to ensure you document, monitor, and take appropriate corrective action pertaining to property loss, damage, or destruction cases.
- Ensure time frames for processing an ROS are met (see AFMAN 23-220, chap. 5).
- Take disciplinary action after consulting with the legal office.

Absent without Leave

Original Author: Maj Jonathan Bland
8th Maintenance Operations Squadron Commander

References

AFI 36-2911, *Desertion and Unauthorized Absence*, 15 October 2009.

USAF JAG School, *The Military Commander and the Law*, 2012.

The majority of the following information is excerpted directly from the above references.

Most forms of unauthorized absence—from simply being late for work ("failure to go") to being absent without leave (AWOL) for an extended period—are punishable under Article 86 of the *UCMJ*. Airmen who intend to permanently abandon their military duties are deserters and subject to prosecution under Article 85 of the *UCMJ*. The unit must satisfy certain requirements and considerations in handling cases involving an unauthorized absence.

When an unauthorized absence is discovered, it is important to note the date and time.

- An absence of less than 24 hours is classified as failure to go.

- When the absence continues longer than 24 hours, the member's unit must change the member's administrative status to "AWOL."
- On the 31st day of continuous absence, the member's unit must change the member's status to "deserter."
- These actions must normally be taken even if the commander suspects that the absence may be legally excused. Consult AFI 36-2911, table 1.1, for a comprehensive list of actions to be taken upon realization of an unauthorized absence.
- Taking these administrative steps will not prove that the member has been absent without authorization. However, they will affect pay and allowances and put the service member's name on a database that civilian law enforcement can access during routine stops.

Regardless of the reason for the absence, if the commander's initial investigation reveals any indication that the absence results from an involuntary casualty rather than desertion or unauthorized absence, a categorization of duty status—whereabouts unknown (DUSTWUN) may be appropriate. Consult AFI 36-3002, *Casualty Services*, the MPF, and the SJA for advice in such cases.

Tips for Success

- Ensure Airmen keep their emergency contact information current.
- Make every attempt to establish the reason for the member's absence by contacting the absentee's relatives and associates.
- Notify the SFS, SJA, and MPF once AWOL is established.
- Ensure documentation continues throughout the entire process.
- If the member had access to classified materials, inventory all material and remove his or her name from the access list and other such locations.
- In the presence of a witness, inventory and secure the absentee's personal effects.
- Consult with the SJA to decide whether court-martial charges should be preferred while the member is absent and, if so, when.
- On the 10th day of AWOL, notify relatives and those paid by allotment of the continued absence.

- When the absentee is apprehended or returns voluntarily, notify the MPF, SJA, and SFS; prepare an AF Form 2098, Duty Status Change.
- If the member is in custody of civilian authorities, it is your responsibility to return him or her to military control.

Unprofessional Relationships

Original Author: Maj Jonathan Bland
8th Maintenance Operations Squadron Commander

References

AFI 36-2909, *Fraternization and Professional Relationships*, 1 May 1999.

USAF JAG School, *The Military Commander and the Law*, 2012.

The majority of the following information is excerpted directly from the above references.

Professional relationships are essential to maintaining good order and discipline. Unprofessional relationships can develop among officers or enlisted members and between officers and enlisted members; they can also exist between military personnel and civilian or contractor personnel.

Relationships become matters of official concern when they adversely affect, or have the reasonable potential to adversely affect, the Air Force by eroding morale, good order, discipline, respect for authority, unit cohesion, or mission accomplishment. Fraternization is an aggravated form of an unprofessional relationship and is defined as a personal relationship between an officer and an enlisted member in violation of acceptable behavior in the Air Force. This prejudices good order and discipline or discredits the armed forces.

Any unprofessional relationship detracts from the authority of superiors and results in, or reasonably creates the appearance of, favoritism and/or abandonment of organizational goals for personal interests. It also creates the impression that personal friendships are more important than individual performance and contributions to the mission. This can erode morale and discipline and affect the organization's ability to perform its mission.

Commanders must be aware of relationships within their organization and be mindful of any relationship that can be perceived as unprofessional. If you detect or perceive that there are unprofessional relationships in the squadron, take immediate corrective actions to remedy both the reality and the perception, including disciplinary action if necessary. As the commander, if you fail to take corrective action, you may be held accountable for failing to act and rectify the situation. You must also carefully consider how a third party might perceive your actions—ask the first sergeant and key squadron leaders for feedback.

Examples of Unprofessional Relationships

- Familiar relationships in which one member exercises supervisory or command authority.
- Shared living accommodations, vacations, transportation, or off-duty interests on a frequent or recurring basis in the absence of any official purpose or organizational benefit.

Examples of Fraternization

- Officers gambling with enlisted members.
- Officers lending money to, borrowing money from, or otherwise becoming indebted to enlisted members (an exception is if an individual forgets money and cannot pay for lunch at a unit function—quick repayment is expected to reduce the duration of indebtedness).
- Officers dating, courting, or becoming close friends with junior members. Subsequent marriage does not preclude punishment.
- Officers making a habit of spending off-duty time with enlisted personnel, regardless of gender or the nature of their relationship.
- Officers engaging in business enterprises with or soliciting sales from enlisted members.
- Supervisors showing favoritism, partiality, or misuse of grade or position.

Tips for Success

- Use your authority to maintain good order and discipline within your unit—clearly explain your standards during newcomer orientations and commander's calls.
- Solicit feedback from the first sergeant and supervisors about squadron members' perceptions.
- If an unprofessional relationship is discovered, discuss the case with the SJA, and quickly take corrective actions.

Standards of Ethical Conduct

Original Author: Maj Jonathan Bland
8th Maintenance Operations Squadron Commander

References

DODD 5500.07-R, *Joint Ethics Regulation*, 29 November 2007.

USAF JAG School, *The Military Commander and the Law*, 2012.

The majority of the following information is excerpted directly from the above references

Airmen are public servants. It is fundamental to the Air Force core values that personnel shall not engage in personal business or professional activity that places them in a position of conflict between their private interests and the public interests of the United States. To preserve the public confidence in the Air Force, even the appearance of a conflict of interest must be avoided.

Commanders must enforce standards and discipline throughout the unit and be on guard against the reality and the perception of unethical conduct. Commanders must understand the spirit and letter of the law to help their people avoid unethical situations. Communication is key because the informal "rumor mill" can quickly spread misinterpretations of ethical regulations. Brief your people about the common rules and any special cases that apply to your mission. Making this clear up front can help to prevent awkward situations in the future.

Ethical Prohibitions

- Making personal commercial solicitations or sales to personnel junior in rank.
- Using inside Air Force information for personal gain.
- Accepting something of value from any person or company engaged in procurement or other business with a DOD agency.
- Using grades, titles, or positions to endorse a commercial product.
- Accepting off-duty employment that is incompatible with government duties or that might discredit the government.
- Soliciting contributions for gifts to an official superior, except gifts of nominal value for special occasions.
- Giving gifts to or accepting gifts from an official superior (i.e., anyone involved in directing and evaluating a member's performance). However,

this is acceptable under certain circumstances, such as organizational farewells. Your SJA can provide guidelines to cover these situations.

Authorized Actions

- Using frequent-flyer miles earned during official travel for personal travel or personal travel upgrades, provided they are obtained under the same terms as those offered to the general public and are available at no additional expense to the government.
- Accepting and giving gifts clearly motivated by family relationship or personal friendship or that are low-value, noncash items.
- Participating in widely attended gatherings that are part of member's duties or further the agency's interests. (Individuals cannot make a determination that an event is a "widely attended gathering"; this has to come through the base legal office.)

Tips for Success

- Annually communicate the standards included in the *Joint Ethics Regulation* to all personnel (e.g., include material in training sessions, in commander's calls, or on bulletin boards).
- Always consult the base ethics advisor at the legal office if you have ethics questions.

Financial Responsibility

Original Author: Maj Jay Stewart
Detachment 5, 67th Information Operations Group Commander

Reference

AFI 36-2906, *Personal Financial Responsibility*, 1 January 1998.

The majority of the following information is excerpted directly from the above reference.

First we make our habits, then our habits make us.

—Charles C. Noble

Air Force members are required to pay their financial obligations in a timely manner. You, as the commander, are responsible for counseling members regarding their financial obligations. The Air Force does not have the legal authority to order a member to pay a private debt (since it is a civil matter), but it is important to advise the Air Force member that continued failure to pay financial obligations may result in administrative or punitive action against the member.

When members fail to pay their private debts, you may receive complaints either directly from the creditor or from the MPF before the complaint is formally lodged. Keep in mind that GTC debts are not considered private debts; therefore, actions to be taken against members for failure to pay are clear-cut (see chap. 4 of this guide).

You can require unit members to attend the Airman and family readiness (AFRF) flight's personal financial management program (PFMP) as a proactive or corrective measure. Continued reminders to your Airmen of AFRF services should solve most financial obstacles before they become problems that you will have to address.

- Financial advisors at the AFRF flight offer the following programs and more. The communication remains solely between the financial counselor and the Airman.
    - Access to the Air Force Aid Society—the Air Force's official charity that provides financial assistance in terms of loans or grants to assist families experiencing emergencies.
    - Financial education.
    - Credit and debt management.
    - Personal budgeting.
    - Car buying strategies.
    - Introduction to investments, mutual funds, and stocks.

Tips for Success

- When you receive a debt complaint
    - Review and assess the complaint.
    - Advise the member and the complainant of Air Force policy, including the fact that the Air Force has no authority to arbitrate disputed cases of nonsupport or personal indebtedness.
    - Attempt to respond to the complainant within 15 days.

- o Monitor the complaint until it is resolved.
- o Don't provide any information to the complainant regarding administrative or disciplinary actions contemplated or taken against the member.
- o Refer members who demonstrate financial irresponsibility to the AFRF's PFMP contact for financial management education and information.
- o Consult the SJA about corrective and disciplinary action for financial irresponsibility, as required.

- Obtain the advice and coordination of the SJA, MPF, finance officer, and IG on complaints involving senior officers.

Additional Resource

- Check out *The Military Commander and the Law*, chapter 7, for more information on finances and financial responsibility.

Protest and Dissident Activities

Original Author: Maj Jonathan Bland
8th Maintenance Operations Squadron Commander

References

AFI 51-902, *Political Activities by Members of the US Air Force*, 12 November 2010.

AFI 51-903, *Dissident and Protest Activities*, 1 February 1998.

AFI 51-904, *Complaints of Wrongs under Article 138, Uniform Code of Military Justice*, 30 June 1994.

USAF JAG School, *The Military Commander and the Law*, 2012.

The majority of the following information is excerpted directly from the above references.

Public demonstrations for and against every conceivable cause have always been part of the American political landscape. Such activities are firmly rooted in our history and cultural values of free speech, peaceful assembly, and the right to petition the government for a redress of grievances. The First Amendment of the US Constitution expressly protects these rights. For commanders, the difficulty in dealing with such activities comes in balancing the free-expression rights of service members and civilians with the needs of the

Air Force mission. Included also are the duty to respect our civilian leaders and the need to maintain readiness, morale, good order, and discipline.

Activities by Military Members Restricted by Law or Regulation

- Distributing written or printed materials on base, other than official publications, without permission of the installation commander.
- Writing for unofficial publications during duty hours.
- Producing unofficial publications, such as underground newspapers, using government or NAF property or supplies.
- Actively participating in organizations that support supremacist causes, illegal discrimination, or the use of force or violence or that otherwise engage in efforts to deprive individuals of their civil rights. Such activities include
    - o Publicly demonstrating, rallying, fundraising, recruiting, or training members.
    - o Organizing a group, holding office in it, or otherwise leading such an organization or group.
- Participating in demonstrations or other disruptive activities on Air Force installations when they could either, in the judgment of the installation commander,
    - o Result in interference with or prevention of the orderly accomplishment of a mission of the installation.
    - o Present a clear danger to loyalty, discipline, or morale of members of the armed forces.
- Participating in demonstrations while on duty in a foreign country or in uniform when the activities constitute a breach of law and order or whenever violence is likely.
- As an officer, using contemptuous words against the president, the vice president, Congress, the secretary of defense, the secretary of military departments, or the secretary of transportation or the governor or legislature of any state, territory, commonwealth, or possession in which the officer is on duty or present.

Tips for Success

- Consult with the SJA in all cases, and consider keeping a memorandum for record (MFR) about the facts of the situation and your decisions.

- You may prohibit protest or dissident conduct by military members on or off base that would harm mission effectiveness, morale, welfare, or national security. (Normally, only the installation commander or above makes this decision.)
- Remind unit personnel of the official channels for addressing grievances—through the wing IG and/or to members of Congress.

Base Driving Privileges

Original Author: Maj Jonathan Bland
8th Maintenance Operations Squadron Commander

References

AFMAN 31-116, *Air Force Motor Vehicle Traffic Supervision*, 9 May 2012.

USAF JAG School, *The Military Commander and the Law*, 2012.

The majority of the following information is excerpted directly from the above references.

Driving Privileges

Driving on a military installation, whether in a government-owned vehicle (GOV) or a privately owned vehicle (POV) is a privilege granted by the installation commander or designee. This authority may be delegated to the vice commander, mission support group commander, or other appropriate official not occupying a law enforcement, investigative, or other position raising the appearance of a conflict of interest.

Implied Consent

When operating a motor vehicle on a military installation, drivers give implied consent in a number of areas, including consent for

- Testing for the presence of alcohol or drugs in their blood, on their breath, and in their urine, provided there is a lawful stop, apprehension, or citation for any impaired driving offense committed while driving or in physical control of a motor vehicle on a military installation.
- Removing and temporary impounding their POVs if
  - o Illegally parked.
  - o Interfering with traffic operations.

- o Creating a safety hazard.
- o Disabled by accident or incident.
- o Abandoned.
- o Left unattended in a restricted or controlled access area.

Suspension

The installation commander can administratively suspend or revoke installation driving privileges. A suspension of up to 12 months may be appropriate if a driver continually violates installation parking or other nonmoving standards. The installation commander will immediately suspend installation driving privileges pending resolution of an intoxicated driving incident under any of the circumstances outlined below:

- Member refusal to take or complete a lawfully requested chemical test for the presence of alcohol or other drugs in the driver's system.
- Member operation of a motor vehicle with a blood alcohol content (BAC) or breath alcohol content (BRAC) of 0.10 percent by volume or higher, or in excess of the applicable BAC or BRAC level in the local civilian jurisdiction, whichever is applicable.
- Commander receipt of an arrest report or other official document showing that an intoxicated driving incident occurred.

Revocation

The installation commander will immediately revoke driving privileges for a period of not less than one year in any of the following circumstances:

- A person is lawfully detained for intoxicated driving and refuses to submit to or complete tests to measure blood alcohol or drug content.
- Conviction, nonjudicial punishment, or a military or civilian administrative action resulting in the suspension or revocation of a driver's license for intoxicated driving.
- The installation commander determines an immediate revocation is required to preserve public safety or the good order and discipline of military personnel.

Procedures

A point system is used on base to provide a uniform administrative device to impartially supervise traffic offenses. Points are assessed for violations of motor vehicle traffic regulations for on- and off-base traffic offenses. Certain procedural guidelines apply before an individual's driving privilege may be suspended or revoked.

- Individuals have the right to a hearing before a designated hearing officer. They must be notified of their right to a hearing, but it is only held if they request it within the prescribed time period.
- A suspension for an offense of driving while intoxicated may be effective immediately if based on reliable evidence. Such evidence can include witness statements, a military or civilian police report, chemical test results, refusal to complete chemical testing, videotapes, written statements, or field sobriety test results.

Civilian offenders may be prosecuted in a federal magistrate's court for on-base traffic offenses. Installation commanders are authorized to prescribe installation traffic rules.

Airman Reassignment Restrictions

Original Author: Maj Jonathan Bland
8th Maintenance Operations Squadron Commander

Reference

AFI 36-2110, *Assignments*, 22 September 2009 (incorporating through change 2, 8 June 2012).

The majority of the following information is excerpted directly from the above reference.

Commanders must take prompt action to prevent reassignment of Airmen not meeting minimum quality standards or those whose performance is substandard. The intent should be to address and correct, whenever possible, the individual's deficiencies in the environment in which they arose and before passing problems off to another commander. If the situation cannot be resolved, separation should be considered in lieu of reassignment. Commanders must work closely with the SJA, MPF, medical group, and/or other base support agencies as appropriate.

Reasons to defer reassignment include individuals who are

- Not recommended for promotion or nonselected for NCO status or reenlistment.
- Not recommended for further upgrade training or removed for failure to progress.
- The subject of a referral evaluation on their most recent EPR.
- Not recommended for overseas duty because of mental instability.
- Undergoing treatment for drug or alcohol abuse.
- Undergoing control roster observation.
- Awaiting trial, serving a court-martial or Article 15 punishment, or serving a suspended administrative discharge action.
- Under investigation by the AFOSI or other law enforcement agency.

Bottom line: Don't PCS a problem to another commander—fix it!

Tips for Success

- Develop a positive review process for PCS assignments to ensure selected personnel are appropriate for reassignment.
- Review AFI 36-2110, table 2.1, for applicable assignment procedures.
- Work with the MPF, the SJA, the medical group, and other base agencies as appropriate to ensure the right steps are taken administratively and for the individual's rehabilitation.

Selective Reenlistment

Original Author: Maj Jonathan Bland
8th Maintenance Operations Squadron Commander

References

AFI 36-2606, *Reenlistment in the United States Air Force*, 9 May 2011 (incorporating change 1, 29 August 2012).

USAF JAG School, *The Military Commander and the Law*, 2012.

The majority of the following information is excerpted directly from the above references.

The selective reenlistment program (SRP) is designed to ensure only enlisted members who consistently demonstrate the capability and willingness to maintain high professional standards are afforded the privilege of continued military service.

- Commanders have total SRP selection and nonselection authority.
- Decisions should be in line with other qualitative recommendations, such as promotion, and must be based upon substantial evidence. Commanders may reverse their decisions at any time.
- The SRP applies to all enlisted personnel eligible for consideration or reconsideration.
- SRP nonselection makes members ineligible for consideration or reconsideration.
- SRP nonselection makes members ineligible for promotion and automatically cancels projected promotion line numbers.
- Commanders will conduct early SRP considerations for members who have not previously received formal SRP consideration, are otherwise eligible to reenlist, and request early separation for reasons including the following:
    - Palace Chase.
    - Early separation directed by HQ USAF (except special separation benefit / voluntary separation incentive).
    - Officer training program, other than Air Force Reserve Officer Training Corps (AFROTC).
    - Early release to further education.
    - Sole surviving son or daughter.
    - Early release from extension.
    - Accepting public office.
    - Pregnancy or childbirth.
    - End-of-year early release.
- Immediate supervisors are responsible for ensuring members meet quality standards.
    - Provide unit commanders with recommendations of a member's career potential.
    - Prepare AF Form 418, Selective Reenlistment Program Consideration.

- Unit commanders consider the supervisor's recommendation, the member's duty performance, and career force potential before making a decision.
  - o If a member is selected for reenlistment, the commander completes the SRP roster.
  - o If the supervisor recommends nonselection or the commander nonconcurs with the supervisor's recommendation to allow the member to reenlist, the commander must
    - ▪ Notify the member of the specific reasons for nonselection, areas needing improvement, appeal opportunity, promotion ineligibility, and the possibility of future reconsideration and selection.
    - ▪ Permit the member three workdays to decide whether to appeal the decision.
- The appellate authority may be the group commander, wing commander, or secretary of the Air Force, depending on the member's length of service.
- A legal review is required only when a member appeals SRP decisions; however, it is recommended that commanders contact the servicing legal office prior to notifying a member of a nonselection decision.
- Coordination with the legal office can identify any potential problems with the package and avoid issues during the appeal process.

Tips for Success

- Discuss each individual's situation with the first sergeant and applicable supervisor before making any decisions.
- Keep the SRP process independent of the Airman's intent to reenlist or the existence of a skill requirement.
- Base your SRP decisions on
  - o EPR ratings.
  - o UIF contents.
  - o Supervisor recommendations.
  - o Potential duty performance.
- Before recommending nonselection, ensure that the decision is fully documented on AF Form 418 and that you understand all collateral effects.
- Personally inform all Airmen of their selection or nonselection.

Chapter 6

Airman and Family Assistance

Commanders are called upon to assist their people in a variety of situations, many of which relate only to mission requirements or military service. How commanders conduct themselves and orchestrate available resources to help their people can have a tremendous impact. Their actions can affect a unit's ability to accomplish its mission and serve as a litmus test to evaluate the effectiveness of the unit's leadership team. More importantly, they can have a profound influence upon the people, service members, and their families who are striving to overcome the challenges these situations pose. Successfully serving members in a crisis can be one of the most challenging as well as rewarding aspects of command. This chapter provides insight into the resources available to assist you when supporting out most valuable resource.

Leading Airmen and Families in Times of Distress

Original Author: Maj Jay Stewart
Detachment 5, 67th Information Operations Group Commander

Reference

US Air Force Medical Operations Agency, Mental Health Division, *Airman's Guide for Assisting Personnel in Distress, Commander Version*, http://www.afms.af.mil/shared/media/documents/AFD-130404-047.pdf. Also see full version on Air Force Portal, http://www.afms.af.mil/airmansguide/index.asp.

The majority of the following information is excerpted directly from the above reference.

Commanders in today's Air Force face incredible challenges while helping their units deal with the stress of a nation at war. The *Airman's Guide for Assisting Personnel in Distress* is a tool you can use to help identify how personnel may react in many types of distressing situations. It summarizes relevant guidance and provides recommended actions and agencies available for consultation to provide maximum assistance to Airmen in times of crisis. Awareness is the key to providing early help to your Airmen. Some of the common problems that you must watch for in all your Airmen are:

- Death of a loved one/unit member.
- Serious illness.
- Changes in relationships (e.g., marriage or divorce).
- Medical, financial, or legal problems.
- Changes in lifestyle (e.g., deploying, PCSing, retiring).
- Promotion (or "passed over" for promotion).
- Changes in job responsibilities.

The situations listed above can result in many problems that manifest themselves in different ways, some of which are severe: withdrawal; impulsive, suicidal, or violent behavior; depression; anxiety; and other interpersonal problems. The *Airman's Guide for Assisting Personnel in Distress* provides detailed checklists for dealing with these and many other common problems. Bookmark the site, and become very familiar with the guide. The tips for success listed below offer some good ideas to help you care for your Airmen.

Tips for Success

- Get to know your people.
- Get to know the resources available for dealing with distressing situations.
- Foster a climate of mutual support.
- Help members build a community, both inside and outside the unit.
- Understand how distress may impact your Airmen and their ability to do the mission.
- Closely watch for signs of distress in your unit! Isolate problems, and provide resources to mitigate issues where possible.
- Decrease the impact of distress by linking individuals with the appropriate support agencies as soon as possible.

Air Force Readiness EDGE and the Integrated Delivery System

Original Author: Maj Jay Stewart
Detachment 5, 67th Information Operations Group Commander

References

Air Force Readiness EDGE: A Guide to Support Commanders and Supervisors with the Services of the Air Force Integrated Delivery System, http://www.afcrossroads.com/famseparation/pdf/ReadinessEdgeCommanders.pdf.

Taking Care of the Families of America's Armed Forces, http://ra.defense.gov/documents/family/Benefits%20Guide%202008%20FINAL.pdf.

The majority of the following information is excerpted directly from the above references.

> *The United States Air Force is committed to taking care of its own. Our Air Force families deserve the best support possible. Steadfast home front support for family members is provided by the Integrated Delivery System (IDS) coalition.*
>
> —Lt Gen Joseph Wehrle Jr., USAF, retired

The Air Force Readiness EDGE program assists Airmen and their families during all phases of deployment, reunion, and reintegration through the services of the IDS—a multidisciplinary team of professionals on each base united in providing seamless services to Air Force families.

IDS Members

- Family advocacy.
- Sexual assault response coordinator.
- Mental health clinic.
- Health and wellness center.
- Airman and family readiness center.
- Wing chaplain.

The primary focus of the Readiness EDGE and IDS programs is to provide Air Force commanders, supervisors, and families with the resources necessary to help cope with the AEF lifestyle—deployment, extended absence, and reintegration upon return. The Readiness EDGE website provides commanders, supervisors, and families guides that contain up-to-date, reliable information to confront the challenges of deployment, family emergency preparedness, and, if needed, survivor assistance.

Ensuring access to services is an important concern. A family's connection to the network of base, community, and national support services can begin with the information in the guide (family version), but the program will only be successful through close involvement of the commander, the first sergeant, and other leaders in the chain of command. Thus, Air Force Readiness EDGE guides are available to help both the leadership and the family members of an organization affected by deployment. For commanders, the commander and supervisor version of the readiness guide will assist your deployment and reunification response efforts.

- Checklists identify challenges, behavior and concerns, and tailored support from the IDS base helping agencies; in-depth resource information is also provided.
- The Air Force Readiness EDGE guide for commanders and supervisors is an easy-to-use resource that outlines the services of the IDS to assist commanders during all phases of members' deployment, reunion, and reintegration.
- The guide is tailored to meet the needs of the commander. The information is displayed in a tabled checklist format, so readers can easily identify the
    - Challenge or event.
    - Behavior/concern they want to address.
    - Available support along with suggested behaviors and helping agencies.

These guides have over 100 websites covering a broad range of topics related to many aspects of predeployment, deployment, and reunion. These websites link to military, DOD, government, university, and nonprofit and private organizational Web pages.

Guidelines for Command

Know the resources—such as the Air Force Readiness EDGE guides and IDS available to commanders and their personnel and family members—when in need of information pertaining to predeployment, deployment, and postdeployment activities and requirements. Encourage your personnel to be aware of and to share the many online resources offered to mitigate burdens related to deployments. Get involved with your Airmen and their families—make appropriate referrals to the IDS team as needed.

Tips for Success

- After a referral, follow up with your troops, their family members, and the IDS team to see how things are going and to determine what you can do to further assist.
- Use the Air Force Readiness EDGE guides and resources to assist you in this process.
- Familiarize yourself with the checklists available in the *Air Force Readiness EDGE* guide.

Key Spouse Program

Original Author: Maj Terri Sheppard
Cadet Squadron 17 Commander

The key spouse program is a partnership among a commander-appointed key spouse, squadron leadership, and the A&FRC. The goal is to address family member concerns and issues during deployments and extended family separations. The volunteer key spouse is empowered by the commander to help address quality-of-life concerns for squadron families, connect families in need with appropriate resources and base agencies, and offer stability and support during times of increased stress.

The program is not mandated Air Force–wide and varies greatly across MAJCOMs and bases. Contact your A&FRC to determine if a program exists at your base or to obtain information on how to start one in your unit.

Key Spouse Role

- Communication link to squadron leadership.
- Connects families with community information, volunteer opportunities, and referral services.
- Peer-to-peer support system for military life experiences, especially in preparation for deployments and family separations.

Some Key Spouse Responsibilities

- Welcomes incoming members and their families.
- Attends and actively participates in squadron and base events.
- Provides and coordinates assistance to deployed members' families.
- Helps keep families informed about local events and initiatives.

- Participates in the basewide community action information board (CAIB), if permitted.
- Maintains a contact list (e.g., phone tree, e-mail list, or website) to ensure information flow.
- Communicates with squadron leadership and provides feedback regarding family readiness issues.

Tips for Success

- Establish, design, and direct a key spouse program to meet the needs of your squadron.
- If you implement the program, appoint your volunteer key spouse in writing.
- Meet initially with the key spouse to articulate your expectations and priorities.
    - o Provide squadron focal points for information.
    - o Define situations you wish reported to you.
    - o Stress the necessity to follow Privacy Act guidelines and protection of sensitive information.
- Provide support to key spouses as appropriate and practical.
    - o Office space and supplies.
    - o Telephone services, use of official mail, and e-mail account.

American Red Cross

Original Author: Maj Jay Stewart
Detachment 5, 67th Information Operations Group Commander

Reference

The American Red Cross, http://www.redcross.org.

The majority of the following information is excerpted directly from the above reference.

An Air Force Partner

The American Red Cross (ARC) links members of the US Armed Forces with their families during a crisis. Twenty-four hours a day, 365 days a year, the Red Cross quickly sends emergency communications to deployed service members on behalf of their families. Military members can have peace of mind knowing that when they are on a mission, in training, or stationed far from home—leaving cell phones and e-mails behind—they are still connected to home.

The ARC and the Air Force enjoy a great working relationship. As a commander, you will find that the ARC can assist you, your Airmen, and family members during conflict or peacekeeping and humanitarian operations.

American Red Cross Services

- Emergency communications. Following the death or serious illness of a family member or other important event, such as the birth of a child, the ARC quickly sends information on behalf of the family. This information can assist you in making a decision regarding emergency leave.
- Financial assistance. Financial assistance is available via the ARC and the Air Force Aid Society program for emergencies.
- Counseling, information, and referrals for various social services are available through a worldwide network of support providers.
    - Holiday Mail for Heroes.
    - Veteran services.
    - ANG and AFRC services.
    - Deployment tips.

Tips for Success

- Meet with your base's ARC coordinator to learn about local programs, capabilities, and procedures.
- Obtain the ARC's *Coming Home from Deployment! The New "Normal"* for Airmen returning from deployment. See http://www.redcross.org.
- Get to know your ARC before you need it.

Alcohol and Drug Abuse Prevention and Treatment Program

Original Author: Maj Tom Smith
42nd MPF Commander

Reference

AFI 44-121, *Alcohol and Drug Abuse Prevention and Treatment (ADAPT) Program*, 11 April 2011.

The majority of the following information is excerpted directly from the above reference.

As a commander, you are responsible for substance abuse prevention and treatment at the squadron level. The ADAPT program is an installation-level resource available to assist you in this effort.

ADAPT Program Services

- Assistance in identifying and referring individuals needing treatment services ranging from counseling to inpatient medical care.
- Substance abuse prevention education, materials, and resources for your Airmen and their families.
- Follow-up care if needed.

Tips for Success

- Refer Airmen for an ADAPT assessment within seven days of when alcohol or substance use is suspected to be a contributing factor in any incident, on or off duty.
  - o The commander or first sergeant should personally review DD Form 1569, Incident/Complaint Report, to screen for evidence of substance use or abuse.
  - o The first sergeant is key in ADAPT-type situations.
- Work with your SJA and ADAPT coordinator for blood alcohol and drug testing as soon as possible after a suspected alcohol-related incident, an episode of aberrant or bizarre behavior, or where there is reasonable suspicion of drug use.
- Refer individuals under investigation for drug abuse to ADAPT for assessment immediately after preferring charges (i.e., sign DD Form 458, Charge Sheet).
- With any ADAPT referral
  - o Inform the Airman of the reason for the assessment.
  - o Advise him or her that the assessment is not punitive in nature.
  - o Instruct him or her to report in uniform for the assessment appointment at the scheduled date and time.
  - o Ensure the ADAPT office is provided all relevant information relating to the referral, plus an assessment of duty performance and behavior as observed by you, the first sergeant, or the Airman's supervisor prior to the first appointment.
  - o Ensure that neither the assessment nor treatment process is delayed due to ordinary leave or TDY.

Exceptional Family Member Program and the Special Needs Assignment Consideration Process

Original Author: Maj Tom Smith
42nd MPF Commander

References

Air Force Special Needs website, https://www.afspecialneeds.af.mil/skins/afsn/home.aspx?mode=user.

vMPF, "Self-Service Actions/Assignments/Exceptional Family Member Program."

AFI 36-2110, *Assignments*, 22 September 2009 (incorporating through change 2, 8 June 2012).

AFI 40-701, *Medical Support to Family Member Relocation and Exceptional Family Member Program (EFMP)*, 15 February 2012.

The majority of the following information is excerpted directly from the above references.

The Exceptional Family Member Program is designed to identify family members of Airmen with special needs (medical, educational, or otherwise) and ensure that these Airmen are assigned to valid manning requirements where suitable military or civilian resources are available for dependent care.

The EFMP is not a separate assignment consideration process, nor does it ensure Airmen are assigned to specific locations. Airmen with family members identified under EFMP are still considered for and selected for assignments, including deployments, in the usual manner. EFMP becomes involved only after Airmen are selected for assignment and request the new location be assessed for its ability to meet their family members' special needs. Detailed information as well as access to the online application process is available to your Airmen through the vMPF.

Tips for Success

- Refer Airmen with questions on EFMP to the vMPF and the EFMP or special needs coordinator (SNC).
- For Airmen desiring EFMP consideration, advise that
  - EFMP deferments or assignments are not automatic and must be requested through the vMPF.

- o EFMP assessments cannot be mandated by the commander or requested by a family member.
- o The vMPF provides information to the sponsor on what he or she needs to submit in the package.
- o AFPC ultimately determines the appropriateness of the request and makes the final decision.
- Ensure Airmen with a dependent having newly identified special needs are referred to the base MPS.
- Ensure Airmen with dependents already enrolled in the EFMP are referred to the SNC at the MTF upon assignment notification for proper clearance and coordination. This is required before PCS orders are finalized.
- Advocate for the Airman, and provide support and encouragement.

Mental Health Flight

Original Author: Maj Tom Smith
42nd MPF Commander

References

AFI 44-109, *Mental Health, Confidentiality, and Military Law*, 1 March 2000 (certified current 20 September 2010).

USAF JAG School, *The Military Commander and the Law*, 2012.

DODI 6490.4, *Requirements for Mental Health Evaluations of Members of the Armed Forces*, 28 August 1997.

The majority of the following information is excerpted directly from the above references.

The mental health flight (MHF) is a section within the installation MTF. It is staffed by trained, professional psychologists, psychiatrists, and social workers to support and assist Airmen and their family members during times of unusual stress or difficulty. The staff provides counseling, therapy, and educational programs on mental health and related issues including, but not limited to, anger and stress management.

The MHF is a tremendous resource to you, as a commander, in three primary ways: (1) it provides your Airmen individual assistance for interpersonal or emotional difficulties, (2) it helps your unit recover in the aftermath of a collective loss or trauma, and (3) it conducts commander-directed mental health evaluations (CDE) of your Airmen should questions arise regarding safety or suitability/fitness for duty. It is important to develop a working relationship with the MHF so you will know who to call when one of your Airmen just "isn't acting right." This is increasingly important during time of war when stress, trauma, and loss can be intense and unavoidable. As a commander, you must ensure your Airmen understand that getting advice from a professional—even just talking to someone who understands—is a healthy behavior and is the right thing to do for themselves, their families, the unit, and the mission.

Tips for Success

- Develop a working relationship with the MHF commander—better to have a relationship before a crisis.
- Put the website for the *Airman's Guide to Managing Personnel in Distress, Commander Version*, in your favorites. Searchable on the Air Force Portal, or go to http://www.afms.af.mil/shared/media/document/AFD-130404-047.pdf. This resource answers many "just in time" questions you might have, especially when a mental health staff member cannot be reached immediately.
- Ensure your Airmen are aware of services and programs offered and that they understand that participation in a mental health program does not equate to having a mental health problem.
- Dispel misperceptions that voluntarily seeking mental health services is detrimental to a military career.
- Encourage Airmen to seek advice and assistance from the mental health clinic (or chaplain*) during times of overwhelming or exceptional stress, trauma, or loss. Emphasize that this is a healthy behavior, not a "sign of weakness."
- Do not, under any circumstance, coerce members to "voluntarily" seek a mental health evaluation.
- Do not request postevaluation feedback from the MHF after encouraging an Airman to "voluntarily" seek an evaluation.
- If you believe an Airmen is an eminent danger to himself or others due to mental or emotional issues, do what is reasonably necssary to safely detain the Airman. Immediately contact SJA and mental health for assistance.
- If you believe an Airman may have a mental health problem that impacts his or her fitness for duty, consult with the SJA and mental health clinic for advice on how to proceed through a CDE.

- Educate your Airmen about Military OneSource. Military OneSource (https://www.militaryonesource.com) also offers free off-base, short-term nonmedical counseling options to help with issues such as adjustment disorders, stress management, decision making, grief, communication, and family issues. Eligible service members or family members receive up to 12 sessions, per issue, at no cost.

*Some Airmen prefer to visit with a chaplain or other spiritual leader during difficult times instead of consulting a mental health provider. This is a personal choice and should be respected. Chaplains regularly work hand in hand with the mental health staff in such cases.

Chaplain

Original Author: Maj Jay Stewart
Detachment 5, 67th Information Operations Group Commander

References

AFI 52-101, *Chaplain Planning and Organizing*, 5 December 2013.

AFPD 52-1, *Chaplain Corps*, 19 December 2013.

The majority of the following information is excerpted directly from the above references.

Chaplains help you watch over the spiritual and moral welfare of members under your command. Chaplains manage the wing's religious programs and are key to assuring accommodation of religious practices by military members.

Base chaplains are key members of casualty notification teams and are expertly trained in ministering to the bereaved. Additionally, they serve on traumatic stress response (TSR) teams to help educate Airmen and, when necessary, intervene in times of intense stress. Chaplains also receive applied suicide intervention skills training (ASIST) and can help you set up training in this vital area for members of your unit. They are an invaluable resource in helping evaluate and understand organizational, institutional, and individual dynamics often involved in problems common to military life.

In addition to administering the wing's religious programs, chaplains provide religious ministry and offer counseling to military members, family members, DOD civilians, and retired military personnel. Your unit should have an assigned chaplain; integrate him or her into your unit. The more familiar unit members are with the chaplain, the more likely they are to use his or her services.

The only person on base who can offer total confidentiality in counseling is the chaplain. The chaplain is often preferred for individuals or families in need of expert advice in the areas of marriage counseling, marriage enrichment, and pre- or postdeployment care. Chaplains also offer confidential counseling to commanders and provide ethical and moral guidance.

Tips for Success

- Meet regularly with your unit's assigned chaplain to discuss the health of your unit.
- Make your unit's chaplain an integral part of the unit.
    - o Invite him or her to commander's call and social functions.
    - o Invite him or her to "walk around" the unit to talk to your Airmen.
    - o Include his or her name and phone numbers on key personnel listings and recall rosters.
- Encourage members to become familiar with the chaplain's counseling services.
- Complete the ASIST course yourself to improve your understanding of when unit members need help.

Sexual Assault Prevention and Response Program

Original Author: Maj Kathy Goforth
898th Munitions Commander

References

AFPD 36-60, *Sexual Assault Prevention and Response (SAPR) Program*, 28 March 2008 (certified current 14 April 2011).

AFI 36-6001, *Sexual Assault Prevention and Response (SAPR) Program*, 29 September 2008 (incorporating change 1, 30 September 2009; certified current 14 October 2010).

DODD 6495.1, *Sexual Assault Prevention and Response (SAPR) Program*, 23 January 2012.

Also go to the DOD's SAPR website, www.SAPR.mil, for more information.

The majority of the following information is excerpted directly from the above references.

Sexual assaults are a major challenge to the United States, and the Air Force is not immune. Sexual violence in the military creates leadership and readiness problems by eroding trust and morale. To counter this problem, the DOD has established a DOD-wide SAPR program, and each service has promoted the program with supporting service instructions and directives. The Air Force's SAPR program reinforces the Air Force's commitment to eliminate sexual assaults through awareness and prevention training, education, victim advocacy, response, reporting, and accountability. Each base has a sexual assault response coordinator. The SARC serves as the installation's single point of contact for integrating and coordinating sexual assault victim care services. The SARC is also available to assist unit commanders, as necessary, to ensure victims of sexual assault receive the appropriate responsive care.

In the event of a sexual assault, active duty members (or anyone on active duty orders) have the option of submitting a restricted (confidential) or unrestricted report. The restricted report allows a victim of sexual assault to access care and treatment without notifying a commander or law enforcement personnel or triggering an investigation. To maintain confidentiality, the victim must disclose information only to the SARC, victim advocate, or a healthcare provider. Reporting a sexual assault to any other person or agency is considered an unrestricted report. An unrestricted report must be coordinated through appropriate command, legal, and law enforcement channels.

Commander's Response to Allegations of Sexual Assault

- Commanders notified of a sexual assault must take immediate steps to ensure the victim's physical safety, emotional security, and medical treatment needs are met.
- Commanders must ensure the sexual assault is reported to the SARC, AFOSI, or appropriate criminal investigative agency.
- Commanders should consider whether no-contact orders or military protective orders (DD Form 2873) are required.
- The victim's unit commander is responsible for ensuring the victim receives, at a minimum, a monthly update on the current status of all investigative, medical, legal, and command proceedings pertaining to the unrestricted case. This action is usually facilitated through monthly meetings coordinated by the SARC.
- Commanders should consider an array of personnel actions available to the victim of sexual assault to include alternate duty locations, hours, or assignments within a unit; PCA on the installation; and PCS (including humanitarian reassignment).
- Refer to attachment 2 of AFI 36-6001 for a checklist of other important considerations.

Tips for Success

- Provide a clear "zero tolerance" policy on sexual assault.
- Establish a command climate of prevention predicated on mutual respect and trust.
- Emphasize that sexual assault violates the core values of being a professional Airman.
- Foster a unit environment that makes victims more comfortable with reporting assaults, and publicize contact information for your installation's SARC.
- Ensure Airmen are aware of their right to make a confidential, restricted report of assault to the SARC, victim advocate, or healthcare professional.
- Ensure all personnel receive sexual assault prevention training.
- Support and encourage squadron members to become victim advocates to assist victims of sexual assault.
- Once you or someone in the chain of command becomes aware of an alleged sexual assault (i.e., the report is unrestricted), action must be taken to investigate.

Death of a Unit Member

Original Author: Maj Jay Stewart
Detachment 5, 67th Information Operations Group Commander

References

AFI 44-153, *Traumatic Stress Response*, 29 August 2011.

AFI 34-242, *Mortuary Affairs Program*, 2 April 2008 (incorporating change 1, 30 April 2008).

AFI 34-511, *Disposition of Personal Property and Effects*, 7 June 2011.

US Air Force Medical Operations Agency, Mental Health Division, *Airman's Guide for Assisting Personnel in Distress, Commander Version*, http://www.afms.af.mil/shared/media/documents/AFD-130404-047.pdf. Also see full version on Air Force Portal, http://www.afms.af.mil/airmansguide/index.asp.

The majority of the following information is excerpted directly from the above references.

When a unit member dies, it is important for the entire base community to work together to provide reassurance and a sense of security for those experiencing the loss. Support for unit members to cope with feelings of loss is essential during this critical time.

In some cases, surviving members may experience distress associated with shock and guilt. They may feel that something could have been done to prevent the death. This most commonly occurs following suicides and accidental deaths. The TSR team is available for use in dealing with the stress. The TSR team's primary function is to consult with unit leaders and provide the initial response when groups or individuals expect to be, or have been, exposed to potentially traumatic stress. Its main goal is to foster resiliency in those exposed to potentially traumatic stress. This is accomplished through preparatory education for those likely to experience potentially traumatic stress (e.g., first responders and search and recovery personnel) and through education, screening, psychological first aid, and referral for those exposed to potentially traumatic stress. A TSR team can also be requested to assist unit members in managing their guilt and grief.

Unit members will look to you, as the commander, and to the first sergeant for answers as to why the unit member died. Survivors are especially sensitive to comments or suggestions that imply their responsibility. Avoid passing judgment, providing simplistic explanations of the death or suicide, or publicly placing blame. Minimize the spreading of rumors by keeping people informed while protecting privacy.

A casualty affairs team will provide guidance and checklists to help you meet mandated timelines for notifications and reporting. Everybody will rely on you for information and direction, so be prepared to provide assistance up and down the chain of command.

Your unit needs to see you as often as possible following the first days after the incident. Keep an eye on your Airmen; be conscious of individuals (especially close friends and teammates) who are taking the incident harder than expected.

Tips for Success

- Immediately establish contact with the force support squadron commander and casualty affairs section (in the FSS); they will assist you with all required actions.
- Always use proper channels to accomplish next-of-kin notification.
- Provide basic information to unit members about the death, and contact unit members away from the unit.
- Consult with the TSR team chief concerning what services may be appropriate to support your unit.
- Announce the details for the memorial and funeral arrangements.
- Appoint an escort to transport remains to a burial site, if necessary.
- Attend the funeral service if possible and if welcomed by the family.

- Hold a memorial service for unit members who are unable to attend the funeral.
- Consult PA and casualty affairs to best determine what to say and what not to say to the member's family or in public statements.
- Make personal contact to express your condolences. Send a condolence letter to the member's family, and visit the member's family when appropriate.
- Recommend to the installation commander a unit member to serve as summary court officer. This officer will
  - o Secure the work and living area once the AFOSI and SFS investigations are finished.
  - o Pack the deceased member's residence, if necessary.
- Periodically check on unit members who were closest to the victim.
- One year after the member's death, send a follow-up condolence letter to the member's family. Consult casualty affairs for assistance.

Violence Involving a Unit Member

Original Author: Maj Jay Stewart
Detachment 5, 67th Information Operations Group Commander

References

AFI 44-153, *Traumatic Stress Response*, 29 August 2011.

AFI 40-301, *Family Advocacy*, 30 November 2009.

US Air Force Medical Operations Agency, Mental Health Division, *Airman's Guide for Assisting Personnel in Distress, Commander Version*, http://www.afms.af.mil/shared/media/documents/AFD-130404-047.pdf. Also see full version on Air Force Portal, http://www.afms.af.mil/airmansguide/index.asp.

The majority of the following information is excerpted directly from the above references.

The two main categories of violence involving a squadron member are violence at home and violence at the workplace. Domestic violence normally refers to the verbal, physical, or sexual abuse of one's spouse or intimate partner but can include child abuse. The risk of domestic and family violence increases when one or more family members is in distress, experiencing high stress, abusing alcohol or drugs, or is diagnosed with mental illness (such as depression). Prevention is the Air Force's primary means of dealing with family violence. You can contribute to prevention and early identification of family violence by promoting

- An overall healthy lifestyle.
- Awareness of the helping agencies.
- An environment that offers assistance without fear of retribution.
- Opportunities for military members and their families to build informal connections within the squadron and their neighborhoods.

Violence in the workplace is the other area of concern. Workplace violence most often involves aggressive behavior toward a fellow colleague, subordinate, or supervisor and can range from verbal abuse to physical violence. Common examples are when an individual faces the loss of his or her job, is passed over for promotion, or perceives favoritism toward others in the work environment.

Possible Indicators of Impending Violence

- Anger over personal or work-related events.
- Recent major change in behavior, demeanor, or appearance.
- Intimidating, verbally abusing, harassing, or mistreating others.
- Escalation of work-related or domestic problems.
- Increasing resentment toward authority.
- Viewing self as a victim; preoccupation with violent incidents.
- Making threats to harm self, others, or property.

Common Violence Triggers

- Perceived rejection or loss of love, status, or advancement.
- Perception of supervisor as unjust.
- Loss of employment benefits or entitlements.
- Feelings of humiliation and rage.
- Projection of blame: "I didn't do anything; they're out to get me."
- Concluding that "they can't get away with this."

Tips for Success

- When dealing with violence at home
  - Create an environment that encourages individuals to seek help. Get people to the help they need.
  - Raise awareness of the signs of domestic and family violence.
- When dealing with violence in the workplace
  - Establish a clear policy that any form of workplace violence is unacceptable.
  - Provide training and education about stress and violence in the workplace.
  - Create an environment of mutual support and open communication.
- If violence seems imminent
  - Remove nonessential personnel from the area.
  - Make sure there is an escape route if the situation escalates.
  - Keep a safe distance (five to seven feet) between you and the person; do not turn your back to the person.
  - Leave the door open, or open a closed door; be sure someone is near to help if needed.
  - Calmly and firmly set limits (e.g., "Please help me understand what you need so that I can try to help you.").
  - If the person is shouting, do not try to talk. When the person gives you a chance to say something, speak in a normal tone of voice.
  - Never touch the individual to try to remove him or her from the area; even a gentle push or holding the person's arm may be interpreted as an assault by an agitated individual, who may respond with violence.
  - Call for help! Safety is paramount.

Chapter 7

Compliance and Inspections

Whether in the preinspection, inspection, or postinspection phase, mastering a major graded event requires time and focus. This chapter provides details on your role in the inspection process and highlights inspection criteria. Further, it outlines programs and actions to help you prepare for inspections and ensure your unit is meeting its wartime and peacetime mission requirements.

Preparing for Inspections

Original Author: Maj Shelley Strong
Commanders Connection Facilitator

As a commander, it is your responsibility to always be ready for someone to come in and evaluate how you are conducting your mission. Whether you are preparing for an IG formal inspection, a functional inspection, or a no-notice inspection, the culture you breed in your day-to-day operations will set the tone for how well you will do.

Tips for Success

- Identify all applicable governing directives and inspection areas.
  - o Your MAJCOM IG Community of Practice (CoP) website and the other commanders in your wing are the best sources for this information.
  - o Paying a visit to both your MAJCOM and wing IGs helps build a good working relationship with these critical agencies.
- IAW AFI 90-201, *The Air Force Inspection System*, implement a solid self-assessment program (SAP).
- Review past assessment reports and crosstell information; identify trends and repeat findings.
  - o Don't look just at your specific manpower data system or career field; most problems can transcend all MDSs and career fields.
  - o Ensure your programs do not have these same problems.
  - o Ensure all previous findings for your unit are closed.
- Request one or more SAVs before the assessment to ensure your programs are in top-notch shape. Sources for SAV teams are other squadrons with excellent programs or group/wing/NAF/MAJCOM staffs.
- Observe another unit during its assessment, if possible.
- Support MAJCOM IG augmentee requests. Augmentees gain valuable insights on IG procedures as well as significant crosstell information.
- Avoid simulations as much as possible. If you simulate everything, it can get you in more trouble than just doing the real task. This helps validate that you have all the required tools necessary to support your DOC statement.
- Fight the war, not the IG. Recognize that the IG has been tasked to observe certain skill sets. While the scenario may not seem logical in your mind, it is important to understand that the inspectors built it into the scenario at the most logical point to observe your ability to complete the skill set.
- Review your DOC statement. By knowing what your wartime tasking is, you won't be surprised when asked to generate X number of aircraft, Y number of sorties, or Z amount of cargo. By familiarizing yourself with UTCs, time-phased force deployment data, and so forth, you can have an idea of what you will be tasked to perform.

- Know how to report SORTS and ART data. If you are C-1 and/or green, don't claim you can't support the tasking. Truthful reporting is key.
- Prepare your Airmen for when the inspectors arrive—stress the following during your preparation:
  - o First impressions are most important!
  - o Focus on doing the mission, not on the assessment requirement or graded task. Demonstrate your unit's capability to do the mission.
  - o Ensure you are following appropriate guidance (tech data, AFIs, etc.)
  - o Maintain a positive attitude.
  - o Exhibit a sense of urgency.
  - o Present information openly; don't make inspectors dig for the data needed to grade your programs.
  - o Emphasize and demonstrate teamwork.

Self-Assessment Program

Original Author: Maj Shelley Strong
Commanders Connection Facilitator

Additional Contributions: 2011 Commanders Connection Team

Reference

AFI 90-201, *The Air Force Inspection System,* 2 August 2013 (incorporating change 1, 10 March 2014).

The majority of the following information is excerpted directly from the above reference.

Self-assessment is your best method for determining your squadron's ability to conduct its mission in accordance with applicable AFIs and directives. The program is designed to provide you with a tool for internal assessment and to complement external inspections. The focus is on how your squadron accomplishes the mission and gives commanders and supervisors an idea of where improvements are needed.

Commander's Responsibilities

Self-assessment provides commanders with a tool for internal assessment of unit health and complements external assessments. MAJCOMs will ensure self-assessment programs are established for subordinate organizations. DRUs and FOAs will develop and implement self-assessment programs that align with Headquarters Air Force (HAF) intent and function in similar fashion as wing programs described in AFI 90-201.

Your SAP should be tailored to your unit and contain mechanisms that ensure adequate coverage of your mission, resources, training, and people programs. While a SAP is most often implemented as a series of periodically administered checklists, other methods for self-assessment include quality-control reviews, internal audits, functional inspections, and SAVs. The following tips will get you started with developing a solid program.

Tips for Success

- Appoint a unit SAP monitor.
- Obtain the most recent HHQ-approved SAP checklist and guidance.
  - o A good source for most recent checklists and program guidance is the HAF and the MAJCOM IG website.
  - o Talk to your wing IG to determine if any NAF, wing, or local checklists complement MAJCOM guidance.
  - o Review any special interest items from HAF and MAJCOM.
- Review previous inspection reports such as SAVs, nuclear surety inspections, safety inspections (SI), and operational readiness inspections (ORI), and ensure checklist steps are included to prevent these problems.
- Get your local supplements approved by the wing IG before any formal inspection.
- In completing the self-assessment
  - o Ensure self-assessments are conducted periodically (quarterly or semiannually, depending on your HHQ); don't wait until right before a formal assessment to run your SAP!
  - o Mark each checklist step, as applicable, with a written explanation. Don't answer just yes or no and move on; cite examples and provide examples on how you conduct business.
  - o Fully document discrepancies and annotate corrective actions.
- Work to correct all identified discrepancies as quickly as possible.
  - o For problems that cannot be corrected immediately, establish a time line for resolution.

- o Monitor progress on all open discrepancies regularly (weekly staff meetings are a good place to do this).
- o Keep discrepancies open until fully resolved.
- o Provide status updates on critical findings, chronic findings, or limiting factors and the progress of corresponding corrective actions, as necessary, to HHQ or the inspection functional agency.

- Keep in contact with your MAJCOM functional manager for any areas that may require a deviation waiver. By keeping your MAJCOM in the loop, it can assist you with corrective actions or administer policy changes.
- Encourage discovery, review, and implementation of crosstell information, lessons learned, and best practices from other units.

Readiness Exercises

Original Author: Maj Kathy Goforth
898th Munitions Squadron Commander

References

AFI 10-204, *Participation in Joint and National Exercises*, 21 April 2010.

AFI 10-2501, *Air Force Emergency Management (EM) Program Planning and Operations*, 24 January 2007.

AFI 90-201, *The Air Force Inspection System*, 2 August 2013 (incorporating change 1, 10 March 2014).

AFPD 10-8, *Defense Support of Civil Authorities (DSCA)*, 15 February 2012.

The majority of the following information is excerpted directly from the above references.

In no other profession are the penalties for employing untrained personnel so appalling or so irrevocable as in the military.

—Gen Douglas MacArthur

Exercises are critical to ensuring our Airmen are prepared for current operations at home and across the globe. They are an important investment in the safety of your Airmen and the successful execution of your mission. Enhancing readiness and improving crisis response, they are conducted to facilitate your ability to get the job done. It is imperative that you accurately identify local and worldwide training requirements for your Airmen and provide the necessary instructions in a timely manner either in person, by formal course, or via computer-based training. Your wing IG, base safety office, and installation deployment officer can help in identifying the requirements for your unit.

Types of Exercises

(See AFI 10-2501 for frequency requirements.)

- Accident response exercises, depending on the base and its mission, may be called major accident response exercises (MARE), full-spectrum threat responses (FSTR), or emergency management exercises.
- Natural disaster exercises.
- Terrorist use of chemical, biological, radiological, nuclear, or high-explosive exercises.
- Operational readiness exercises (ORE).

Tips for Success

- Build your unit exercise program IAW these key concepts.
    - Embody the "train the way we fight" concept. Don't develop disparate exercise and real-world methods of doing business.
    - Ensure all unit personnel participate in exercises. Resist the temptation to "stack the deck" with an "A-Team" of exercise participants.
    - Apply real-world command structures and local community relationships in exercises when possible.
    - Keep simulations to a minimum.
    - Integrate logistics, support, force protection, and operational security requirements with mission requirements.

  - o Develop exercise scenarios to validate actual plans, policies, procedures, processes, and doctrine using existing command, control, and communications systems.
  - o Incorporate and institutionalize homeland defense concepts into training activities and exercises.
  - o Plan, prepare, and exercise with local communities in local emergency or disaster recovery actions to support AFPD 10-8.
- Support the installation deployment plan and exercise plan (if any).
  - o Provide input during exercise planning. Decide which objectives or tasks you want tested, which UTCs you want tasked, and which actions and requests from other units your Airmen can support.
  - o Understand your unit's responsibilities IAW the deployment and exercise plan, and ensure that your Airmen are postured to meet the requirements.
  - o Appoint unit and base EET members. If you appoint more than one EET member, then you will designate one as the unit's EET manager. EET members should be the most qualified managers, leaders, or technicians to provide an effective evaluation of exercises.
  - o Appoint a UDM and unit EM representative. Ensure they receive the proper training.
- Identify requirements and budget for and also obtain, store, and maintain exercise equipment, to include individual protective equipment (IPE), personal protective equipment (PPE), communication devices, shelter supplies, and contamination control materials.
- Conduct a review, or "hot wash," after each exercise.
  - o Ensure key unit members attend.
  - o Publish an after action report containing identified discrepancies and corrective actions.
  - o Establish a plan to get the unit back on track.
  - o Attend group- and wing-level postexercise meetings; provide input as required.

Additional Resource

- AFPAM 10-100, *Airman's Manual*, 1 March 2009 (incorporating change 1, 24 June 2011), contains information to help your unit deploy, employ, fight, and survive. Ensure each of your Airmen has a copy.

Staff Assistance Visits

Original Author: Maj Shelley Strong
Commanders Connection Facilitator

Staff assistance visits are provided to assist commanders in assessing their organizations' effectiveness. MAJCOM and NAF agencies conduct SAVs to ensure compliance with DOD, Air Force, MAJCOM, NAF, base, and unit guidance and commander's programs. Checklists are available to guide commanders in preparing for SAVs. Base-level agencies provide SAVs for specific programs such as the CSS, MEO, safety, or security. A SAV team is comprised of functional experts from staff agencies and is augmented with support personnel from field units. Often these visits identify deficient areas, providing valuable tools for assessment that should be included in your inspection preparatory plan.

Tips for Success

- Review copies of past SAVs.
- Schedule a SAV early.
- Ensure there is sufficient time to correct deficiencies.
- Before the SAV
  - o Plan the same way you would plan for a major inspection.
  - o Ensure the purpose of the SAV and the areas to be assessed are clear.
  - o Review the checklist.
  - o Pay particular attention to "special interest items" and ensure compliance.
  - o Establish the duration of the visit.
- During the SAV
  - o Request an in-brief, and set expectations for the visit. Invite key leaders from your unit.
  - o Review findings daily, and do on-the-spot corrections when possible.
- After the SAV
  - o Request a clear and concise report identifying strengths and weakness of areas assessed and recommended improvements.
  - o Track deficiencies and recommended improvements until closure.
  - o Report status to HHQ as required.
  - o Maintain a copy of the written report.

Formal Inspections

Original Author: Maj Thomas Kirkham
509th Munitions Squadron Commander

References

AFI 90-201, *The Air Force Inspection System,* 2 August 2013 (incorporating change 1, 10 March 2014).

Chairman of the Joint Chiefs of Staff Instruction (CJCSI) 3263.05, *Nuclear Weapons Technical Inspections*, 4 June 2010.

The majority of the following information is excerpted directly from the above references.

Three major types of formal inspections that you may experience during your command tour are ORIs, compliance inspections (CI), and nuclear surety inspections (NSI).

You should become familiar with several functional area inspections, such as health services inspections (HSI], the logistics compliance assessment program (LCAP), and so forth. It is important to identify the interval, when the last inspection was conducted, and the results. A successful SAP can help you achieve positive results in all inspection arenas.

Operational Readiness Inspections

ORIs measure the ability of a unit to perform its assigned operational mission. An ORI assesses how well a unit meets its designed operational capability, mission-essential task list (METL), and assigned DOC statement(s) and/or OPLAN taskings.

An ORI generally consists of two phases. Phase 1 evaluates three key functions: the ability to (1) transition from peacetime readiness into a wartime posture, (2) deploy forces and materiel, and (3) maintain and sustain essential home-station missions during and after the deployment of forces.

Phase 2 evaluates a unit's ability to meet its wartime taskings and mission in a wartime environment. While optimum frequency varies among the MAJCOMs, ORIs are conducted no more than 60 months (three full AEF cycles) apart for any unit. MAJCOMs may waive ORI Phase 1 activities for units that have recently demonstrated capability through an actual deployment.

ORIs are graded on a five-tier rating scale—outstanding, excellent, satisfactory, marginal, and unsatisfactory. Each major graded area (MGA) receives a tiered grade, and the wing receives an overall grade.

The four MGAs in an ORI are (1) positioning the force; (2) employing the force; (3) sustaining the force; and (4) the ability to survive and operate

(ATSO) in a hostile environment and/or contaminated chemical, biological, and nuclear environment.

Subareas evaluated in each of these categories include the following:

Positioning the Force

- Command and control.
- Preparation for operations.
- Deployment planning and processing.
- Reception and beddown.

Employing the Force

- Command and control.
- Information operations.
- Intelligence.
- Maintenance.
- Operations.
- Weather.

Sustaining the Force

- Communications and information systems operations.
- Manpower, personnel, and services.
- Civil engineering.
- Security forces.
- Logistics readiness.
- Medical/health services.
- Rules of law.
- Contracting.
- Safety.
- Chaplain.
- Public affairs.

ATSO

- Command and control.
- Preparation.
- Protection.
- Contamination avoidance and control.
- Response.
- Mission continuation/restoration and sustainment.

Compliance Inspections

Compliance inspections are conducted to assess areas mandated by law as well as mission areas critical or important to the health and performance of organizations. Unit failure to comply with the established directives in these areas could result in legal liabilities, penalties, or mission impact. At a minimum, CIs will be conducted on all wing/wing equivalent units at an interval of no more than 60 months. MAJCOM commander approval is required to exceed the 60-month inspection interval. MAJCOM IGs notify the Air Force Inspector General (SAF/IG) when a unit will exceed the inspection interval and provide anticipated inspection dates.

CIs assess unit programs for compliance with current guidance in three general categories: (1) mission areas, (2) common core compliance areas (CCCA), and (3) special interest items (SII). MAJCOMs can identify their MGAs. Consult your MAJCOM IG for inspection areas.

Nuclear Surety Inspections

Nuclear weapon systems require special consideration because of their political and military importance, their destructive power, and the potential consequences of an accident or unauthorized act. NSIs are performance- and compliance-based inspections conducted to evaluate a unit's ability to manage nuclear resources while meeting all nuclear surety standards (DOD 3150.2-M, *DOD Nuclear Weapons System Safety Program Manual*, December 1996; certified current 8 March 2004). Technical Order (TO) 11N-25-1, *DOD Nuclear Weapons Technical Inspection System*, is the governing instruction for the conduct of NSIs.

There are three types of NSIs:

- Initial NSI—used to evaluate and certify
    - o a unit's ability to assume its assigned nuclear mission.

  - o a unit's ability to resume its nuclear mission following unit decertification.
  - o that portion of a unit's mission that has been decertified.
- NSI—designed to certify a unit's continued capability to perform its assigned nuclear mission.
  - o Inspects a unit's capability to manage nuclear resources while complying with applicable nuclear surety rules governing its nuclear mission.
  - o Inspects a unit's capability to safely and reliably receive, store, transport, secure, maintain, load, mate, lock/unlock, test, and render safe nuclear weapons. Missile launch crews, aircrews, command post controllers, and release teams must demonstrate their knowledge of weapon acceptance procedures, nuclear weapon system safety rules, and nuclear weapon control order handling and authentication procedures.
- Limited nuclear surety inspection (LNSI)—limited in scope and does not evaluate all NSI areas applicable to the unit.
  - o Designed to assess sustained performance of nuclear surety while minimizing the inspection footprint on a unit's operations.
  - o While LNSIs may be scheduled, no-notice, or minimal-notice inspections, each nuclear-capable unit will receive at least one no-notice or minimal-notice LNSI every 18 months.

Tips for Success

- Fully understand all potential taskings from your DOC statement and other sources.
- Appoint squadron EET members; utilize them wisely to help prepare the squadron.
- Identify key war-fighting positions, and ensure primary and alternate personnel are properly trained in their responsibilities.
- Review previous assessment reports to ensure there are no repeat discrepancies.
- Conduct squadron exercises and in-house training to enhance wartime skills and to identify deficient areas. Continue to train.
- Talk to squadron commanders at recently inspected bases to obtain insight on the inspection process and potential taskings.

Postinspection Activities

Original Author: Maj Thomas Kirkham
509th Munitions Squadron Commander

After an assessment is complete, it is critical to ensure the timely correction of any findings or discrepancies identified by an inspection team. An electronic spreadsheet is an excellent way to track the status of write-ups and ensure appropriate follow-up actions are taken.

Equally important is to capture lessons learned and incorporate safeguards in your programs to prevent repeat (or similar) problems in the future. All program managers and the unit SAP monitor should maintain a continuity book containing historical data on past inspections to prevent repeat discrepancies and to provide continuity for new personnel. You may also want to keep a copy of inspection reports for future commanders to review.

Tips for Success

- When possible, correct findings on the spot—this will ensure that item meets the inspection team's standards. Work to correct all findings or discrepancies identified by the inspection team as quickly as possible.
    - o Consider appointing an action team to monitor/manage correction of inspection findings.
    - o Talk to the IG, MAJCOM staff, or inspection team members for clarification on required actions, if necessary.
    - o For problems that cannot be corrected immediately, establish a time line for resolution.
    - o Monitor progress on all open discrepancies regularly; weekly or monthly staff meetings are a good place to do this.
    - o Keep discrepancies open until fully resolved.
    - o Ensure any inspection continuity books are updated with any corrective actions.
- Update HHQ regularly.
    - o Provide status updates on critical findings, chronic findings, or limiting factors and the progress of corresponding corrective actions, as necessary, to HHQ or the inspection functional agency.
    - o Provide a formal response to the wing commander (via wing IG) for fix actions on minor discrepancies.

- o Provide a formal response to MAJCOM IG through your wing commander (via the wing IG) for fix actions on major discrepancies.
- Take care of your Airmen.
  - o Recognize outstanding or superior performers.
  - o Ensure EPRs, OPRs, and civilian appraisals reflect superior performance.
  - o Your unit has worked hard to prepare for the inspection. Consider holding a unit sporting event, picnic, or down day to reward and rejuvenate your Airmen.

Documenting and Sharing Best Practices

Original Author: Maj Shelley Strong
Commanders Connection Facilitator

References

Air Force Handbook (AFH) 38-210, *Air Force Best Practices Clearinghouse*, 9 April 2001.

Air Force Manpower Agency (AFMA), "Air Force Best Practices Clearinghouse," https://www.my.af.mil/afknprod/community/views/home.aspx?Filter=AF-DP-00-30.

The majority of the following information is excerpted directly from the above references.

A "best practice" is a superior method or innovative practice that contributes to improved performance as agreed upon by multiple sources. The "best" moniker is subjective, based on several factors such as an expert review or breakthrough efficiencies (e.g., saving money or manpower).

The AFMA is the clearinghouse and repository for best practices identified by MAJCOM IG teams. The AFMA sets the criteria for retention, removal, and archiving best practices. Before implementing a best practice, you need approval from the chain of command, process owner, or functional OPR. Remember, not all best practices can be adapted to every Air Force working environment.

Tips for Success

- Scan the AFMA's best practices website periodically for new ideas to improve how your squadron manages its programs and executes its mission.
- Visit your IG, and review crosstell information on best practices applicable to your wing.
- Visit your local manpower office, located in the FSS, at your base for information on this program.

Abbreviations

AAA	antiaircraft artillery
A&FRC	Airman and family readiness center
A/OPC	agency or organization program coordinator
A1C	Airman first class
AAC	assignment availability code
AAR	after action report
ACSC	Air Command and Staff College
ADAPT	Alcohol and Drug Abuse Prevention and Treatment (program)
ADC	area defense counsel
ADP	Airman Development Plan
ADPE	automated data processing equipment
AEF	air and space expeditionary force
AEFC	Air and Space Expeditionary Force Center
AETF	air and space expeditionary task force
AFAS	Air Force assignment system
AFFMS	Air Force Fitness Management System
AFGM	Air Force guidance memorandum
AFI	Air Force instruction
AFIT	Air Force Institute of Technology
AFMA	Air Force Manpower Agency
AFMAN	Air Force manual
AFMS	Air Force manpower standard
AFORMS	Air Force operations resource management system
AFOSH	Air Force Occupational Safety and Health
AFOSI	Air Force Office of Special Investigations
AFPAM	Air Force pamphlet
AFPC	Air Force Personnel Center
AFPD	Air Force policy directive
AFRC	Air Force Reserve Command
AFRF	Airman and Family Readiness Flight
AFROTC	Air Force Reserve Officer Training Corps
AFSC	Air Force specialty code
AFTTP	Air Force tactics, techniques, and procedures
AGR	Active Guard and Reserve
AIB	accident investigation board
AIDS	acquired immune deficiency syndrome
ALC	assignment limitation code
ALS	Airman Leadership School
AMS	assignment management system

ANG	Air National Guard
AO	approving official
AOR	area of responsibility
APC	agency program coordinator
APOD	aerial port of debarkation
APOE	aerial port of embarkation
ARC	Advanced Riders Course, Air Reserve Component, American Red Cross
ART	AEF reporting tool
ASBC	Air and Space Basic Course
ASIST	applied suicide intervention skills training
AT	antiterrorism
ATOC	air terminal operations center
ATSO	ability to survive and operate
AWC	Air War College
AWOA	absent without authority
AWOL	absent without leave
BAC	blood alcohol content
BDE	basic developmental education
BER	budget execution review
BITS	base information transfer system
BPA	blanket purchase agreement
BRAC	breath alcohol content
BRC	Basic Riders Course
BTM	base training manager
C2	command and control
CAA	career assistance advisor
CAFSC	control Air Force specialty code
CAIB	community action information board
CBRNE	chemical, biological, radiological, nuclear, and high-yield explosive
CCM	command chief master sergeant
CCT	contamination control team
CCTK	Commander's Toolkit
CDC	career development course
CDE	commander-directed mental health evaluation
CDI	commander-directed investigation
CE	civil engineer
CEMP	Comprehensive Emergency Management Plan
CES	civil engineering squadron
CFETP	career field education and training plan
CFMT	career field management team

CH	cardholder
CJCS	chairman of the Joint Chiefs of Staff
CLC	Chief Master Sergeant Leadership Course
CLEP	College-Level Examination Program
CMI	classified message incident
CMSgt	chief master sergeant
COCOM	combatant command
COMPUSEC	computer security
COMSEC	communications security
CONPLAN	concept plan
CONS	contracting squadron
CONUS	continental United States
CoP	community of practice
CPO	civilian personnel office
CPTS	comptroller squadron
CS	communications squadron
CSA	controlled spend account
CSAF	chief of staff, US Air Force
CSS	commander's support squadron
DANTES	Defense Activity for Non-Traditional Education Support
DBMS	director of base medical services
DCAPES	deliberate and crisis action planning and execution segment
DD	designated driver
DE	developmental education
DEERS	Defense Eligibility Enrollment Reporting System
DFARS	Defense Federal Acquisition Regulation Supplement
DFAS	Defense Finance and Accounting Service
DNIF	duty not involving flying
DOC	designed operational capability
DOD	Department of Defense
DODD	DOD document
DODI	DOD instruction
DODM	DOD manual
DPAA	Airman Assignment Directorate
DRU	direct reporting unit
DUI	driving under the influence
DUSTWUN	duty status—whereabouts unknown
DV	distinguished visitor
EA	epidemiological assessment

ECAMP	Environmental Compliance Assessment and Management Program
ECD	estimated completion date
ECS	expeditionary combat support
EEO	equal employment opportunity
EEOC	Equal Employment Opportunity Commission
EET	exercise evaluation team
EFMP	Exceptional Family Member Program
EM	emergency management
EML	environmental and morale leave
EO	equal opportunity
EOC	emergency operations center
EOD	explosive ordnance disposal
EOR	explosive ordnance recognition
EP/FPM	exercise physiologist/fitness program manager
EPR	enlisted performance report
EPTS	existed prior to service
EQUAL	enlisted quarterly assignments listing
FA	fitness assessment
FAC	fitness assessment cell
FAM	functional area manager
FAR	*Federal Acquisition Regulation*
FIP	fitness improvement program
FM	financial management
FMB	financial management board
FOA	field operating agency
FP	force protection
FP	fitness program
FPCON	force protection condition
FSS	force support squadron
FSTR	full-spectrum threat response
FTAC	First Term Airman Center
FW&A	fraud, waste, and abuse
FWG	financial working group
FY	fiscal year
GCM	general court-martial
GFM	global force management
GO	general order
GOV	government-owned vehicle
GPC	government purchase card
GS	General Schedule
GSA	General Services Administration

GSU	geographically separated unit
GTC	government travel card
HAP	high-aptitude personnel
HAWC	health and wellness center
HAZMAT	hazardous material
HHQ	higher headquarters
HIPAA	Health Insurance Portability and Accountability Act
HIV	human immunodeficiency virus
HLP/HLPR	healthy living program/healthy living program reserves
IA	information assurance
IAW	in accordance with
ICE	Interactive Customer Evaluation
IDE	intermediate developmental education
IDO	installation deployment officer
IDS	Integrated Delivery System
IDT	inactive duty training
IG	inspector general
IMA	individual mobilization augmentee
INTRO	individual newcomer treatment and orientation
IPE	individual protective equipment
IPR	individual personnel readiness
ITT	information, tickets, and travel
JA	judge advocate
JLLIS	Joint Lessons Learned Information System
K	thousand
LAN	local area network
LOA	letter of admonishment
LOAC	law of armed conflict
LOC	letter of counseling
LOD	line of duty
LOE	letter of evaluation
LOR	letter of reprimand
LRS	logistics readiness squadron
MAJCOM	major command
MARE	major accident response exercise
MCM	*Manual for Courts-Martial*
MDS	manpower data system
MEB	medical evaluation board
MEO	military equal opportunity
METL	mission essential task list
MFR	memorandum for record
MGA	major graded area

MHF	mental health flight
MilPDS	Military Personnel Data System
MISCAP	mission capability statement
MPF	military personnel flight
MPFM	military personnel flight memorandum
MPS	military personnel section
MRC:RSS	Motorcycle Rider Course: Riding and Street Skills
MRE	military rules of evidence
MSF	Motorcycle Safety Foundation
MSG	mission support group
MSgt	master sergeant
MSRC	Military Sportbike Rider Course
MTF	medical treatment facility
MTP	master training plan
MW	major war
NAF	nonappropriated funds
NBC	nuclear, biological, and chemical
NBCC	nuclear, biological, chemical, and conventional
NCO	noncommissioned officer
NCOA	NCO Academy
NIPRNET	nonsecure Internet protocol router network
NJP	nonjudicial punishment
NQP	not qualified for promotion
NSI	national security information
O&M	operations and maintenance
OCONUS	outside the continental United States
OI	operating instruction
OJT	on-the-job training
OPLAN	operation plan
OPM	Office of Personnel Management
ORI	operational readiness inspection
OPR	officer performance report
ops	operations
OPSEC	operations security
ORE	operational readiness exercise
ORI	operational readiness inspection
ORM	operational risk management
OS	overseas
OSHA	Occupational Safety and Health Administration
PA	public affairs
PAD	program action directive
PBD	program budget decision

PCA	permanent change of assignment
PCS	permanent change of station
PEB	physical evaluation board
PERSCO	personnel support for contingency operations
PFE	promotion fitness examination
PFMP	personal financial management program
PFW	performance feedback worksheet
PHA	preventive health assessment
PIF	personnel information file
PIMR	preventive health assessment and individual medical readiness
PME	professional military education
POC	point of contact
POV	privately owned vehicle
PPE	personal protective equipment
PRD	personnel requirements display
PRF	Promotion Recommendation Form
PRM	personnel readiness management
PRP	personnel reliability program
PRT	provincial reconstruction team
PSDM	personnel services delivery message
PT	physical training
PTL	physical training leader
QIC	quarters improvement committee
RA	resource advisor
RAC	risk assessment code
RAM	random antiterrorism measure
READY	resource augmentation duty
RFF	request for forces
ROMO	range of military operations
ROS	report of survey
RPT	reclama processing tool
RRT	reclama reporting tool
RST	readiness support team
RTFB	Return to Flying Board
SABC	self-aid and buddy care
SAPR	sexual assault prevention and response
SARC	sexual assault response coordinator
SAV	staff assistance visit
SCM	summary court-martial
SDA	special duty assignment
SDE	senior developmental education

SECAF	secretary of the Air Force
SFIP	self-paced fitness improvement program
SFS	security forces squadron
SI	safety inspection
SIB	safety investigation board
SIF	security information file
SII	special-interest item
SIP	self-inspection program
SIPRNET	Secret Internet Protocol Router Network
SJA	staff judge advocate
SKT	specialty knowledge test
SME	subject matter expert
SMSgt	senior master sergeant
SNC	special needs coordinator
SNCO	senior noncommissioned officer
SNCOA	Senior NCO Academy
SORTS	status of resources and training system
SOS	Squadron Officer School
SOT	status of training
SPCM	special court-martial
SrA	senior Airman
SRP	selective reenlistment program
SSgt	staff sergeant
STEP	Stripes for Exceptional Performers
TAFCS	total active federal commissioned service
TAFMS	total active federal military service
TDRL	temporary disability retired list
TDY	temporary duty
TIG	time in grade
TIS	time in service
TMF	traffic management flight
TPFDD	time-phased force deployment data
TSgt	technical sergeant
TSR	traumatic stress response
TTR	total trip reimbursement
UATO	unit antiterrorism officer
UCA	unit climate assessment
UCC	unit control center
UCI	unit compliance inspection
UCMJ	*Uniform Code of Military Justice*
UDM	unit deployment manager
UFPM	unit fitness program manager

UGT	upgrade training
UIC	unit identification code
UIF	unfavorable information file
UMD	unit manning document
UPAR	unit public affairs representative
USM	unit security manager
USR	unit safety representative
UTA	unit type code availability
UTC	unit type code
UTM	unit training manager
VA	victim advocate
VML	vulnerable to move list
vMPF	virtual military personnel flight
WAPS	Weighted Airman Promotion System
WGM	work group manager
WHMC	Wilford Hall Medical Center
WMD	weapon of mass destruction
WMP	War and Mobilization Plan
WRM	war reserve materiel